ANNA WICKHAM was born i[...] of six she went with her paren[...] educated in Brisbane. In 1904 she [...] period studying singing at the [...] Hepburn, a London lawyer and [...] four sons, the first, James, born in 1907: their third son died at the age of five. From 1905 she lived in Bloomsbury and, from 1909 until her death in 1947, in Hampstead. She had a long friendship with the lesbian writer and patron of the arts, Natalie Barney. Other friends, who included Kate O'Brien, Dylan Thomas, Malcolm Lowry, Ezra Pound, David Garnett, and D.H. Lawrence often spoke of her immensely powerful effect on people.

Anna Wickham started writing at the age of six, and wrote compulsively, producing over 1400 poems in her lifetime, encouraged by Harold Monro of the Poetry Bookshop and Louis Untermeyer in America. Her collections included *Songs of John Oland* (1911), *The Contemplative Quarry* (1915), *The Man with the Hammer* (1916), *The Little Old House* (1921). In 1971 her *Selected Poems* was published by Chatto & Windus. Nevertheless, her neglect by critics is, as Kunitz has said, 'one of the great mysteries of contemporary literature'. Virago publish this collection of her writings, which includes poetry, prose and an autobiographical fragment, on the centenary of her birth.

R.D. Smith was born in Birmingham in 1914, where he was brought up. He worked for the British Council from 1939 to 1942, first in Bucharest, later in Athens and Cairo. He married the novelist Olivia Manning in 1939. From 1942 to 1945 he was Director of Broadcasting for the Government of Palestine, and was a BBC Senior Writer-Producer for twenty years, winning the acclaimed Italia Prize for Radio. He now teaches Literature at the University of Surrey.

THE WRITINGS OF
ANNA WICKHAM
FREE WOMAN AND POET

EDITED AND INTRODUCED BY
R.D. SMITH

PREFACE BY JAMES HEPBURN

Published by VIRAGO PRESS Limited 1984
41 William IV Street, London WC2N 4DB

This arrangement, Memoir and Notes copyright © R.D. Smith 1984

Preface copyright © James Hepburn 1984

Copyright © James and George Hepburn: *Songs of John Oland* 1911; *The Contemplative Quarry* 1915; *The Man with the Hammer* 1916; *The Little Old House* 1921; *Richard's Shilling Selections* 1936; *Selected Poems* 1971. All unpublished writings copyright © James and George Hepburn 1984

All rights reserved

British Library Cataloguing in Publication Data
Wickham, Anna
  The writings of Anna Wickham.
  I. Title   II. Smith, R.D.
  828'.91208   PR6045.I25
  ISBN 0-86068-482-2

This book has been published with subsidy
from the Arts Council of Great Britain

Printed in Great Britain by litho at The Anchor Press,
Tiptree, Essex

In memory of
John Hepburn
and
Olivia Manning

CONTENTS

FRAGMENT OF AN AUTOBIOGRAPHY:
Prelude to a Spring Clean

From *Songs of John Oland:*

From *The Contemplative Quarry:*

From *The Man with a Hammer:*

PREFACE

One of my first memories is of waking in the early hours and hearing my parents arguing in the room next to mine. My mother was trying to persuade my father not to press his objections to his sister's marriage. She said: 'Nell is thirty-two, not likely to get another chance and anyway she loves the man.' My father rumbled on saying that Edgar was only a bank clerk, his family connections were negligible, and his health was poor. My mother's view prevailed. And I know now that the marriage was a great success.

Anna's championship of her sister-in-law was entirely character-istic; she did not particularly like Nell, but she felt that she should not be deprived of the chance of happiness by the exercise of a male prerogative supported only by prejudice. Anna did not regard men as rivals, nor did she seek conflict with them. She was prepared to leave the mining of coal exclusively to men, but she was not prepared to accept that they were inherently superior. Men and women were different, equal but complementary. She saw marriage as a partner-ship and all her life she hoped to find a man with whom she could collaborate fully, utterly.

Anna was a good friend. She gave an immense amount of energy in sustaining her friends at their times of trial. 'Better than a Continental holiday', wrote one on the kitchen wall. Another wrote:

Only dear Anna with large Attic rhymes
Creates and celebrates my sweetest times.

But Anna was a strict disciplinarian in everything concerning personal relationships. To anyone who offended her code she could be devastatingly rude. Such offences usually concerned third parties. Anna was protective, possibly over-protective, of the creative imagination of her sons and of the young artists who looked to her for encouragement and support. Any attack, real or imaginary, would be emphatically resisted. Thus occasionally a long-standing and affectionate friendship was terminated. But no one who had known her ever forgot her; many loved her.

From my early years I remember my mother as an amiable presence, kind, reassuring and always attentive to the things which interested us. My brother John was two years younger than I. Our house seemed always full of people, and of the sound of singing, for Anna had a truly remarkable voice with a range of three octaves and a very full tone in the upper register. She played the piano too. I remember cascades of arpeggios and chromatic successions of chords coming from the drawing-room above. 'What's she playing now?' the housemaid asked the cook. 'Picture music,' the latter replied with a knowing look.

My father seemed a remote figure but later in our teens we boys made many excursions with him, boating, walking, climbing, and we were hard put to keep up. He was immensely strenuous. As a young man he had bicycled great distances; throughout his life he walked, sailed small boats and climbed mountains. He had great powers of concentration. For years he slept only four hours a night so as to make time for astronomy as well as his practice at law. His interests were wide. I remember that, becoming dissatisfied with the available translations of the Psalms, he learnt Hebrew and translated them for himself. He was not a conventional man, save only in his concept of what should be the role of a wife. I have no doubt that Anna and Patrick loved each other. But their conflict was bitter; neither was prepared to lower their flag to the other. Nonetheless, there were moments of tenderness and periods of tranquillity.

In the winter of 1921, Anna was devastated by the death of her third son, Richard. It seemed to her a judgement because she had allowed her attention to be diverted from the family: *The Little Old House* had recently been published and also the American editions of *The Contemplative Quarry* and *The Man with a Hammer*. Richard contracted septic scarlet fever, which at the time was nearly always fatal. It was a long illness and Anna seldom left his bedside. She willed his recovery with the whole of her energy. When the crisis approached he was moved to the fever hospital in Lawn Road. The crisis passed and he seemed set for recovery. Anna and I visited the hospital every day, although I was not allowed into the ward. For five days he gained in strength. On the sixth she was stopped as she was about to enter the ward and told that Richard was dead. The shock was shattering.

Christmas was over, the New Year stretched bleakly ahead. Anna felt that she must have a break to get herself sorted out. She decided that she would go to Paris, and that I should go with her to be her companion and possibly learn a bit of French. In early January we went over on the night ferry via Dieppe. We breakfasted at the Rotonde with Lett Haines whom we encountered on the boulevard outside. I remember he was wearing his army officer's tunic, but with or without badges of rank I cannot say. My mother and I spent about five months in Paris, and lived together in amity and accord in a hotel in the rue d'Odessa. Our lives took up parallel courses which, however, converged at frequent intervals. I remember one morning Anna came back before lunch to the hotel where I had been studying, and told me that she had spent the morning with Ezra Pound on the terrace of the Café du Dôme. That afternoon she wrote her poem, 'Song to Amidon'. It begins:

> Dear fragrance,
> Be no more a man
> But a small hill of herbs.

American writers were coming over in numbers to join their expatriate countrymen who had remained in France throughout the war. Anna found many old friends and made many new ones. She met Natalie Barney at this time although their friendship did not begin until later. Sylvia Beach, Bob McAlmon, Djuna Barnes, Griffen Barry, Berenice Abbott (who photographed her), Beatrice Hastings, Nina Hamnett, Tommy Earp, Ezra Pound, George Slocombe and Aleister Crowley were all in her circle of friends. Tommy Earp fought a duel with Van Loo, the art dealer, in the Luxembourg Gardens over some real or imagined slight to Anna (the swords were made of wood). After the confrontation we all went to the Café Flore where I had my first encounter with pink champagne.

Often in the evening I would go to the Cirque de Paris or a cinema. Sometimes Anna would come too. At others she joined friends at the Boeuf sur le Toit or one of the 'boites' in Montmartre. Late one afternoon I had come up to Montparnasse after a late lesson at the Berlitz school and found Anna at the Dôme talking to Aleister Crowley. I joined them and he suggested a game of chess. The board was set up, the game started, and Anna and Crowley continued their conversation while a circle of friends and acquaintances gathered to listen to the discourse. Crowley rather casually made his moves without much consideration. Suddenly I saw that I had checkmate in two moves. He was furious, Anna delighted.

Back in Hampstead, Anna took over the management of the house. At times the going was easy, at others a black tension pervaded. The periods of tranquillity became fewer. In 1926 Patrick engineered a judicial separation. Anna was to leave the marital establishment taking her children, John, myself and the youngest, George. Under the deed she was to have £400 a year, but if she made any attempt to approach her husband the allowance would cease. We moved in to Prospect House off Heath Street in Hampstead. The day after the move, Patrick called. He stayed for hours, and he and Anna had an entirely amiable − if lengthy − conversation.

My father died on Christmas Day 1929 and, since he had no surviving partner, Anna and I spent the next two years winding up his practice. The decade moved on towards the outbreak of war. Anna managed the house, cooked, received friends, sometimes descended on the town like a sheep-shearer knocking back a pay cheque, wrote poetry when she had to, gave more of her energy to others than she could spare. Many loved her; few would deny her quality as an artist.

Anna felt keenly about the war; she thought it inevitable that the three of us should be involved. She stayed put in Hampstead. When it was over, in due course, after many months my brothers and I were demobilised. Each was preoccupied with new interests and associations. In 1947 Anna committed suicide (I was in Australia). She killed herself because she was tired (she had recently had a bad attack of bronchitis), and because she felt that we were well set up and no longer needed her — that we would be better off without her. In this she was wrong. She had sat at home, often alone, throughout the war weaving her spells to promote the survival of England and her sons. Now she thought the task achieved, the last battle won.

James Hepburn, London 1983

EDITOR'S NOTE
AND
ACKNOWLEDGEMENTS

From the published verse, which covers the years 1911 to 1936, I've omitted some poems that are superseded by later and better workings of identical themes and/or forms. There are over 1100 unpublished poems, in MSS and Anna Wickham's own typescript; of these 100 are included.

The poet's titles are usually apt and make a contribution to the poem, but there are dozens of 'Songs', 'Notes' and 'Comments'. To avoid tiresome repetition, occasionally I have provided a title from an appropriate phrase taken from the poem.

Her punctuation was impatient and erratic — dashes do for colons, semi-colons, commas and even full-stops. This was particularly so in 'The Little Old House' which was sloppily edited. I've corrected evident nonsenses.

Of the prose, the 'Autobiographical Fragment' and 'The Spirit of the Lawrence Women' (posthumously published in 1966) were written straight onto the typewriter and had obviously not been revised or prepared for publication. I have heavily cut the first two chapters of the former to remove long-winded historical speculations. In the latter, I have tightened up the first pages, but have taken care not to obscure individuality of phrase and image. The short prose pieces were written early, probably between 1910 and 1915. For lack of space, only five have been included apart from the two *Lecture Notes*.

Many of her letters and papers were destroyed in 1943 by a fire-bomb on her Hampstead house. Again for lack of space, it has not been possible to include any of her own letters to her friends, particularly her long correspondence with Natalie Clifford Barney. Her letters are quirky, acute, passionate and funny.

My thanks are due to Berenice Abbott for permission to use the photograph she took in 1926. To Oswell Blakeston, Eliot Bliss, Edward and Gwen Marsh, Robert Pocock and Heather Sherrie. Also to M. Chapon and Mme Prévot of the Bibliothèque Jacques Doucet in Paris, the Librarian of Reading University Library and Miss Sally Hine of the BBC Reference Library. And finally to the Hepburns – Margaret, George and James whose 'mingled banners' have aided me in my editorial task.

ANNA WICKHAM
A MEMOIR BY R.D. SMITH

ANNA WICKHAM (born Edith Alice Mary Harper)
1884-1947

> Here is no sacrificial I,
> Here are more I's than yet were in one human,
> Here I reveal our common mystery:
> I give you *woman*.

Anna Wickham said that these lines must preface all her books. In this, as in many things, she was frustrated; her thousand and more poems, most of them dashed off in pain, for fun, in anger, with glee, for cash or in desperation, are largely a record of her frustrations and her triumph over them. W.B. Yeats said that out of the quarrel with others we make rhetoric (or in our modern sense, propaganda); that out of the quarrel with ourselves we make poetry. He might have had Anna in mind. She was a bonnie fechter for freedom — especially freedom for women — for children's futures, against cant hypocrisy, and, more significantly, within herself against her fierce, contra-

1

dictory nature. Lust, love, duty, will, restraint, passivity, ambition and a mistrust of ambition warred within her. So did a social rebelliousness with a need to conform. Since poetry with her came out of living, out of her immediate uncensored experience, and since her experience was simultaneously felt, thought about and analysed, it is not surprising that (as with all major artists) early experiences of parental conflict resulting in a crippling tension and areas of insecurity were lived out in both later relationships and her poetry.

Some of these deep contradictions were apparent in her own person. She was a woman with a strong, sensitive face and a sturdy body, who appears in photographs both observant and withdrawn. She gives an impression of being sunk in reflection while tensed for action. The poets, Louis Untermeyer, Oswell Blakeston and Paul Dehn, and the novelist David Garnett, who all fell in love with her at first sight, over a long span of years have described her appearance and manner. They agree to a remarkable extent, which indicates the consistent naturalism of her manner, and her 'star' quality, the breath-taking effect she had on people: even Harold Acton, whose aesthetic preciosity found her not *comme il faut*, and American celebrity-hunters were taken by the force of her personality.

She is remembered as handsome, big, and dark, of nectarine colouring, with flushed cheeks, and very humorous eyes. 'A magnificent gypsy of a woman, who always entered a room as if she had just stamped across the moors', she was careless of her appearance. Although she loved magnificent clothes, she had, as she indicates often in her writings, a touch of the slattern, which her more doting friends called 'a gypsy carelessness'. Garnett, though fascinated, was uneasy with her 'rag-bag' coterie. Acton was snooty about her performance at an upper-class lesbian poetry soirée in Paris, and an American culture snob called her 'a burly lady fortified in advance with garlic and wine'.

In England, 'struggling between dreams and domesticity', she enjoyed café and pub life as natural extensions of her curiosity about and care for all manner of people from Hampstead tramps to Lord Northcliffe eating a meat pie off the kitchen table; from obstreperous Betty May and Silvia Gough and Nancy Cunard at the Fitzroy, to the diligent social works of the School for Mothers; from the cramped economy of Harold Monro's Poetry Bookshop to the aristocratic, plutocratic and indeed artistic splendour of Natalie

Barney's Temple of Sappho. These inner contradictions gave thought to her poems: like MacNeice she felt 'the drunkenness of things being various'. But in life they often made difficulties: 'Her personality was tremendous: she could build up or she could destroy.' As in an old Shropshire saying, 'She was like a cow who gave a good pail of milk, and then kicked it over.'

Anna was a worker for peace, but supported the Great War effort. She quarrelled bitterly with her husband, but stayed faithful to her marriage till her husband's death. In her children she found her only unspoiled happiness, in her vocation of poet her unshakeable centre, and in her passion for freedom and intellectual clarity, strength to endure long years of sexual, artistic and economic privation. But not without paying a heavy price. Her mother's manic and histrionic energy, overacted emotional scenes, rages, physical violence and her effusively demonstrated love for the infant Edith, had imposed on her child a too heavy load of emotional responsibility. All through her life a letter from her mother would cause Anna to retire to bed. She drained herself in support of other people: she had no means of conserving her energy, deeply as she wished to, both for her family, and for her art.

The inner contradictions expressed themselves in her social and political activities. Paul Dehn, as good a journalist as he was a poet, brings her before us in her energy and charm. He met her at Muriel Dean Paul's. 'Much of her verse is delicate as the wind on a saucer of milk,' he wrote. But Anna herself was beetle-browed, leonine, shaggy and unashamed, with a heavy hunch in her bearing like that of a peasant bowed down after centuries of toil. And, in an earthy way, beautiful at that.

She read her poems in a voice deep as the bittern, interrupting herself constantly with odd conversational asides and explanatory phrases: ' "Twenty nine years of Hell are dying in me" – can I have a drink? Thanks. Now here's an intelligent bit. . .'

This habit of instant self-criticism, of on-the-spot rejection of what had just flowed from her pen persists in her letters, and in her manuscript poems, of which there are over eleven hundred. 'Bunk'; 'Rubbish, but there it is'; 'Not much sense but some rhythm.' Written of herself, these remarks justify her often savage criticisms of her friends' unsuccessful poems. Her incisive analytic intellect complemented her tumultuous feelings.

3

She told Dehn, 'Young man, all men are theorists and all women are practical'. (She thought this, in a Shavian way, about G.B. Shaw.) 'If you wanted to feed the nation, you'd do nothing but scribble figures on your blotting-pad at an office desk. But a woman would be thinking in terms of beans and broccoli, Ribstone pippins and potatoes. *She'd* get it *done!*' After twenty minutes she wrote him a poem:

> Paul Dehn
> Must not refrain –
> But conjure doves:
> He must defy
> Such menace of the sky
> As shall control his loves.
> He shall be faun
> On Leonora's lawn –
> God grant me gratitude for slaves.

'Not so hot that last bit,' said Anna. 'Bit obscure, what?'

It's clear that she had a strong dramatic sense. 'The bittern voice' reminds us that had she not married she would certainly have triumphed as a singer; the leading London and Paris voice-coaches, including Randaegger and De Reszke, had the highest opinion of her future. Her voice was matched by an electrifying stage presence. She wrote of her mother, 'you could imagine a ray coming out of her!' So it was with Anna. Indeed, the novelist, Eliot Bliss, in her frightfully titled *A First Meeting with God* speaks of 'her genius a kind of major star' and of the 'tremendous electric force which emanated from her. At night I felt through the walls what I can only describe as powerful magnetic rays, disturbing and exciting even terrifying.'

Certainly Anna owed these gifts of a magnificent natural voice with a star's magnetism and a talent for performance to her mother; from her father, she was blessed with an artist's sensitivity, intelligence and integrity. From both parents she inherited a facility for charming, encouraging and teaching others.

GEOFFREY HARPER
1860-1929

As her autobiography tells (see pp. 49 – 157), Anna was brought up to pity, and later, despise her father, Geoffrey, as an ineffective failure. Alice, her mother, was a dazzler in public: 'She looked marvellous, big and impressive in a very beautiful evening dress, and with a lot of golden hair piled in a crown on her head.' She ran her home efficiently: with guests she reserved her energies for the evening's entertainment. A child remembers with fascination how she would, just for the two of them, put on an evening of Shakespeare or *The Ingoldsby Legends* (adapted for dramatic presentation). 'She was really wonderful . . . her complexion was like a beautiful rose.' From this enchanting mother she learned that her father had failed as a businessman, and, evidently, as a husband and father. By the time she was fifteen her parents slept separately. As Anna grew older Alice became more hostile to Geoffrey, and increasingly independent as a bread-winner. This Geoffrey admired, saying that if she were dropped into the middle of the Sahara she would quickly be making a good living by teaching the Arabs something or selling them something. She was a goer, if not quite a bolter. Her energy, beauty, tumultuous love for the child, her remarkable talent for reciting, teaching, fortune-telling, managing and money-making, above all, her energetic eccentricity and inventiveness fascinated young Anna. Her love was not shaken by Alice's often farouche behaviour, or by her sometimes savage discipline, which included use of stick and later a strap. All this left an unhealed unconscious wound that expressed itself in the poems, and probably in some aspects of her life, in various sado-masochism symptoms that showed in episodes of depression, and in extravagant outbreaks, and from time to time, in her emotional sex life. The hammer and the whip recur as images in her poems and so do extremes of abasement, domination, and exaltation through suffering. 'As she beat me, I cried to her "Beat me, mother, but love me – O love me." ' (p. 80).

When Anna was ten, the Queensland poet Brunton Stephens told her anxious father: 'She will be a poet on a condition you can hardly wish her since you are her father: she will be a poet if she has pain enough.'

Her education at the Roman Catholic convent also gave her a precocious preoccupation with Christ's wounds and the virtues of suffering, as well as a heightened, if repressed, sensuality. It also provided a substitute for her often withdrawn mother-love.

Her father she loved for his tenderness, care, and passionate will for her to be successful. She may have been influenced by his encouraging her 'boyishness'. Anna, no doubt taking entirely her mother's point of view, shows a true but pitying affection for Geoffrey, and always felt an obligation to make an acknowledged success of her writings in order to gratify his ambitions for her, and no doubt to assuage the guilt she must have felt for her own ambivalence to him whom she both loved and in some respects despised.

Certainly the leaving of Sydney incident is embarrassingly funny. As the boat begins to pull away from the wharf taking the daughter off, on a £4 weekly allowance, to conquer Europe with her art, father shouts, '*Punch*, Anne, *Punch*!' Twenty years later, one of her best-known poems was parodied in *Punch*, and she was written up by Humbert Wolfe in the 14th edition of the *Encyclopaedia Britannica*, so Geoffrey had some gratification at least.

But this picture of her father as an ineffectual salesman hawking in the Queensland bush his grand pianos in vain always seemed contradicted by other facts that existed independent of her mother's impatient complaining and dismissals.

He never aspired to be a musician: he would have liked to have been a writer. In this certainly he failed. So do most aspirants, after all. But he was a sensitive intellectual, respected as an independent mind, an amateur philospher and a Rationalist, a crony of men of intellectual repute, and a close friend and adviser, in the early stages of his rise to fame or notoriety, of George Riddell, later Editor of the *News of the World*, and Lord Riddell. (He saw Geoffrey off on the boat to Australia with a present of a copy of the *Origin of Species*.)

Evidently there was much more to Anna's father than her mother put about. Moreover, whether or not the music shops in Haverstock Hill and in Wimbledon did provide a decent living for the family, the job he obtained when he decided (no doubt with some reluctance) to move on led to growing success. It was to manage a music shop in Maryborough, South Queensland, with two branches in nearby sugar towns, Bundaberg and Gympie. (See p. 92 for their way of life and the marital quarrels, in their house on stilts on the

Mary River.) Floods wrecked the branches and piano selling in Maryborough was supplemented by piano-tuning.

Life in Queensland was tough, and primitive, but the settlers were beginning to 'civilise' themselves. A piano (or pianola) was becoming a necessary pleasure, an educational tool, and a symbol of respectability.

After a year or two, Geoffrey moved to Brisbane as tuner and repairer in the leading music shop there. No doubt the ruinous floods of that time meant there was a deal of repairing to do. Alice set up as Mme Reprah, Physiognomist and character-reader-by-the-face, 2/6 for spoken reading, 5/- if written down.

Typhoid brought him close to death, and he gave up his job while he convalesced. He then moved to a firm in Sydney and went on the road selling pianos. He proved an able salesman and made a good thing of it. He earned enough to buy a house and to send Anna to England with an allowance of £4 a week – no doubt partly provided by Alice's thriving elocution practice (see p. 118).

Geoffrey was handsome, well-turned-out, and generally thought of, outside the family, as a live-wire, charming and kind. This is, of course, in flat contradiction of the contemptuous cracks put about by Alice and repeated in three written memoirs by David Garnett, in a good deal of pub gossip, and, to a considerable extent, by Anna in the Autobiography (pp.101-3). An Australian friend who first met him when she was ten years old is much distressed by what she feels is a wrong and slanderous picture. She writes that he was a brilliant conversationalist, with a wonderful sense of humour, witty, an intellectual inspiration to all her family, and a fascinating promoter of new movements in the arts and new ideas generally. Her father, a prominent newspaper editor, used to say, 'he should have a Boswell'. 'It was always a real treat when he came to dinner. . . It wasn't that he held the floor, but . . . in fact he opened the door on a new world for us.'

So he did for Anna. She adopted her professional name Wickham because of an evening of passionate rapport with him, when at the age of ten she stood with him in Wickham Terrace, Brisbane, half-way between an Anglican Church and a Presbyterian Church from both of which sprayed showers of emotional hymn singing, and he urged her to promise him that she would be a poet. (Her first, immediately-to-be-ditched pen name was John Oland, chosen because of a visit to the Jenolan Caves with her feminist friend May Mukle, the cellist.) The return to a close family association was characteristic of Anna's behaviour: she took all vows and commitments as binding, even when they were not formalised. (W.H. Auden was blessed with the same quality.)

As we see later, Anna makes clear the social antagonisms that divided her mother's family, the Whelans, and her father's family, the Harpers, and takes great stock of each side's ancestors as far as she knew them, which she did mainly from family tradition and gossip. The rival traditions became part of her poetic apparatus, and their complex antagonisms often settled the direction of her political values and activities. She wrote at great length about all this in her autobiography, but told the Harper tale with more impact and precision in a poem at different times entitled 'Descent of Dorelia', and 'Eugenics'.

Descent of Dorelia

My great-grandfather was a pious man,
He lived carefully and well as a Methodist can.
He was thrifty and laborious, he made no waste,
He closed his house at nine at night, was faithful and
    chaste.

He was just to all men according to degree,
He went to class meetings, and had the minister to tea.
From birth to death he rose two grades in rank,
Born a labourer, he died a farmer with savings in the
    bank,
But all the calculations of his life-time were undone
By my grandfather, who was his only son.

My grandfather was naturally addicted to sin,
At the age of eight he bought a violin.
Alone he learned to play that instrument of evil,
Though well he knew that music was the language of the
    devil.

Sweet sounds and sin were wedded joy
To the perverted sense of that farm-boy.
He practised waltzes in a barn, using a mute,
When he had fiddled long in secret, bought a flute.

One day his Father found his fiddle and in ire
Broke the vile thing, and threw it on the fire.
Savage and unpersuaded, the mad fellow
Begged, stole and starved, until he bought a cello.

The rogue, my grandfather would never stop
On any farm, or patient in a shop;
He wished the spade and yard-stick both to Hades,
And took the road with a tragedian, and two light ladies.

The minister never knew, all his poor life,
Whether one or both of these women was my grand-
    father's wife.
I, a Conservative, am descended from their communion;
And I am married to the Squire.
My Grandfather died in the Union.

'The Little Old House' (p. 244) is a variation on this subject.

    The Harpers had been tenant farmers in Shropshire at least since
the sixteenth century. Some broke away and succeeded in the professions or even in commerce. One, Andrew, married the daughter
of a Knight and Alderman of the City of London. She treated him
ostentatiously as her social inferior, a piece of history that (like the
Boyne in Ulster) stayed naggingly alive in Anna's head. When this
lady died in the last of her many confinements, Andrew busied himself with the scientific improvement of wheat. He left most of the
fortune he had inherited to found the Harper Adams Agricultural
College, which exists to this day.
    When Anna married into a family of aristocratic lineage, now
settled in the upper-reaches of the professional middle class, she
found its conventionality oppressive in every aspect, and especially
in its 'Victorian' attitude to women. The themes of Them against Us
– the Villa-dwellers against the struggling poor; Men against

9

Women; and the Artist against the Philistine – are central in much of her writing, and, therefore, in much of her best work. Sometimes, though, as in the poem 'Nervous Prostration' (p. 210), she conforms to Yeats' 'rhetoric' in the way Betjeman does in *Come Friendly Bombs*: she makes good propaganda, but it feels strident, and at the last, unfair.

The events of her father's family history became part of her poetic equipment, so that she could unselfconsciously use the effect of genes *and* the effect of past environments to create poems and explain present situations.

ALICE WHELAN

The picture Anna gives of her mother, Alice Whelan (pp. 70-1), needs little comment from me. Her influence dominated every aspect of the poet's life, not least in the painful ambivalence she felt for her father.

Anna's great-grandmother, Joanna, used the name Burnell, but this was an Anglicisation of the Italian Bournelli. Illiterate, in youth a lady's maid at the Belgian Court, she died at a great age in a work-house, leaving only some beautiful needlework pieces. Her husband had been a courier: when her daughter, Martha, was born she had the King of the Belgians for godfather. Inevitably, in the common romantic habit, the family hinted at royal bastardy. The courier died two months after Martha's birth: Joanna then came to England and married a shoe-maker. Martha stayed in Belgium for fifteen years before coming to England. There she married Michael Whelan, a poor but decent plumber, and by the age of twenty she had three children: Helen, George, and Anna's mother, Alice. When her husband died of T.B., Martha was helped by George Cruikshank who paid for the funeral, and made it possible for her to become an artist's model. She was beautiful and 'middle-Victorian pictures seem full of [her] head and hands and feet'. Charring, home-working on chenille hair nets, and letting rooms, saved the family (now augmented by an illegitimate girl) from destitution.

The School Board for London was established in 1870 and Martha seized this chance of giving her daughters a future. Helen and Alice became teachers, two of the first lot of working-class people to escape economic insecurity and to enter the uncertain status of the Board School teacher. (If many doctors, clergymen and ushers were not fully socially acceptable, what could one make of a Board School teacher? Anna, with her experience of Board Schools, and D.H. Lawrence, who had been a Board School teacher, found common ground here when they first met.)

The ruling classes used the new Board School-educated and de-classed teachers and bureaucrats as cadets for maintaining the status quo, just as the products of the minor public schools founded two generations before had produced a new class of 'acceptable gentry' to keep the Empire going. Anna saw this stage in maintaining upper-class hegemony as operating 'by penalising imagination and putting genius under restraint. They have allowed no heroes to rise to save the citadel of democracy, for no hero after his contact with popular education has ever been wholly himself. The Board School castrated the mind of my father, as it did later that of D.H. Lawrence.'

The painter, Frank Potter, became engaged to Helen and his *The Music Lesson* in the Tate shows Alice teaching a young girl. Aveling, to whom Alice became secretary, made his usual pass at Helen, and being refused went off to wreck the life of Eleanor Marx.

Her mother's family took only a minor place in Anna's ancestral mythology: nevertheless their (and her own) class position influenced crucially her social and political reactions, and the Irish/Italian and artistic connections played their roles too. Alice, her mother, courter of disasters and diseases and deaths, seemed to transcend all class barriers, being more a force of nature than a social being.

PARENTS' COURTING AND MARRIAGE

Alice was already a stunning performer; although an amateur she had been praised in the *Illustrated London News*. An improbable and modest stage-door Johnny became her Boy in the Gallery. He was Geoffrey Harper, who had met her at a dance in the Holborn Town Hall. Her family tried to prevent their wedding, but Geoffrey, in direct contradiction of his later family reputation of being 'ineffectual', persisted, and they got married on a shoestring, the loan of a few pianos to sell if possible, and practically no cash at all. He was twenty-one. They went to live over the Wimbledon music shop.

In what Anna liked to call 'domestic economy' they were Jack

11

Sprat and his wife in reverse. Geoffrey was for spending, laying out for the future: Alice for lean living, and building up a cash reserve. The best room over the shop was let to a curate. Geoffrey adored books; Alice needed people, or at least an audience.

A stillborn son led to increased help from grandfather William: he also caused Geoffrey to use Anna, born a year later, as a substitute son, and so established a longing for Anna to stay 'boyish'. 'My strong impression was that it was Geoffrey who felt the grief and Alice who manifested it,' writes Anna with antenatal confidence.

Quarrels between her parents became more violent, and, when Anna was eighteen months old, Alice quit – first to a furnished room, then on to a sailing ship for Australia. She worked her passage, possibly as the skipper's mistress (see p. 79).

In Australia Alice caught pneumonia and Anna was put into an institution. The authorities got in touch with Geoffrey, who had not a clue about where they were. His family offered help with fares, and a year later Alice sailed back with the now two-and-a-half-year-old Anna. At the age of four she wrote her first poems for her father. Her parents' quarrels became more vicious and when she was five, they took separate rooms, her father the attic.

An imposing new piano shop opened near Wimbledon Station, and Geoffrey realised he would have to get out. Two of Geoffrey's sisters, May and Beatrice and an Uncle Charles had gone to Australia. Geoffrey followed, leaving Alice teaching at a school near Primrose Hill. She soon made up her mind to follow him, arranged to travel as mother's help for a well-off family, rowed with them en route, and swapped her servant status for passenger. From Sydney they set off to join Geoffrey in Maryborough, Queensland. The autobiography gives details of the rest of their married life, though not of Alice's later escapades and exploits that took in the U.S.A., Mrs Annie Besant, a new 'religion' to whose 'community' she invited Geoffrey as a disciple. All of this followed logically from her fortune-telling as Mme Reprah and her own gargantuan appetite for drama and domination.

Nor does it tell of Geoffrey's remarriage. Heather Sherrie writes, 'We were not told whether they were divorced or if Mrs Harper had died, or if he was committing bigamy. When he brought his new wife to see us, we were amazed. Mother and I were very shocked, and felt she wasn't worthy of him, but Mother said wisely, "I expect

Geoffrey is tired of living in hotels, and wants someone to look after him".' I wonder if it was not more a case of 'some shy gazelle, some gentle dove, something to love, something to love', for Geoffrey's married life seems to have been an eternity of being denied love, and being deprived for most of the time of his adored Anna. From the series of economic ups-and-downs and the bruised feeling of not having his considerable talents decently recognised, I imagine his good nature and his brains provided him with shelter and healing.

ANNA IN LONDON AND PARIS
1905-1906

Of this period Anna gives a lively account (pp. 121-38). The determination to succeed shown by her pertinacity at the various stage and music auditions did not fade as she grew older. Nor did the need she had taken from her mother for performing. In London, in addition to her efforts to get on, she had to renew family contacts, and in Paris she was busy with her music, quite apart from the exciting enchantments of that capital, and no doubt as on the boat from Australia a growing urge to enlarge her experience with men-friends.

Her astute observation of the feuds and jealously preserved social distinctions between the Harpers and the Whelans was undimmed. Harper Aunt Matilda, or Tid, as she was known, thought Anna too self-possessed and bossy for so young a lady. The Harper grandparents, Alicia and Edwin, seemed old, but he played Mozart beautifully. The Aunts Matilda and Muriel sang a duet in cracked voices that had never recovered from their training (Anna was relentlessly hostile to uninspired routine teaching).

She renewed her old friendship with the cellist May Mukle and, through her, met the Goossens. She felt some envy of their technical efficiency, which she knew she lacked: 'I could never work at an art: I could either do it, or refrain from doing it'.

Next she won a scholarship at the Tree Academy of Acting, and soon, while on a trip to His Majesty's Theatre to hear G.B. Shaw talk on 'The Economics of Art', she was picked up by, or got off with, a freelance reporter called William Ray. At that time she felt lonely, rejected by both sides of her family and slighted by her old friend May, and by the Goossen girls. He chatted her up with a conventional line in lying about his posh connections, but once she had got

13

this out of the way, they became engaged. (So she acquired a second engagement ring, having had a brief fling in Australia.) Her fiancé's work took her to Wonderland, the Whitechapel boxing ring – not for a fight, but for a Russian Exiles' protest meeting about St Petersburg's Black Friday (see p. 126).

Soon William introduced her to Patrick Hepburn, a thirty-two-year-old solicitor with a passion for Romanesque churches, for marathon rides on his push-bike, and for star-watching. His obsessional devotion, devoid of ambition, to architectural photographs, the absorbed pleasure he took in making them into lantern slides to be used for modest lecture engagements touched her, for it reminded her of her father's pure passion for his books. Also Patrick was of a superior class, and much as Anna despised the villa-dwellers, she felt that they had in most ways greater possibilities for independence, neglected or stifled though these were by the blanket of conformity. 'He was high bred, and beautiful, though prematurely bald' (see pp. 127-9).

However, encouraged by the highest praise from her singing tutor Randaegger, she decided to chance her luck in Paris. William followed her and they became lovers. (This was the first time Anna records going to bed with anyone: for a woman who had had so many adventures and such a rackety life she was rather innocent sexually.)

Patrick now asked Anna if his sister Ellen could come over and stay with her. Anna agreed: 'It was the most disastrous decision of my life' (see pp. 133-7). To her, Ellen was the archetype Croydon villa-dweller, though the worst crime she seems to have actually committed was to take Anna 'to the Bon Marché to buy woollen combinations'. Whatever the rights and wrongs of this heavily dramatised antagonism, Ellen went deep into those inner springs from which Anna's poems sprang, while reinforcing her already formed views on the class struggle.

Anna was by now in Jean de Reszke's Master Class. The public success which was her father's life-long ambition would not be delayed too long!

Ellen and Anna left Paris to spend Christmas in England. William was still around, but happy to 'lend' Anna to Patrick for a visit to Oxford where Patrick kissed her and they decided to chuck William. They left immediately for Paris, and Patrick, after one night in a different hotel, asked her to marry him: 'You'll never leave me, will you? It would be such a shock to my family.' Later, on a visit to some cousins in Watford, he said, 'You won't show me too much affection before Eleanor, will you?'

Anna ignored these danger signals (they were both much in love) but continued her relentless recording of class habits and conventions. 'I was struck by the narrow range of the Hepburn family. Their habits were set and their circle limited. They would have as soon asked the baker to dinner as get to know the peerage.' It did not occur to her that the insecure, that is most people, are on the make: security generally brings with it complacency and self-satisfaction.

MARRIAGE
1906-1929

Anna and Patrick were married at St Margaret's Church opposite the Bank of England, a fitting place for Patrick, a Freeman of the City of London. The marriage was almost private: no best man, Ellen as bridesmaid, and a congregation of a one-eyed man and the pew opener. They took twenty-two books with them on their honeymoon, during which they were to visit and photograph twenty-two Romanesque churches.

For the first few months they were happy − 'not a single crumpled rose-leaf'. Anna became pregnant. Then Alice announced that she was coming home to see her dear daughter and Anna cried all through the night: her brief peace of six months she felt had now gone. She was right. Her child, a girl, died in premature birth. Alice rampaged, until deciding on a return to Australia. Before she left, Anna had a miscarriage. Patrick had taken her on several strenuous holidays, and she determined the third time was to be lucky: to make sure she insisted on rest. She went to full term, and James, an eleven-pound boy, was safely born: it was the happiest day of her life. James always 'sustained my imagination and my craving for tenderness and beauty, and I had always my pre-occupation of my dream for him'.

She took up baby-training with scholarly passion: 'For a year no other subject entered my mind'. With her mother's energy and bossiness she broke nurses into her ways. She joined the St Pancras School For Mothers, though not so much to instruct the poor, as to learn what she could from them, for she remembered how well her own grandmother had coped. She began, against the wishes of the

15

Committee, to give away new saucepans so that milk could be clean and boiled: she took sick babies into her own nursery.

The school was one of a number of similar organisations, set up to fight the evils of infant mortality by instructing and training mothers in better methods of hygiene and diet. (The first National Conference for the Prevention of Infant Mortality took place in 1906.) It was a move to promote self-help in place of the Victorian doctrine of institutional philanthropy and benevolent guidance of the poor or 'slumdwellers' by the well-to-do. The Medical Officer for Health for St Pancras, Dr J.P.T. Sykes, enlightened, energetic, able and articulate, was also a friend of many influential middle-class and aristocratic liberals and socialists. He promoted the principle of the mother as 'the centre round which all the agencies revolved for the protection and preservation of the health of both mother and child'. All this Anna later realised she had plunged into with far too much hysterical commitment: 'I overtaxed [James] and induced a nervous stammer that will inconvenience him all his life.'

What she was doing without being aware of it was running away from the cloud over her marriage that began to loom with her mother's arrival. It was now swelling and darkening as the incompatibility of Anna's and Patrick's natures led to suspicion, aloofness, and soon to open hostility. Anna was passionate, impulsive, intensely fixed on motherhood: Patrick was guarded, controlled, and disliked the way babies stole Anna's attention which he needed for himself. Both were inhibited by different senses of duty, she by the duty that coition should be without pleasure, he by the duty that coition should be frequent. She thought fucking was to make the babies she loved, and who fulfilled her; he thought fucking was part of a husband's obligations, and what a man was expected to do. She lived for the present and the future: he lived in, and by, and off the past.

There were other, some less serious, points of conflict. Their ideas on holidays and housekeeping were different; she was ambitious for him to be publicly successful as a lecturer while he thought that kind of success ostentatious; she loved to shine in company, he thought that bad form; she basically lacked confidence and he was brought up with too much of it. Their bitterest clash was caused by Anna's need to write and publish her poems, and Patrick's insanely furious reaction to her insistence on this — unjustifiable in a man who was himself a loner, rejecting success in the law for his private passion of astronomy.

Despite this, however, a tether of regard, at least, and probably of passion, was twisted tightly. Anna defended him against all outside criticism, and much of her best poetry celebrates the violent struggles of their relationship which, after all, despite outrageous affronts and vengeful separations, lasted until his death twenty-two years after James' birth.

Early in her next pregnancy, they decided they needed a garden for the children, and moved to a beautiful house, 49 Downshire Hill, Hampstead, where John was born in 1909. Here she established a kind of salon, with music and entertainments in the garden and lectures on women's suffrage. Patrick resented this further diversion of her attention from him. Anna replied that he should enlarge the range and scope of his lectures, which she thought too piffling. They continued to grow apart.

In five years of marriage, Anna had suffered two disastrous accouchments and given birth to two children. She poured out her energies in looking after her babies and in her enthusiastic work with the School for Mothers. From her preoccupation with this came in 1909 and 1910 two interesting lectures: 'The School for Mothers' and 'Notes for a Lecture' (see pp. 372-3 and pp. 374-6).

All this, and her unresolved conflict with her husband, made her run-down and nervously exhausted. Her doctor recommended a sea voyage. She decided to meet her father in Ceylon, and they toured that island, and parts of South India. They returned together: Geoffrey and Patrick got on well enough. Soon after Geoffrey's return to Australia, Alice arrived, but was not put up in the home. Then burst out an insanely violent battle over Patrick's forbidding Anna to publish poems which she had had printed for her father (see *Songs by John Oland* pp. 161-71). James Hepburn writes: 'Patrick and Anna quarrelled, Patrick showed violence, Anna, in resisting, accidently pushed her hand through a glass panel and cut her wrist. Patrick called in a doctor to attend to the injury, and Anna soon found herself certified and confined to a private asylum near Epping, where she spent about six weeks. She was discharged a few days before an inspection by visiting doctors, discharged subject to a "probationary month". Anna and Patrick shared their marriage bed that night, "It is good to have you back," he remarked. When recalling this time, Anna thought it odd that Patrick should risk her conceiving if he considered her to be mad.' If any proof is needed of their passion, this surely is it.

The 'probationary month' had barely passed before Anna made her way to the Poetry Bookshop, which Harold Monro and his wife, Alida Klementaski, were running in Red Lion Square, Bloomsbury. She asked, ' "Have you any free rhythms?" He looked at me, interested, realising I meant Free Verse. He said, "We've all been trying to write them". I gave him my *Songs*.' In the next months Anna also widened her acquaintance with distinguished writers, and artists in the studios of Chelsea and the Hampstead Road. She met Augustus John, Jacob Epstein, T.E. Hume, Ezra Pound, Hannen Swaffer, Nina Hamnett, David Garnett and a chirrup of young poets.

Anna's forays to the watering holes of the intelligentsia were not rejections of her husband and children: she always put them first in her practical and moral priorities. She was trying to assuage the complicated anguish she felt as her husband (whom she loved, as he, in his somewhat immature way, loved her) tried to force her to give up her writing and social activities because he felt they were diverting her energy from himself. He would have been proud of her success if only it could have been complementary to his own life but he felt that her poetry, like her children, was depriving him of the total attention he needed.

Meanwhile Harold Monro printed nine of her poems in *Poetry and Drama* (summer 1914) for which he paid her the not bad sum of £9. She wanted to buy Patrick a sextant with the money, but he would not have it. This rebuff did not dampen her pleasure that this success of hers would delight and fulfil her father's lifetime longing for her to make a 'meritorious' public triumph. (Maurice Hewlett, then a name to conjure with, was a fellow-contributor.) 'Here I was, from the pit of obloquy to the pinnacle of pride.' Anna was only twenty-five and already had had two fruitless and two successful pregnancies as well as a triumphant period as an aspirant professional singer. Yet she told Oswell Blakeston, 'Harold Monro ruined my life by encouraging me to be a poet. I should have been a maker of popular mottoes!'

18

Her work to this point had been privately printed. *The Seasons — A Speaking Tableaux for Girls (100 Performers)* and *Wonder Eyes — A Journey to Slumbertown (For 80 Little People)*, written when she was 17, were printed by W.A. Pepperday and Son, Sydney, under her real name, Edith Harper. And, 1911, *Songs* by the Women's Printing Society Ltd, Brick Street, Piccadilly, under the pseudonym John Oland.

WAR-TIME
1914-1919

Patrick was in Siberia, observing an eclipse of the sun with a scientific expedition, when the Great War was declared on 4 August 1914. It took him some months to get back to England for they had to travel via Japan. Although over forty, he volunteered as a Kite balloon observer in the Royal Naval Air Service, and later became an original member of the Royal Air Force.

Civilians did not have such a bad time in the Kaiser's War as they did under Hitler's buzz-bombs. I mean, materially, for they suffered infinitely more from the mass killings on the Western Front, and, of course, wives and mothers suffered most. Anna, who gave birth to a third son, Richard in 1917, had a busy war. In her house in Hampstead she continued to meet artists of all kinds, and made friendships that lasted till her death in 1947.

Her reputation grew with the publication in 1915 of *The Contemplative Quarry* (Poetry Bookshop) and a year later of *The Man with a Hammer* (Grant Richards). Louis Untermeyer, the American man-of-letters and busy anthologist, caused both volumes to be printed as one by Harcourt Brace & Company, New York, though the volume did not appear till 1921.

Early in the war she became closer friends with Frieda and D.H. Lawrence. In 1915 she worked on the production of *Princess Marie-José's Children's Book* brought into this by a friend, Carmel Haden Guest, mother of David Guest who was killed in the Spanish Civil War. She contributed two poems, 'Baby Marigold' and 'The Bad Host', written to provide captions for a series of drawings by W.K. Haselden of the *Daily Mirror*:

19

The Bad Host

When Archibald Percival Minns turned three
His mother invited his friends to tea;
She bought chocolate and cakes and cook made toast,
And they all told the boy he must be a good host.

The artist has drawn his behaviour. Just look!
While his nice friends are dancing he's reading a book;
When they have 'Hunt the Slipper' he won't play at all,
But goes off and stands on his head near the wall.

Then his kind cousin Maud starts a fine tug of war,
But Archibald Minns just behaves as before:
The queerest of hosts, and the rudest of boys,
He's under the table alone with his toys.

So his mother sent up for the naughty boy's nurse,
Which makes a sad end to the tale and this verse;
For they put him to bed with no tea for his sins
Which serves him well right − wicked Archibald Minns.

As the war went on, her husband being away, Anna became more 'Bohemian'. One night at the Café Royal she heard some news about Russia which seemed to connect with the revolutionary contacts she had made when she first came to London (see pp. 125-6). She rushed off to her aunt Gertrude Chester's house to pour out the story in a histrionic style worthy of her mother. Gertrude's daughter, Peggy, a child at the time, writes: 'She was sure she was going to be shot . . . we had to lock ourselves in the bathroom while it was being related. My mother let me go and sleep the night with her. I was years younger and small, and she was six foot. It was moral support that was required.' The next day Anna went down to Fleet Street and persuaded Lord Northcliffe to see her. He took the story seriously. That night he drove Anna home. On the way they bought a meat pie which they ate together at the kitchen table.

At the end of the war, Anna, not worried about what would have been a sharp fall in income, suggested that Patrick give up the law to join the Meteorological Service. But Patrick's partner, George Cutcliffe, who had carried on the practice alone throughout the war, wanted to retire, so Patrick had to return to an occupation that now bored him. He and Anna were often at loggerheads, but agreed on finding a new house. They left the decaying Downshire Hill residence for a fine and larger house with a garden and a view, in Parliament Hill, Hampstead, where the family still lives.

In December 1919, the youngest son, George, was born, and together with the two-year-old Richard, gave Anna the happiness she had enjoyed ten years earlier with the infants, James and John.

DEATH AND PARIS
1921-1922

In 1921 the Poetry Bookshop brought out *The Little Old House*, and Harcourt Brace & Company published in one volume *The Contemplative Quarry* and *The Man with a Hammer*. The feminist drive in her verse was now much praised. In an introduction, Untermeyer wrote, 'But already a small and widely-scattered group of women are taking stock of themselves – appraising their limitations, inventions and energies without a thought of man's contempt or condescension. Searchers like May Sinclair, Virginia Woolf, Rebecca West, Willa Cather and Dorothy Richardson are working in a prose that illuminates their experiments. In poetry, a regiment of young women are recording an even more vigorous self-examination. The most typical, and in many ways the best of these seekers and singers is Anna Wickham.'

Then came disaster. The four-year-old Richard caught septic scarlet-fever. After removal to the Fever Hospital in Lawn Road, Hampstead, he rallied but six days later he was dead. In agony and despair Anna decided to get away to Paris to sort out her problems, which, apart from the death, were mainly concerned with the war inside her between her irreconcilable and unassuaged obsession to be an artist and her duty to devote all her energy to her family. She had happy associations with Paris, from the days, now seventeen years past, when she had been a student there. She used this time to restore her vigour, to 'get the smell of the sickroom from her nostrils', and to make new acquaintances in the arts, including a talented, wealthy lesbian, Natalie C. Barney, who was soon to become the emotional centre of her life outside the family. Outside it had to be, for Anna was adamant about the sanctity of the family, as her poetry clearly shows.

HOME, AND PATRICK'S DEATH
1922-1929

Back from Paris, Anna determined to become a model housewife. She had a cook and living-in housemaid, and an aspiring ballet dancer to look after George. Patrick had even blacker moods, and Anna felt he was suffering from melancholia. However, his fame as an astronomer increased. At various times Jeans and Eddington came to dinner; Patrick made important discoveries connected with the Rings of Saturn and became treasurer of the Royal Astronomical Society, and President of the British Astronomical Association.

Anna kept up her literary contacts, indeed, she increased them. Through Mrs Dawson-Scott she had joined P.E.N. which gave her a dinner shared with Edith Sitwell. 'Anna thought Edith would turn up in brocade so she wore a woollen jumper out of devilment.' She began to use Kleinfelt's, as the Fitzroy Tavern was generally known, to keep up her pre-war acquaintance with Nina Hamnett and Augustus John. Betty May was also about at this time, singing at the Crabtree Club. Though into cocaine and booze, she was still strikingly beautiful and worthy of her soubriquet 'Tiger Woman'.

Apart from these Bohemian forays, Anna gave poetry readings, and had a wide 'respectable' circle of friends through her social, charitable and political activities. Also she had great compassion for down-and-outs, often employing them to give them a 'fresh start'. 'If she saw an old tramp on Hampstead Heath looking at the sky, she would talk to him and tell him to go to her husband's lectures on astronomy at the Observatory. Where he did go — for a nice warm — but was not popular with the rest of the class or her husband.'

Preparing to go off to Hull for a poetry reading she could not find her silk stockings and fine blouse. 'The cook was wearing them in the kitchen — incidentally we had to hunt everywhere for her good velour hat, and eventually found it in the waste-paper basket. She rang up from the station to say she had missed the train, but found a machine which told fortunes.'

The rows with Patrick became more frequent and more violent. In 1926 Patrick engineered a judicial separation, and the family moved to a little house in Hampstead. After a few months the family moved to stay in Alida Monro's house in Bloomsbury, while Patrick lived alone at Parliament Hill. This form of solitude was too much even for Patrick, and it was agreed that the adolescent James and

John should keep him company, while Anna and the eight-year-old George should lodge in High Street, Hampstead. Next year, 1928, the judicial separation lapsed, and the family reunited itself in Parliament Hill. Relations were more peaceful, though Patrick became difficult about money. He had no partner in the practice, and was running it with the help of an aged managing clerk.

Just before Christmas 1929 he went (as he had done before) on a solitary walking holiday in the Lake District. On Christmas Day he fell off a mountainside and died of exposure. Anna's poem of 1921, 'The Homecoming' (see p. 256), now became deadly fact, and suggests that she may have inherited something of her mother's clairvoyant powers.

WIDOWHOOD, NATALIE C. BARNEY, AND THE GREAT SPRING CLEAN
1926-1935

It took the next two years for Anna and James to wind up Patrick's law practice. By 1932 she found herself a widow with two sons able to start earning their own living, and a boy of school age. There was little cash. What was she to do with her life now that she was, in a way, free to choose?

She had an international reputation as a poet: improbable as it seems today, anthologies printed more of her poems than they did of such greater poets as de la Mare, Graves, and even in some volumes, W.B. Yeats. She was in *International Who's Who* and Humbert Wolfe had written of her in the great 14th Edition of the *Encyclopaedia Britannica*. She was proud of their recognition, but sensible enough to realise that it was not enough to ensure her a living as a professional poet. She had long realised that her talent was special, intensely personal, slapdash and essential to her sanity. Though the odds were against proper financial reward, what else could she do but try to promote her career as a poet? As almost all of her correspondence, and goodness knows how much verse and prose of her own, were destroyed by a fire-bomb that burnt out the attic in Parliament Hill in 1943, it is impossible to know what she may have intended to put out if she had found a willing publisher. There is evidence that in 1919 she had projected a volume entitled *The Disorderly Shepherdess* and that around 1928 she had planned a dramatic poem, 'The Boy and the Daffodil'. We know too that she did try, or said she tried, to write a novel, at the request of Horace Shipp, talent scouting for Sampson Low, Marston & Co.

But the centre of her hopes and the place to which she directed her energies, while not failing to keep up her U.S.A. connections, was Paris, and Paris meant Natalie C. Barney, and the Temple of Sappho.

After meeting Natalie Barney in 1922, she had made fairly frequent trips to Paris and increasingly they centred on Natalie's house and salon in the rue Jacob. The attraction was emotional, sexual and artistic, three areas in which Anna had been parched for years by her fidelity to her husband and devotion to domesticity. Her love for her children was always unclouded, but naturally could not fulfil these other needs, although her children always gave her perfect happiness.

She maintained from 1926 to 1937 a correspondence of passionate love-letters (which was also a passionate discussion of the problems of being a woman and an artist).

Natalie Barney was a cosmopolitan personality, very American, and very French. Born in Ohio in 1877 she was bilingual, a patron, hostess, propagandist for lesbianism, and later for peace, poet (in French) and writer, mainly of aphorisms. Not as discriminating as Sylvia Beach or as rich and pushing as Peggy Guggenheim, but more talented than either, she gathered round her in her Temple à l'Amitié, leading scholars, academicians, intellectuals, artists, and socialites with sapphic and aesthetic enthusiasms. 'She represented the *Mercure de France* as Gertrude Stein represented *transition*.' Remy de Gourmont was a close friend and collaborator. Great figures included Anatole France, Rilke, Paul Valery, Rodin, d'Annunzio, Colette, Ezra Pound, Sinclair Lewis, Proust; and lesser personalities were Alan Seeger, Paul Geraldy, Sherwood Anderson, Richard Aldington, Gertrude Stein and Janet Flanner (for so long Gênet of the *New Yorker*). Her immediate circle of friends and lovers included the painter Romaine Brooks, the poets Lucie Delarue Mardrus and Elizabeth de Gramont, who concealed her artistocratic family under the by no means plebeian *nom de plume* of Lily de Clermont-Tonnerre.

Natalie in her *Pensées d'une Amazone* (Emile-Paul, 1920), refers to '*Cette catastrophe; être femme*', a sentiment that Anna shared, and that led her to attempt translations of some of the poems written by Natalie's friends. She also read her own poems at the Temple, as Natalie translated spontaneously with a running commentary. 'She is only a *demi-revoltée* − has four sons but no daughter − reared a family of males of which she is both pelican and nightingale [loud applause]. Feminist leagues have inscribed her poems on their banners. One of them has been used by the Women's Movement against corsets.' (Anna herself wore old-fashioned whale-bone stays. In the gallery of the Holborn Empire she once wrestled them off herself and enjoyed the show in relaxed comfort. They were pink.) Lucie Delarue Mardrus brilliantly translated some of Anna's poetry, which appeared in 1935 in *Edition des Poèmes Choisis de Lucie Delarue Mardrus* which gave Anna great pleasure. Another saying of Natalie's evidently impressed Anna as she struggled to order her life:

> *Si mes études furent nulles c'est que*
>   'My only books
>   Were woman's looks'
> *Mes amours? Multiples,*
> *Mes amitiés? Fidèles et loyales,*
> *Ma jeunesse? Elle dure encore, comme pour le vieux Goethe: que de premières amours vont à la rencontre de nos dernières amours. Et que défuntes elections s'y retrouvent!*

Anna was fascinated by Natalie, though never subdued by her. Natalie, even after Anna's death, continued her admiration for her poems, but their correspondence reveals that Anna's mainly long-distance passion for Natalie was not reciprocated. More satisfactory was their artistic rapport. Anna was looking for a collaborator in various literary ventures, and, insofar as the activities at the Temple made her personally and artistically known, she found one. But the lover-soulmate-fellow worker in the arts she hoped for was not there, despite Natalie's true affection, admiration for the poems and, in times of crisis, financial help.

The letters they exchanged were equally concerned with love and art. Anna enclosed hundreds of what she called Post-card Poems (*Des Cartes à l'Amazone*). Having noticed an old spelling of the philospher's name as Des Cartes, Anna thought she might make something out of playing off Descartes' thought against her own problems, but nothing came of it.

In America, Untermeyer remained a faithful promoter, and she found in London an effective admirer and impressario, the poet, John Gawsworth, pseudonym of Fytton Armstrong, later to succeed M.P. Shiel as King of Redonda. He included her work first in *Edwardian Poetry* (1937) and then in *Neo-Georgian Poetry* (1937). The adjectives in the title refer to the change in monarchs, not to poetic styles. In 1936 Gawsworth also edited *Thirty-Six New Poems* (Richards' Shilling Selections): there were thirty new poems actually; six came from an earlier volume.

The year before, 1935, was the year of *The Great Spring Clean* (see pp. 49-157), a year in which Anna struggled to exorcise her complicated guilt feelings over having done those things she might not have done, and having left undone those things she ought to have done for so many years in all matters concerned with domesticity. She longed for a clean slate on which she could, without inhibition, write her poetry. But the quarrel with herself was 'never quiet': she 'found no discharge' in the war between her two opposites, family and art, nor in the war between her 'biting lust' and her essential fastidiousness, nor in the war between her indifference to social forms and her sense of what was permissible and decent.

LA TOUR BOURGEOISE AND THE LAST YEARS
1935-1947

Anna continued to watch over her sons, to play the generous hostess, and to make occasional forays to Fitzrovia. In these years her interest in theatre and the ballet intensified. Her friends ranged from Anton Dolin (see pp. 42-3) to Bud Flanagan (see p. 42), who enjoyed and admired her poems. The 'gypsy' or, as she referred to it, the 'slattern' part of her became more prominent. She had always suffered from bouts of nervous exhaustion, bronchitis, and other, possibly psychosomatic, upsets, and from time to time had drunk a good deal, but always in company. In these years café-pub anecdotes began to accumulate, mostly very much to her credit.

In the Fitzroy she knocked down a silly poet to prove that ' "I am more immortal then he is". Then she picked him up, saying, ' "tonight I'm not a witch but a warlock" '. She could be

26

frighteningly dismissive if she took against anyone. One gushing admirer begged, 'Anna, dear, do ring me up soon. We're on the 'phone now.' Anna replied, 'Oh yes – any particular number?' At an art show where she had been scornful in too loud a voice, the art dealer whispered to Oswell Blakeston to take her away: she stood up to her full height and muttered, 'You'd better retract, my good man. I may be a minor poet, but I'm a major woman!'

She knew that war was approaching. She had been a pacifist, but when it came, she expected her sons to do their bit and was unmoved by the Phoney War arguments. She knew evil when she smelt it.

After a period of professional eclipse, which was not surprising given the violent change in poetic fashion brought about by Auden, and given her unbiddable originality, which was rooted in Victorian values, Edwardian social aspirations and Fabian politics, she was beginning to have a revival.

On 18 April 1938, Friends of the Library of Chicago wrote to her as one of a select group of poets asking for a message celebrating the memory of the editor of *Poetry, a Magazine of Verse*, Harriet Monroe, who had died the year before, climbing in the Andes. She collected signatures including those of Beatrice Kean Seymour and Carmel Haden Guest, and sent a cable 'Honouring a valiant woman, celebrating a courteous spirit, and remembering Harriet Monroe'. (The slightly old-fashioned use of 'courteous' here is typical of Anna and, I think, derives from her youth in Australia.)

She also busied herself gathering the support of seven feminists who signed, on 16 June 1938, a manifesto she had drawn up *The League for The Protection of The Imagination of Women. Slogan: World's Management by Entertainment.* Professor J.B.S. Haldane lent his considerable weight to the project. Anna was beginning to buzz again.

The BBC contracted her to take part in a television programme (probably through Royston Morley). She almost certainly would have been a tremendous performer in this infant medium, but the date was 3 September 1939. War was declared and the programme cancelled.

I went to work for the British Council in Bucharest soon after Munich in 1938. Anna's elder sons, James and John, had for some years been a successful dance-act as the Hepburn Brothers, and played Bucharest at this time. My first wife, Olivia Manning, wrote

The Spoilt City, which vividly recreates the exotic, if seedy, background to their engagement. Now they were to travel wider, James as an R.A.F. navigator, John as an artillery officer. The youngest, George, now nineteen, soon went off to the Middle East.

Anna stayed at the house in Parliament Hill for the duration of the war, unshaken by a fire-bomb that destroyed some of her manuscripts and almost all the letters she had kept, including what would have been of great interest to us, most of the Natalie Barney half of their long correspondence. She had always rated courage as the central virtue: she thought it her duty to help maintain morale. She was lonely, for she missed her sons badly.

On 27 April 1946 *Picture Post* did a feature on her, 'The Poet Landlady'. This recalled the time after Patrick's death in 1929 when she had let off parts of her house, and hung in the hall this notice:

Tour Bourgeoise 68 Parliament Hill, N.W.3
ANNA WICKHAM'S
Stabling for Poets Painters and their Executives
Saddle your Pegasus here
Creative Moods respected Meals at all Hours.

Dylan Thomas slept there from time to time, once with Caitlin. Then, in a not uncharacteristic way, he later bit the hand that had fed and watered him. Different in his generous thanks was Malcolm Lowry, a frequent visitor in the early thirties.

The sons were demobilised, but James was still flying and John preoccupied with learning Chinese. In April 1947, Anna hanged herself. George found the body, and was amazed that she, so clumsy with her hands, had succeeded in tying an efficient knot. This came to him at the first moment of shock: later he ran into the street howling wordlessly like a dog.

WOMAN AND POET:
NO DISCHARGE IN THE WAR

Like many poets Anna was a just and ruthless critic. Unlike some she was so with her own work:

> The tumult of my fretted mind
> Gives me expression of a kind;
> But it is faulty, harsh, not plain –
> My work has the incompetence of pain.

'Self Analysis' (p. 192)

And also of haste, impatience with working on, or working up, her material. Direct expression, spontaneous speech, instant form were what she wanted: 'a poet rediscovers all creation; this instinct gives her beauty, which is sensed relation.' 'The Egoist' (p. 173.) Sometimes, rather wistfully, or in rage because she could, with some justification, blame her husband for her lack of time and peace of mind she would dream of what might be, if:

> If I had peace to sit and sing,
> Then I could make a lovely thing;

'The Singer' (p.173)

but she knows most of her work is botched, fine lines, vivid images, original themes, a personal voice, are not brought to completion in the finished poem; so

> Let it be something for my song
> If it is sometimes swift and strong.

'The Singer' (p. 173)

She both envied and despised professional technique: 'I could never learn to study technique: with me it has to come spontaneously, or not at all'. There are many reasons for this reluctance to work to make perfect. First is her loathing of all dull conventional teaching that inhibited creative shoots: then her contempt for personal showing off, for displays of virtuosity that falsified the truth of what was being expressed: most important perhaps her passionate intellectual commitment to immediate feeling, from which all truth is inseparable.

Her remark about writing mottoes for Christmas crackers is apt. She had considerable dexterity in versifying, and could readily and easily do parodies and, like Louis MacNeice, 'Knew and could write in all the classical metres'.

> Of the dead poets I can make a synthesis,
> And learn poetic form that in them is;
> But I will use the figure that is real
> For me, the figure that I feel.

'The Egoist' (p. 173)

And:

> I first wrote poetry to please my Dad
> Who wanted to write novels and was sad;
> He never could write more than the first pages,
> And then he wrote so slowly that it took him ages
>
> But I wrote easily
> Although in poetry;
> And when I was a girl at school,
> When I learned grammar and was taught a rule
> Or I was taught the meaning of a word such as
>   inanimate,
> I'd write a poem out upon my slate,
> With all I knew of words and grammar to that date.

'Letter to a Boy at School' (p. 37)

Her vocation as poet came rather late: music, or rather singing, was her first vehicle, and the detailed work she put into her singing training, influence her poetic values.

> Tone
> Is utterly my own.
> For less exterior than skill,
> It comes from the deep centre of the will;
> For nobler qualities of Song
> Not singing, but the singer must be strong.

'Comment' (p. 195)

And:

> If my work is to be good,
> I must transcend skill, I must master mood.
> For the expression of the rare thing in me
> Is not in *do*, but deeper in *to be*.

'Examination' (p. 193)

It is not surprising that her first professional poet venturings (to the Poetry Bookshop) started with a discussion of 'Free Rhythms'.

> A varying energy and lethargy
> Sets contrast in the speech . . .
> When the creative depths are stirred,
> There are new rhythms, like a primal word.

At this time she was suspicious of the constraining and distorting effect of rhyme, which she saw as something arbitrary and mechanical:

> Likeness of sound,
> With just enough of difference
> To make a change of sense:
> So we have contrast,
> A piquancy,
> And a certain victory of contrivance:
> But Heaven keep us from an inevitable rhyme
> Or from a rhyme prepared!
> Rhymed verse is a wide net
> Through which many subtleties escape.
> Nor would I take it to capture a strong thing,
> Such as a whale.

'Note on Rhyme'

She hammered away at this problem:

> And now of this matter of ear-perfect rhyme,
> My clerk can list all language in his leisure time;
> A faulty rhyme may be a well-placed microtone,
> And hold a perfect imperfection of its own.

31

Knowledge of G.M. Hopkins, Wilfred Owen and Louis MacNeice, and the widespread use of assonance and half-rhyme, made her original formulation seem dated and over-anxious. But in 1915 she was pioneering in this field, which probably contributed to the high regard she gained, especially in the U.S.A., in the years after the First World War.

Another of her characteristics now so commonplace it needs an act of imagination to realise that she was considered to be pioneering, is her quickness to use images from industrial progress. This, of course, is all of a piece with her practice of giving tongue whenever she saw or felt, or heard, or smelled anything that fired her mind or her curiosity, or her emotions.

> It was as fit for one man's thoughts to trot in
> iambs as it is for me,
> Who live not in the horse-age but in the day of
> aeroplanes, to write my rhythms free.

'The Egoist' (p. 173)

More important, though, was what was then considered her daring in writing of a woman's passion, and in doing so in the way of frank autobiography. She describes war in marriage, her own marriage to a man of decency, intellect and principle, indeed of courageous unconventionality and daring originality except in his attitude to his wife, where he was crushingly, obliteratingly conventional. Anna's poems on this war are of two distinct types: those that generalise, or even mythologise the middle-class, convention-bound bourgeois husband as the killing opposite of the working-class and imaginative wife, and those that transcend social categories and feminist appeals, to achieve a depth and completeness she only rarely brings off, even when writing of sexual frustration or fulfilment, or of her children.

Both types were essential to, indeed means to, her sanity. The struggle in her writing for freedom, for immediate expression, was the kind of self-cure against despair, annihilation, and the dark-night of the soul so vividly described by Ionesco when speaking of his own art. Anna called this 'Mad Song'.

Sometimes I think my head is a spider
Built with a little loom inside her
She spins a web so thin and long
That is my simple song
Alas! Alas! at the full of the moon
I think in tune.

Fear of defeat, of total breakdown, recurred throughout her life. She was aware of the strain that had driven other women poets — Sappho, Lawrence Hope, and Charlotte Mew — to suicide, and of course, in the end, she took her own life, a generation before Sylvia Plath.

Like Ionesco, Anna relieved the choking fear of annihilation with a humour that ranged from black to gay: 'she could improvise a verse that cut the air into witty packs of cards'. Witty but not frivolous: truth was the core of her. Her work was generally unfinished, unworked on, rough notes and sketches for poems, like D.H. Lawrence's 'Pansies' only without his preaching and self-pity. She dashed them off as the image, or rhythm, or thought or joke or aperçu came to her. Some like 'Inelegant Evangelist' came out as knockabout:

For you can't keep a good man down . . .
Paul — Paul, think of old St Paul,
He had hardly any clothes at all,
Yet he was a gentleman by birth
And managed the best advertised
Syndicate on earth.

He walked into Nazareth
In his only coat,
Left it by the railings
It was eaten by a goat,
He bivouacked a moment
To rebuke the goat for sin,
Then walked right on to Galilee
And preached there in his skin
For you can't keep a good man down . . .

Others, like 'Concerning the Conversation of Mr H—', were satiric:

> This gentleman will only talk to us of *dogs*
> Because he wishes to disguise that he's a poet,
> If he should mention lions, dolphins, frogs,
> He thinks by misadventure, we should know it!
>
> He tells us things of white dogs, and of brown,
> Of curious breed with one distinctive spot,
> Of all the dogs that ever walked this town,
> Of dogs of his acquaintance that have not.
>
> I cite a dog I once set eyes upon
> Which, lacking doggy lore, I say looked like a swan;
> He takes me, says, 'That hound was bred in Russia,
> Three such are owned by Henry, Prince of Prussia.'
>
> O, modest violet! cowering in your green
> Your scent betrays you though you are not seen!
> Only unveterinary wights, like you and me,
> Would see in dogs a swanny quality!

Many were polemical, like 'Biology for Breakfast' (Nine hundred and ninety-nine types of domestic argument):

> Why does the peacock spread his jewelled tail,
> And walk so proud a prince of gentlemen?
> Has he not hopes his beauty will prevail
> With that small critical brown hen? . . .
>
> Why does the throstle clear his mellow throat,
> Till all the wood a magic draught receives?
> Has he not faith some individual note
> May yet convince Herself among the leaves?
>
> Think of the tiger and his fiery zest,
> Of all hot fights the wilds among,
> If she who waits approves not of the test
> She'll brook the lover, but devour his young.

> Good scientist, review all things alive,
> And for male strength and beauty you will find
> If not a cause a fixed co-relative
> Within the female mind.

Some, though comparatively few, were of their time, trailing an echo of de la Mare, or, as in 'Direct Interpretation', of W.B. Yeats:

> I heard two splendid simple sounds today,
> The singing of some little ribald boys at play.
> These songs were not good songs and not well sung,
> But they were frank and faithful, and the boys were
> > young.
>
> Then, when the evening kissed the sun-loved land,
> A poor man took fiddle in his hand
> And flung the honest joy of his poor tune
> To the high night, and to his friend the moon.
>
> I heard two splendid simple sounds today,
> A madman's music and young boys at play.

Others are fantasies, at times recalling fairy or folk tales, as does 'A Wizard Considers a Lady':

> This woman is an apple-tree,
> And a small yellow cat.
> Her gracious genius is dear to me,
> And I thank God for that.
> But the indolent cat, with the prey in its mouth
> Is a spirit of sloth, and death, and drouth,
> And the sight of that beast is so loathed by me,
> I go from the orchard, and run from the tree,
> And yet if I tarried a Queen would be free.
> But the beast sits up in the gracious boughs,
> Mouthing its prey in a sullen carouse.
> Till I hate the tree its sap and its root,
> And I will not stretch my hand for fruit.
> Yet could I eat, for my hunger's sake,
> A beast would perish, a Queen would wake.

Anna's children inspired a number of charming yet perceptive and accurate anecdotes. As in the many poems about her husband and their marriage, 'The Impressionist' is straight autobiography: James is Roman, John, Greek.

I have two sons,
One is born of my content,
The other born of sorrow.
Though they are still quite little sons,
I know that one is Roman and the other Greek.
I know this from the boys' looks.

When these two children play with clay
Rome will build bridges, but the little Greek
Will form a pixie.
The first will fill the garden
With real boys with sticks.
The second has made my garden quite untidy with his
      fairies;
These throw early apples down from the trees
And so are proved for my sake.

Lately my Greek son, being turned three,
Found his true medium:
He happened on a piece of brown chalk
And scored his first interpretation on the garden wall.
With gold hair ruffled like fire at a shrine, he called
'Brother come and see,
I have made this very beautiful picture of the black
      night'.

Rome came, muddy-handed from an aqueduct,
'It is a splodge,' he said, 'there are no differences in your
      picture.
Where are the houses? Where are the trees? And where is
      the blue sky?'
Greece drew himself up in infinite contempt,
'There is no blue sky in a black night,' he said.

Years later, for her youngest son, she wrote 'Letter to a Boy at School':

George and me
We'll sing to one another
Like two birds upon a tree.
And that has seldom happened
With a boy and his own Mother.

That George and me
Both write poetry
Shows there's a sympathy
More than in every family
Between George and me.

I first wrote poetry to please my Dad
Who wanted to write novels and was sad;
He never could write more than the first pages,
And then he wrote so slowly that it took him ages.

But I wrote easily
Although in poetry;
And when I was a girl at school,
When I learned grammar and was taught a rule
Or I was taught the meaning of a word such as
    inanimate,
I'd write a poem out upon my slate,
With all I knew of words and grammar to that date.

But when I wrote for my dear father,
I always used to worry rather
And think that for a girl it might be waste of time
To spend her life and love in making rhyme;
And I thought, maybe
I should be better knitting for my baby.

And now my dear and youngest son
Has brains enough to find my verses fun;
And so my head's no longer in a whirl
Wondering if I ought to write them, being born a girl.

And so I'll make,
For George's sake,
As soon as I have time,
The very finest thing I can in rhyme;
And everything I know
And dream and hope will go
Into this book,
Which will be a good pie,
Since I write better than I cook.

And George and me
Will sit and sing to one another
Like two birds upon a tree.
And in our pie
I'll not write 'George and I',
Though both are in the nominative case;
Our poetry will be a pleasant place,
Where grammar is most right when it is wrong,
In ways that sound well, in a song.

From time to time Anna has a quirky, cheeky, wry truthfulness that recalls Stevie Smith, as do the many poems she wrote to be sung, and as does this cautionary tale 'The Tigress':

There was a man who kept a young, tame tigress.
He loved her because she was beautiful;
It pleased him to stroke her neck.
He said to her, 'Tigress, my time is much occupied
But, because you are lovely,
I will see you on the last Thursday of every month,
And, because you are tame,
I will bring you a biscuit'.

With the passing of time the tigress grew strong,
More lithe and full of courteous love.
One morning she rose early and came to the man's
    house.
He was in bed. By his bedside
Was shaving water and a safety razor.

38

The tigress said to him, 'My Lord,
This is the first Friday of the month
And I am come because I want meat'.

The man said to her, 'I am a vegetarian'.
The tigress blinked at him
Like a complacent, slightly squinting woman.
Puzzled by the word 'vegetarian' she took to kissing the
    man's feet.
She kissed with the concentration of a strong thing that
    has been idle,
She was also irritated,
A dilettante offended by a word.
In the end she broke a vein in the skin of the man's
    instep,
Then, quick as fire, she ate the man.

She left nothing of him
But the smallest of his vertebrae.

Stevie Smith had no voice at all, and fitted her lyrics to hymn
tunes, but Anna wrote her own melodies. I can hear Stevie creak-
crooning these lines from 'Anne's First Exercise in Adverbs'.

Maiden where is the Mayor
Is he gone to shoot the swan
Her who held our Lord in thrall
Not at all and not at all
Mayor was seen with Maggie Mean
Herding turkeys on the green
Oh the poor Queen! Woe the poor Queen.

A surprising number of verses celebrate her domestics, whom for
the most part she loved, and nurses whom she execrated, as in 'Conflicting Occupation':

If the baby playing typewriter would only let me write,
I might compose him something on the spirit of delight,
Something as accurate and rhythmical as Shelley's.

But if I turn my back, my young fill their small bellies
With ink and sealing-wax and tacks,
So I forget my emotions and my facts.
I've even lost my sense of rhyme
By this time.
As for sustaining couplets on things Greek,
I cannot chant, I've scarcely strength to speak
After I've chased this pair of bandits up the stairs,
Lassoed them into bed, or bullied them to prayers.
Nurses? An ugly noxious race,
Soft in the head, and hard in heart and face.

Not so Emily in 'The Housemaid':

A natural satirist was Emily,
She saw the weakness of our life, and had her fun with it!
And when she left me for the munition factory
I asked, 'You don't like service?' 'No', said she
'I find the work so chronic slow', said she
'I might as well be married and have done with it'.

And some, like 'The Little Love' are lyrics such as a poet might have
written in any period:

At the height of the May
Your excellence thrilled me,
For a night and a day,
The love of you filled me;
But when the sweet weather
Resolved to the rain,
Like a colt on the tether
My heart felt a strain;
And back to the pasture
That God had ordained me
I lept, with the pleasure
My straying had gained me.

Unique to her seems the compulsion to set down in verse each
passing thought and sensation. The poems on the kitchen wall, and

in what she called her Butcher Book, the ones she called Post-card Poems, and enclosed in letters to her friends, Natalie Barney and John Gawsworth (leaving aside many failures, fragments and botched exercises in various forms of metre), are often more interesting than some of the more finished and more predictable published poems.

Because she attracted so many different kinds and classes of people, and because of her music activities she had a myriad continuing impressions to write about. As shown above, although her voice was always her own, in manner she sometimes echoes other poets. An uncharacteristically bad poem, 'A Love Letter', catches D.H. Lawrence's hectoring sententiousness; these lines show why I find it the least pleasing of all her writings.

> It is well I cannot eat with you all my days,
> I would not take my soup from a consecrated cup.
> I have before me a wealth of happy moments when I
>   shall see you.
> They are like holy wafers, which I will eat
> For stimulation, for absolution, and for my eternal hope.

This is untypical too of her general acute appraisal of D.H. Lawrence (see p. 355). She expressed her affection for him in 'Multiplication (For D.H.L)', while pulling his leg about his monstrously absurd machoism:

> Had I married you, dear, when I was nineteen
> I had been little since but a printing machine
> For before my fortieth year had run
> I well had produced you a twenty-first son.

'Multiplication (For D.H.L.)' (p. 318)

Along with her delight in her children went a kind of fearful joy in the possibility of their growing up to be artists. The heavy load she felt such a vocation had imposed on her would fall with all its painful pleasure on them. 'The Boy and the Doom' records a fine image as well as an anxious recognition.

He looked out over the sunset
And said, 'It is a fire sea'.
Should I most treasure or regret
This charming phantasy?
I see him with my burden on his back,
The love of beauty, the inevitable lack,
And him − just three!

She was not so besotted by her love and ambition for them as to lose
her sense of humour and response to facts, as the charming 'The Boy
and the Dream' shows.

I thought of the delicate things he had said,
And, ruthless marauder, I went to his bed:
'You'll be a poet one day, maybe,
I'm hoping a far better poet than me.'
With a catch in the throat the thing was done,
I had thrown my load to my slip of a son.
He thrilled, and sat bolt up in his bed,
'Will you *really* buy me those soldiers?' he said.

Her interest in the theatre, ballet and music hall was intensified
by her two elder sons' tap-dancing success and by her friendship
with C.B. Cochran, Anton Dolin and Bud Flanagan:

Oi! Flanagan:
Joy! Flanagan:
Not a goy! Flanagan.

When Dolin was fighting to keep ballet alive in Britain in the mid-
thirties, he and Markova (as Pavlova had done earlier) played the
halls from time to time. She wrote 'For Anton Dolin in Carnival
(Golders Green Hippodrome 1936)':

Poor lily in a turnip field
Don't yield!
Stand out for Beauty,
Do not succumb to duty.
Feed middling things to cattle.

Now, join the battle
Spirits of British dead
With Shakespeare at their head
To stir your bitter skies
To winds worthy of your enterprise,
Rains of inventions new,
Fit for a flower like you.

'Middling', as used here, suggests Irish associations, which, of course, could have been acquired only through her maternal family, or picked up in Queensland or New South Wales. Her outback life and later education in Australia (after all, it lasted for years from the age of six to twenty), in my view imprinted in her some of the old-fashioned Empire patriotism, which her more intellectual friends found surprising in a poet of feminist rebellion, and an opponent of the old, class, bureaucratic establishment. These years also strengthened her certainty that courage and will were the two essential virtues, and this the passion of her poetry abundantly illustrates.

From her mother's violent physical punishments (pp. 93-6) and her Roman Catholic schooling with its emphasis on Christ's suffering, His wounds, self-humiliation, redemption through pain and so on (pp. 108-9), she developed and retained a strong sado-masochistic streak. The images of whips, hammers, 'gay love with rods' and battles to death recur throughout her long life as a writer. Most significantly, they are central, though sublimated, in some of her few completely achieved poems, such as 'The Man with a Hammer':

My dear was a mason
And I was his stone.
And quick did he fashion
A house of his own.

As fish in the waters,
As birds in a tree,
So natural and blithe lives
His spirit in me.

And they show more obviously in many of the lesser poems, such as
'The Cruel Lover':

> I ask your pardon that your pain
> Should be so quick your lover's gain.
> But when I know your love's distress,
> My heart leaps high with happiness.
> It sends kind tincture to my lips,
> I walk with a new rhythm . . . from the hips.

They also appear with odd ambiguity in 'The Cherry-Blossom
Wand (to be sung)', which was very popular when published in
1915:

> I will pluck from my tree a cherry-blossom wand,
> And carry it in my merciless hand,
> So I will drive you, so bewitch your eyes,
> With a beautiful thing that can never grow wise.
>
> Light are the petals that fall from the bough,
> And lighter the love that I offer you know;
> In a spring day shall the tale be told
> Of the beautiful things that will never grow old.
>
> The blossoms shall fall in the night wind,
> And I will leave you so, to be kind:
> Eternal in beauty are short-lived flowers,
> Eternal in beauty, these exquisite hours.
>
> I will pluck from my tree a cherry-blossom wand,
> And carry it in my merciless hand,
> So I will drive you, so bewitch your eyes,
> With a beautiful thing that shall never grow wise.

Sometimes the infliction of pain is a scourge to stiffen the sinews and
summon up the will to intolerable effort: sometimes it is naturally
part of pleasure, as in 'The Marriage' (p. 178):

What a great battle you and I have fought!
A fight of sticks and whips and swords,
A one-armed combat,
For each held the left hand pressed close to the heart,
To save the caskets from assault.

The reverse of this fierce joy in marriage is expressed in poems about the stifling mediocrity of bourgeois values and routine. They tend to be rather journalistic, but when Anna is touched personally by unexpected contacts she produces odd, lively verses, such as 'Meditation At Kew':

Alas! for all the pretty women who marry dull men,
Go into the suburbs and never come out again,
Who lose their pretty faces and dim their pretty eyes,
Because no one has skill or courage to organize.

What do these pretty women suffer when they marry?
They bear a boy who is like Uncle Harry,
A girl who is like Aunt Eliza, and not new,
These old dull races must breed true.

I would enclose a common in the sun,
And let the young wives out to laugh and run;
I would steal their dull clothes and go away,
And leave the pretty naked things to play.

Then I would make a contract with hard Fate
That they see all the men in the world and choose a
    mate,
And I would summon all the pipers in the town
That they dance with Love at a feast, and dance him
    down.

From the gay unions of choice
We'd have a race of splendid beauty and of thrilling
    voice.
The World whips frank, gay love with rods,
But frankly, gaily shall we get the gods.

When she transcends her faults of hastiness and carelessness of finish, there is a metaphysical quality in her work, the thinking, analysis and feeling being fused in the poem. Although her own opinions, prejudices and principles were strongly, indeed aggressively, maintained in her social life, she showed a sympathy and understanding that made her loved by a wide range of people. In her work she had the true poet's gift of empathy: she picked with the sparrow in the gravel. Freedom is the dominant theme in her work, a freedom that abhorred licence and recognised necessity. She was preoccupied with the tension between the exact, though 'free', form she worked for, and the spontaneous flow of inspiration. (Her singing training had focused her mind on the problem of freedom of rhythm, of intonation within strict musical limits: she did not write seriously till marriage had terminated her singing career.)

She desperately wanted 'to achieve one perfect thing'. There are poems where she came nearer to it than we might, after all this criticism, have expected.

Envoi

God, thou great symmetry
Who put a biting lust in me
From whence my sorrows spring,
For all the frittered days
That I have spent in shapeless ways,
Give me one perfect thing.

There is a Brechtian tone about 'Domestic Economy':

I will have few cooking-pots,
They shall be bright,
They shall reflect to blinding
God's straight light.
I will have four garments,
They shall be clean,
My service shall be good,
Though my diet be mean.
Then I shall have excess to give the poor,
And right to counsel beggars at my door.

46

'Tribute to the Nursing Staff' seems to me a summing up of her character, and of her personal style:

> Let me die unafraid
> Beyond the reach of aid.
> Let me lie proudly dead
> Where no efficient smooths my bed –
> A lion in the wilderness
> In all my lovely loneliness,
> Unsoiled by science or the least
> Contamination of the priest.

'The Fired Pot', too, could not have been written by anyone but Anna:

> In our town, people live in rows.
> The only irregular thing in a street is the steeple;
> And where that points to, God only knows,
> And not the poor disciplined people!
>
> And I have watched the women growing old,
> Passionate about pins, and pence, and soap,
> Till the heart within my wedded breast grew cold,
> And I lost hope.
>
> But a young soldier came to our town,
> He spoke his mind most candidly.
> He asked me quickly to lie down,
> And that was very good for me.
> For though I gave him no embrace –
> Remembering my duty –
> He altered the expression of my face,
> And gave me back my beauty.

To end this section, here is a poem that can stand with the best love lyrics in the language, 'The Mill':

I hid beneath the covers of the bed,
And dreamed my eyes were lovers,
On a hill that was my head.
They looked down over the loveliest country I have seen,
Great fields of red-brown earth hedged round with green.
In these enclosures I could see
The high perfection of fertility,
I knew there were sweet waters near to feed the land,
I heard the churning of a mill on my right hand,
I woke to breathlessness with a quick start,
And found my mill the beating of your heart.

FRAGMENT OF
AN AUTOBIOGRAPHY

FRAGMENT OF
AN AUTOBIOGRAPHY:
PRELUDE TO A SPRING CLEAN

It is the fourth of March, 1935, and a fine early Spring morning. I begin my great house-clean.

For twenty-nine years I have been attempting to order the house. For twenty-five years of my misery, it has been my passionate pre-occupation. I began in the first year of my marriage with a sort of amiable unction. Three years after my marriage, my domestic happiness was in ruins and I had committed myself to giving birth to two boys, James and John. I have very little doubt that I loved these children, certainly James, the elder of them.

It was during my pregnancy with the second that the shades of the prison house began to close in on me. My husband, Patrick Hepburn, from being my devoted lover seemed to become my enemy and my judge. This synchronised with the reawakening of his intellectual life. He was thirty-three years old when he married me and had only known the embraces of a working-class whore: his real passion had been given to the study of the Romanesque.

Every weekend and always on his holidays he cycled about the country taking photographs of cathedrals. He cycled immense distances, and very fast; in England, Italy, Spain and even as far as Constantinople. He returned with photographs. With infinite care and enthusiasm he worked these up into lantern slides. His lectures on them to the Watford Archaeological Society contained no aesthetic theorising, but were concerned meticulously with detail and dimension.

During the first two years of his marriage with me this passion for architecture abated. He did little more than re-arrange the slides and show them to his acquaintances, seeming to substitute an enthusiasm for me for his enthusiasm for the churches, but he took me to see the cathedrals. During these two years and during my first three pregnancies, I saw a great many. I had no natural interest in cathedrals, but a quite irrational enthusiasm for pregnancies.

For twenty-nine years I have been attempting to order the house; because of the pathological weakness of a betraying untidiness, I have not succeeded. For twenty-nine years I have been putting things away in loathsome sets of drawers. This year I shall conquer the sets of drawers: my self-discipline is complete enough. I shall have every pin, rag, tot and tittle in the villa in its place, and everything will be splendidly clean. But I am finished: I am utterly defeated: there is nothing before me but suicide. I order the villa for my death. When the stove is clean enough I shall turn on the gas.

As I perform this *tour de force* of ordering and house-cleaning I shall write an analysis of myself and of the twenty-nine years of my futile attempt. I shall do this because I am still unhousewifely enough to be immensely irritated by my duty of ordering and cleaning. The relief of writing will give me nervous and physical energy to continue with my task. I write also because I am a woman artist and the story of my failure should be known. I have a European reputation: my poetry is mentioned with honour in the *Encyclopaedia Britannica*: that should give me a right to live. I have very little newspaper reputation: I have always avoided it as part of my phobia.

By the sacrifice of myself I have attempted to serve three generations of men. I seem to have ruined them all. My great energy has been attacked by every man with whom I have been in close relationship. I have never resisted these attacks.

In spite of my long endurance and impotent courage, I have made some profound mistakes. I feel that I am myself a profound mistake and that I was doomed from my conception by being myself: I feel

52

that women of my kind are a profound mistake. There have been few women poets of distinction, and, if we count only the suicides of Sappho, Lawrence Hope and Charlotte Mew, their despair rate has been very high.

I know what has happened to me, and have still the energy and resource to set it down. It is even an expedient for my survival that I set it down. Self-knowledge and self-expression are the only techniques of my continuance. I have never believed in my art. I have never been interested in it. I have been interested in men. My desire has not been to make art but to create an artist. I have believed in being a woman, and my notion of my *métier de femme* has been to stay in my family, and order my house.

For the whole twenty-nine years my resources have been decreasing, and the tragedy growing more complete. It is with loathing I see that the destruction originated with my father. Its root was in his preoccupation with my powers of expression, and in his ambition for my fame and success. Until the time of his death I thought his pride in my poetry was from his love of me, but I then saw that he was bitterly jealous of my work and was interested in me only as a justification of himself, who had failed in self-expression. My writing was his fulfilment and his excuse: this fills me with utter hopelessness, and sense of doom. I obeyed my father by expressing something important to him and ruined my husband, because it diverted my energy from him and involved us in bitter contest. Just as it was necessary to my father's *amour propre* that I should express something, it was necessary to my husband's male integrity that I should not. That poor man made the most heroic attempts to cover his hen and batter the love of words out of me. He failed and died of it. His failure and death have stricken our sons. Their splendid promise will be blasted in the universal ruin. Our story is of a decadence of which my verses are the index. Let me consider if there is any strength in my blood to redeem them.

While my husband's family, the Hepburns, were filling the great Croydon villa with their pride, their efficiency and their gloom, my people were in Wimbledon, at war with all that villas stood for. My father, from his small music shop, made a precarious living by selling sheets of music, a few instruments on the time-payment system, and by tuning the pianos of the local bourgeoisie.

The Wimbledon shop was poor cousin to the Croydon villa in as much as it was built of the same grey Victorian brick. But, whereas the villa was ornamented with carvings of apples and foliage round the windows, a fine tiled approach, an over-elaborate contrivance for the scraping of boots and a general look of being the whelp of a feudal deer-hound out of a Gothic pug-dog, the shop was built with great economy of bricks. Both dwelling places were statements in brick; crystallisations in clay of what was strong and enduring in the blood of the respective families. The villa was a bastardisation of the castle and the great house: the shop was a stabilisation of the hut and the booth. In the villa privilege was burlesqued and put to sleep: in the shop the mountebank was given a resting place and the peasant an airier abode.

CHAPTER I

The Harpers, my father's family, had lived on Shropshire land as tenant farmers for generations.

In the time of Queen Elizabeth, Mathew Harper, inflamed by the adventurous spirit of the times, travelled to London where he improved his fortunes and entered the church.

William Harper the first joined a troupe of mummers and played the fiddle in Shrewsbury, when Charles Stuart visited the town: William did not receive the six and eightpence due to him for his performance. This default may have coloured Harper politics which became radical in the nineteenth century in spite of their tenantships. William had issue, but only bastards by a tragedienne. No Harper condoned the bastards, and the music was a satisfaction only to Edwin who was not born till eighteen thirty-four.

In the time of George the second Andrew Harper followed his most distinguished kinsman to London where he made a considerable fortune. He left the bulk of his considerable fortune to found the Harper Adams Agricultural College, which exists to this day.

After the death of old Andrew, came a reaction from worldliness in William Harper the second. That strain of vagabondage, expressed in the fiddle playing and lechery of the first William, appeared as religious enthusiasm in the second. He sacrificed his family to the preaching and reforms of John Wesley, following the master round England, his good sense drugged by the lovely new hymns. By his absence, William neglected the farm: by his rabid nonconformity, he offended his landlord. He sacrificed his savings, some family silver, and three small freeholds to his enthusiasm, and left his family destitute. His son sank to be a farm labourer and starved in the fields with *his* son − the third William − during the worst days of the Napoleonic wars.

But in the third William, faith had become steady enough to be a source of strength. In spite of an early diet of mangel-wurzels, he had the vigour to obtain the tenancy of a farm ten miles away, across the county. Hitherto intelligence and adventure had left the farm. In William intelligence and adventure clung passionately to the land.

He married Mary Hobart, the daughter of a great contractor of Shrewsbury, Henry Hobart, who had made a fortune building bridges and canals. He lost the greater part of it in speculation, but not before Mary had received the best education that Shrewsbury could provide which included maths and Adam Smith. He joined the Wesleyan Methodists, compensating for the loss of his fortune by an enthusiasm as entire as that which had ruined the second William Harper.

William Harper the third was, by this time, a local preacher of considerable eloquence. Most steadfast of the Harpers, he had a virtuosity in religious soliloquy equal to the fiddle virtuosity of the vagabond Harper who had been owed money by his King. He had a long, lithe body, a mop of bracken-coloured hair, fine eyes. His features were pure like those of a woman who is maternal even to masculinity. His eloquence brought many female penitents to God.

Henry and Mary Hobart heard him preach in the Shrewsbury Bethel. Their passionate sympathy was intensified by their common admiration for William. Henry Hobart lost, in his enthusiasm for William, some of the anguish he felt for his dead son. Mary Hobart appreciated the soundness of William's doctrine. She also, in imagination, compared him to St Paul and, if sensual feeling had been possible to her, it would have been neutralised by the association of her sensations with what she felt about the great apostle: but sensual feelings were not possible to Mary Hobart. Her emotions had been strained by pity for her desolate father, and her imagination had been usurped by a religious enthusiasm that had been impregnated by a strong and mature will. It is probable that Mary Hobart was a natural virgin of the type that has made certain convents places of true peace, but her father transmitted to Mary the idea of marriage as he had transmitted certain ecstacies of religious feeling and faith. Mary, with uncharacteristic lack of reserve, talked the matter over with William and he agreed that they should only share a bed when she desired conception. She agreed to have a numerous family. After their marriage she drove over to the farm with William prepared for a decision. When she dismissed him to his bedroom on their wedding night, she said 'If I don't like the life here, I shall not remain'. William showed no sign of weakness, but he developed a slight tremolo when leading the congregation in prayer. After a year Mary had a guidance from the Lord that she should conceive, and requested that her parents' marriage bed should be brought over from Shrewsbury. Six months earlier old Henry Hobart had died in it.

The Lord was inscrutable in the fruit he granted from what was almost an immaculate conception. Young Edwin pushed himself into the world breech first, and could not afterwards be relied on for any conformity of deportment. By the end of his first year he had developed a mop of black hair, fierce eyes and an infrangible will. No chastisement could shake him from his purpose, but his attention could be diverted by unexpected sounds. Edwin listened, not to the voice of reproof or command, but to sounds of his choosing. Disturbingly, at the end of his second year he could sing any tune that was whistled to him though he was backward in speech. At the end of the child's third year, he could sing a part, and invent harmony to any tune. It was then his father began to regard him with revulsion.

There was no place in William's scheme of things for music, except for hymns sung in unison in the Bethel. There was no hint of the Bethel in the gaiety of young Edwin's harmonisation of *Lillibullero* to the whistling of the ploughmen. William whipped Edwin for making music with them. In good time a delicate, gentle boy was born, with one foot twisted in a manner which would always make him lame. Two years later a third boy was born, almost without pain. He was whole physically but became distinguished only by his conformance with every norm. Of the disciplined loves of William and Mary was issue; a man of potential genius, a consumptive ascetic, and an utter fool.

Lust still lurked in William, but so metamorphosed by the pressure of his will to continence that it was unrecognisable. His mind formulated but was not aware of lust's argument. If Mary ruled William in bed, he could control her in her connection with the farm. William brought in a manageress, a blood relation. Mary's province was narrowed to the parlour.

There Mary's heart and mind starved. She knew she had taken harm from her too passionate relationship with her father, and she determined to save her own children from the assault of her unpolarised energy. Edwin, early, began to woo for her attention with a precocious appreciation of what was authentically woman in her. William did not beat the angel of music out of Edwin: he beat the devil of revolt into him. Mary knew fear for the first time, in her awareness of that devil. An adult Edwin might have awakened and controlled her senses. The better part of Mary's valour was in flight from the advances of her sons. Edwin did not resent this evasion any more than he resented the beatings from his father. He reacted healthily and directly to his parents. Melody was to Edwin a specific against moral inflammation and heat. His precocious senses registered the nature of his mother's flight from him, and induced in him a humorous tenderness, an aseptic which would keep his spirit clear through adolescent adventures and a score of ugly loves.

In the meantime, Mary spent herself in pity for her second, crippled son; and occupied herself with her religion, and ritual philanthropy, stitching endless garments for the poor. In the evenings she read the Bible with William, but there was very little peace for her until, driven by a weight of idleness, she began to write down her thoughts and impressions. She moulded these into short essays written out on the thinnest of notepaper and gave the sheets to William – pathetic *témoins d'amour*. William received the sheets reverently, read them, did not understand, but put them away in his fine brass-bound desk. A generation later, Geoffrey, one of Edwin's sons who loved words as his father loved tunes, opened the desk and read the papers. On the morning after old William's death, he went again to the desk to find nothing but ash. One of the old man's last actions had been to destroy the evidence of his wife's love for him. It is as well for good prose that Jane Austen had no delicate-minded husband.

When Edwin was seven he met a cobbler in a neighbouring

village, a virtuoso on the bassoon. Delighted with the boy's singing, and his sense of perfect pitch, he fired the boy with a desire to play the fiddle. Edwin scraped together every penny he could to acquire one, and at last had saved enough to buy a fiddle, which they brought back to the cobbler's shop. Soon the boy could play simple tunes.

When Edwin was proficient, the cobbler offered to take him to play at a servants' ball. He stole back to the farm late that night, and hid his fiddle in the hay loft. Next morning, William heard of his son's appearance at the ball. He found the fiddle, brought the boy into the parlour where Mary was sitting at her knitting, broke the fiddle across his knee, and thrust it into the fire. He told Edwin to remember Hell-fire from the fiddle flames, and to forget music and all lewdness. Mary made no sort of protest, merely detaching herself by closer attention to her needlework.

There is no evidence that William's brutal action blackened the boy's mood against his father. Edwin knew, instinctively, that, in burning the fiddle, William was in tune with himself. Rather he blamed Mary, who had not the energy or the courage to defend her standards, for Edwin knew that it was not in Mary's scheme of things to have property destroyed.

Some months later Edwin set fire to the farm when he was reading Macaulay in bed with a forbidden candle. This was not an attempt at revenge by the boy; but William feared revenge, and must therefore have been capable of it. He made arrangements for Edwin to go to the Grammar School in Shrewsbury, to be educated until he was old enough to be apprenticed to a tradesman. Edwin could not study music in school, but he read precociously, and by the time he was fifteen he was an agnostic – an infant Ingersoll. Apprenticed to a linendraper, he had so little feeling for buttons and tapes that he lost the job after a few weeks, and went to work at the bakery.

He felt more at home among the cottage loaves and jam tarts. Jeremy, the baker, a deaf, kind man who loved his horses, had one sorrow: a regret that he had never qualified as a veterinary surgeon. Among the lumber at the bakery Edwin found an old clavichord on which, when he had it mended and tuned, he would play bits of Mozart. The baker was too deaf to hear the music, but he enjoyed the happiness of his apprentice. Edwin made quite a passable young baker.

He made love to a number of women, never giving any great

offence. He was even wooed by the squire's daughter, a bobby dazzler, in Shropshire parlance.

Mary heard of this friendship and turned the whole of her energy towards heading Edwin into a safe marriage. She chose Alicia – the daughter of the workhouse master, a natural son of the lord of the manor. He had lived it down by marrying a lovely Puritan wife, who washed the feet of the paupers with her own hands. One day in drink he had gone as usual into the inn and was reaching for a plate of fine black cherries on the bar, when the barmaid snatched the plate away, saying 'Buy your own cherries'. The lord's bastard, wounded that the public-house *bonhomie* he had taken to be real was spurious, swore that he would never enter an inn again. He kept his word, and became so good an economist that the paupers appeared ever afterwards in second-hand tall hats. 'Buy your own cherries' became the theme of a famous temperance tract.

'There is more joy in Heaven over one sinner that repenteth . . .' Mary felt that Edwin would have contantly before him the example of conversion. Alicia was tone-deaf, with no particular physical attractions, but she had a great natural turn for chastity, due perhaps, to her awareness of her father's illegitimacy. To Edwin one woman was very like another. Moreover the workhouse master had considerable savings, since he had long been at no expense for beer. Edwin extracted from him a dowry with Alicia, left the bakery and set himself up as a musician. He taught music, played the organ at an Anglican church, herded all the girls and boys for miles around into his choral society to sing the 'Hallelujah Chorus' – for the glory of Handel, and in defiance of the fires of Hell for ever.

In Shropshire his most intelligent companion was the editor of the local paper, the son of a Staffordshire potter. The parson, the only man with a university education, had been withheld from communication with Edwin by the strict divisions of sect and caste.

Edwin's musical genius, and great, though undisciplined, energy saved him from the common forms of fear that are expressed in envy and imitation of social betters. An artist does not imitate – he discovers. His innate feeling of being a freeman of the great commonwealth of art saved him from a sense of inferiority. He had no resentment at going into houses, where he was despised even by the servants, to tune the pianos of savages who had never heard of Johann Sebastian Bach. His pride was that his ear was true, and it was necessary to him that things should be in tune. In that was the foundation of his unassailable dignity.

Alicia, a dyspeptic, with an ugly habit of breaking wind, was a bad housekeeper but a devoted wife. Unable to appreciate his music because of her tone-deafness, she became fiercely proud of his music, the very weakness from which she had been chosen to defend him, because it distinguished him from other village husbands. She had a most intemperate pride in distinction. On a new schoolmaster from Cumberland, who set up in rivalry to Edwin at the local Presbyterian Church, Alicia composed a lampoon beginning with the line 'A hoarse bull-frog from the North he came', a reference to the schoolmaster's very raucous voice. The satire is said to have been poignant enough to drive the schoolmaster from the village. Alicia was not the only poet in the village. On the tomb of one of the farmers are these lines written by himself:

> With sweat and toil I long have tilled the ground,
> And in it now a resting place have found.
> God gave command, and rest from toil I must;
> He stopt my plough and turned me to dust.
> But as the finest wheat from dust does spring,
> I hope to rise again with Christ, my king.

Alicia gave birth to endless children, with an ugly accompaniment of belching, her plain face pulled awry with privation and pain. As soon as they could walk and speak, Edwin taught them the elements of music. In the eighth year of her marriage, Alicia developed arthritis. She had, by this time, six children and a seventh on the way. Nevertheless, fired with great energy and great enthusiasm, Edwin raised enough money to open a music shop in Hampstead's Haverstock Hill, opposite 'The Load of Hay'. The spirit of these migrating Harpers was expressed by the already half-bedridden Alicia. When some villager mocked Edwin's hope of succeeding in London with 'Aye, and he'll find his level in London', Alicia replied to him, 'Yes, he'll find his level in London, and maybe he'll level up'.

In London, he became organist at a Catholic church. He loved the fine three-manual organ as his father had loved his farm, and the shop pulsed with the sensuousness of Catholic music, rather to the discomforture of the very Protestant Alicia. Her temperance blood stirred uneasily to the strains of 'Kyrie Eleison', the more so after she had caught sight of a tousle-haired, big-bosomed barmaid outside 'The Load of Hay' for she still hobbled out to take the air. With the increasing torture of her arthritis, Alicia became more and more intolerant of errant loves.

Edwin realised that his modest success as an organist was quite disproportionate to the special talent he had been born with. But he did not wreak his disappointment on his children. He scanned every new pair of hands for technical facility, and looked down every throat for a great voice. Geoffrey, his eldest son, had inherited his father's taste for general reading, but could be taught to play ponderously only Schumann's 'Merry Peasant' on the piano. The younger Harpers were passably musical and somehow Edwin found the money to educate them. He sent Mary and Beatrice to the Royal Academy of Music, one to study the piano, the other composition, and throughout their lives these two good virgins taught arts they could not practise, with great insistence on the perfection of routine technique.

Charlie, the second son, had enough talent to be a performer, but he was kept for years uninstructed because he had cut off the top of a finger in a chaff-cutter. Sent to the city to be a stockbroker's clerk, he remained for two weeks, then came home and threw his top hat out of the window. He began working on a difficult sonata of Beethoven, compensating for his stump of a finger by never stopping practising, and made the best teacher of them all.

Edwin established a dance band; piano (himself), fiddle and viola, for which he wrote waltzes which were published, so that everybody was proud and delighted.

Gertrude, the third of Edwin's girls, had a true talent for flower-painting. Trained at an art school she drew marigolds with the strength and precision of a man. But nothing came of it, for she married the son of a baker and went back to Shropshire.

The musical virgins – Mary and Beatrice – felt that Gertrude had betrayed them. Transplantation to London and qualifications from the Royal College had done nothing to alter their essential type. With the long patience of the farm worker, the shrewdness and passion for survival of the shopkeeper, they worked at the piano as their forefathers had worked with the plough, their labours rewarding them with the smugness and feelings of self-establishment experienced by an older generation which had believed in 'salvation by election'. They believed in salvation by correct method. With what feelings of superiority they practised piano gymnastics, a penny balanced on the back of the hand to suppress the joint of the first finger. Years of this ended in a tentative rendering of a Chopin prelude, in which everything was present but the Chopin. But O the glory of the WORK that had gone before!

The sisters were not strong enough to be sincere. Envying and wishing to enter the professional class, at the same time they despised it.

But there was sincerity in Geoffrey. He it was who had tried to preserve his grandmother's writings. To see Geoffrey touch a book was to witness a caress. He had no special love of bindings: but the pleasure he had from beautiful work, an illuminating argument, a keen piece of observation, made him love the page which presented it. Books were to Geoffrey what music was to Edwin, and the farm to old William. By reading, he separated himself from the narrow efficiency which was the condition of his ordinary living.

Geoffrey had an almost womanish desire to merge himself in some admiration, to destroy himself in some worship, so that his zeal for great writers sapped his creative energy, and paralysed his own very considerable talent. He read *Origin of Species*, rejoicing in what he considered to be the final overthrow of Jehovah by Darwin's observation of the stick-insect and the battling butterflies of Borneo, but he never attempted the hard ways of the biologist, or came to personal grips with the butterflies of Borneo. If he had known anything very definite about butterflies, it would have spoiled their beauty for him, and made dry as dust the magic of their appearing so aptly in an argument. He read Herbert Spencer for the narcotic of the phrases. 'The Spirit of Truth in things erroneous', he repeated the words in an ecstasy, as his grandfather had savoured the sentences of St Paul. He was too awed for imitation. To have become, himself, a man of science would have involved Geoffrey in self-worship. To his essentially religious temperament, this was impossible.

Edwin had turned from Methodism in a passionate reaction because it menaced the very life of his spirit. But for Geoffrey, agnosticism had already begun to develop rituals. The reading of Comte, Hegel and Herbert Spencer began to have a semi-magical value like that found in early religious practices. Geoffrey had inherited the worship-desire of his forefathers. The Postitivist Society met in Essex Hall, and there the spirits of great men were held to be more rational objects of adoration than the deity. They were saints of the machine, rather than saints of God. God was, by this time, like certain of the apes, called anthropomorphic. This putting God right into life did not bring Him any nearer, and it thrust great men further away. They became a hierarchy, privileged by their well-advertised attainments, to strike a respect, a religious fear, into such natural worshippers as Geoffrey.

In the shop parlour there was always conversation. Alicia was still periodically pregnant, in spite of her crutches. She wore a stained black dress with a pink cameo of Venus at the neck, which kept in place a dog-eared piece of real lace. She exploited her pregnancies to arouse in Geoffrey a brutalising antagonism to his father. She won Mary and Beatrice to her side in loathing Edwin's provincial manners. Alicia associated his irritability and his shortcomings as a tradesman with his passion for music. It was certainly necessary for Alicia to see that Edwin earned enough to supply the family with food, and herself with liniments, which she had rubbed into her joints, though without noticeable abatement of pain or stiffening. Piano tuning, and the sale of fiddle strings and sheet music showed more profit than did enthusiasm for John Sebastian Bach. Once again, the Harpers honoured the craftsman to the exclusion of the artist.

Alicia held Edwin to the service of her family by the power of her intellect. She undermined his position with the children by substituting her own values for his. That apart, she allowed him all the liberties of the Victorian father. He stormed, he bullied, he kicked the walnut what-not. Once an eye-enticing barmaid at the 'Load of Hay' led him to tear up his Will – the Will in which he had transmitted to his dependants the mill, the grocer's shop, the ten acres of freehold land and his father's savings. Alicia herself was not in fear of these fits of rage, but she exploited them to discredit Edwin with his family. Still, she listened to her husband as he poured out everything that was in his mind. To her, he read Comte, Hegel, J.S. Mill and Herbert Spencer. Perhaps she did not understand everything, but she made a great audience. Once a weakness of the flesh overcame her, and she dozed a little. 'You're asleep,' shouted Edwin – like

Othello, at this infidelity of her attention. 'No, I was only resting my eyes.'

New, grander, acquaintances of the Harpers fell into three groups. First were students the girls brought home from the R.A.M. and the Art School, friends chosen for their superior social standing. Sophy and Mabel Carruthers were the daughters of an artists' supplier in the Charing Cross Road. Carruthers *père* was a master mason, with endless aprons and dignity-endowing little pieces of ribbon, displayed in a glass-covered box in the parlour.

Mrs Carruthers kept a good table: Gertrude was a born guest, with her flow of high spirits, and cheerful amiability. She had the charming accomplishment of being able to high-kick in the best manner of the nineties, a trick learned from the maid-of-all-work who had been in a pantomime chorus and lightened her dungeon of an underground kitchen by spirited renderings of 'You can go to the deuce and the girls don't care', with an appropriate mime and dance. Gertrude began to learn about more luxurious forms of food, and, as her talent for cooking was as distinguished as her talent for water-colour painting, a new scale of living developed at the Harpers.

Mary and Beatrice were now bringing in money from their music teaching: Geoffrey was helping his father, so doubling receipts from the piano tuning. An occasional pheasant, with brown breadcrumbs and a rich sauce, a lobster salad, and a complicated pudding, kept Edwin in good humour, and reinforced the family's feeling of social well-being. But it was Mary and Beatrice who made the first contact with the professional classes. Jessie Matthews, daughter of a deceased land-agent, and sister to a doctor in the Navy, was attracted to Beatrice. She admired her stonily unemotional rendering of *Ich Grolle Nicht* and the purity of her German. The youngest of Edwin's girls, Matilda, unlike her sisters was quite a beauty; she played the 'cello in the new ladies' orchestra at the St James Restaurant, and had a good enough figure to have been a mannequin at Lady Warwick's pioneer dress shop in Bond Street. Matilda (also known as Tid) married a rich, young German merchant and so escaped from retail trade for ever.

The second group was made up by musicians and singers. The contralto had sung on the same platform as Sim Reeves, and an oboist had played in the orchestra at the Milan Opera House.

The third, consisted of customers who, having first entered the shop for some sheet music or a fiddle string, had been attracted by Edwin's skill as an organist, and by the character and peculiarity of the Harper family. Among these were folk of real distinction of birth. For the most part, eccentrics, renegades from their families which they had found lacking in vitality and interest, they assumed to the Harpers an attitude of polite patronage. They would have explained their attraction in terms of the artistic talents of the family, but in truth they depended on the Harpers' upthrusting energy to supply them with the vigour that had been bred out of their own class. In these contacts, the spirit of descending aristocracy, and the spirit of ascending peasantry meet as in a love embrace. Both are bisexual, and have alternating powers of conception and impregnation. If the aristocrat spirit begets, the peasant gains in fineness and pliability of energy, and begins to establish a new master class. The Harpers were not at all aware of what made them attractive to their patrons, but they were impressed by the idiom of their new friends. There is no better school of manners than among the descending gentility.

Miss Sumner, who played the oboe, was a daughter of a late Archbishop of Canterbury. Her Scottish family was immensely distinguished. She had found Canterbury dull, and now made a point of knitting in the shop parlour on Sunday evenings, while the talk ran high against Paley. There had been no knitting on Canterbury Sundays; and Dorothea jabbed away her old boredom, with every thrust of her needles, working her way to freedom with every movement of her hands. She taught Mary and Beatrice genteel speech, but Gertrude, more talented than her sisters but with negligible powers of imitation, when she married the baker's son, fell back into her Shropshire accent, which the Harpers held against her for the rest of her life.

Dr Spencer, rich from an inherited gold-lace business, had taken his medical degree late when he was nearly forty. He was a Fellow of the Royal Astronomical Society, a fact very much admired by Geoffrey, and a fact which was to have a determining effect on his daughter's life. His wife, a large, good-looking woman, had no children, and held her husband by good housekeeping and her impudent vitality. She was a dilettante in all the arts, and, having strayed into the shop for a sheet of music, she remained to play Mendelssohn with Mary, and to sing *Liede* with the lugubrious Beatrice. The three women shared a fierce exaltation of chastity.

Dr Spencer, cheated of a son of his own, became a powerful influence on Geoffrey, who began to think of taking a medical degree. Alicia, approached her brother, a country doctor contributor to the *Lancet*, and an authority on diseases of the ear. He was also childless. His wife, a stout churchwoman, opposed Geoffrey's application because, she said, he was undisciplined and irreligious. Disappointed in his wish to be a doctor, Geoffrey went to work at a piano factory, where he became very efficient with the insides of the pianos, and began to learn organ building. He suffered feelings of inferiority at being little more than a factory hand, became melancholy, nervous, and was afflicted with an outcrop of boils. Looking back self-pityingly at this period, he said that he lived chiefly on badly fried steak and slabs of shop-made plum cake. He continued to read with a fretted and angry mind. It was at this time that Geoffrey – my father – met my mother, Alice.

CHAPTER II

My mother had also been a factory hand. For six dismal weeks at Hart and Weatherby's in Kentish Town she had learned to paint, on superfine notepaper, those heavy black edges which were demanded by Victorian bereavement. Mother was a very good 'black-borderer': she had large, beautiful hands, sensitive and individual in shape. I only once saw hands like them: those of Sarah Bernhardt. My mother's thumbs turned back a very long way, which gave her an extra turn of speed with the black-bordering. The six weeks at the paper factory took away, for the rest of her life, all the pleasure she might have had in craftsmanship.

My maternal grandmother, Martha Whelan, was of problematic origin. Her father was a cobbler. Her mother used the surname Burnell, but this was thought to be an anglicisation of an Italian name. Jonanna Burnell died in a workhouse in England at an advanced age, leaving some beautiful examples of her needlework.

She was said to be quite illiterate and to have shown great servility to the church ladies, which was very much at variance with the independence of character of the rest of the family. My mother would not have called the Queen her aunt.

Martha had been adopted and lived in Belgium until she was fifteen. Then something happened in Belgium and Martha was sent to her mother − in London. She was a beautiful girl in the Florentine manner.

Later, Martha married Michael Whelan, my grandfather, a plumber of Irish peasant stock, who had left Ireland at the time of the expropriation of the cottagers. He made Martha a kind husband, sang charmingly, and left a treasure of beautiful folk stories as the only inheritance to his children. Martha soon adapted herself to living in two backrooms in Camden Town and became a notably good manager. By the time she was twenty, she had three children: first a girl Helen, then a boy George, and then a girl, Alice, who was to be my mother. Michael developed pthisis and died, as seven out of eight of his family had died, of this disease. But the disease never attacked Martha's children. Martha was left without a penny, to face the situation alone with her beauty and her three small children.

Martha had got to know George Cruikshank who lived, at this time, in Mornington Crescent. George lent her five pounds, to pay for the poor funeral, and to start herself and her young family in life. Michael Whelan, taken in a plain deal box, to Highgate Cemetery, was lowered into a hole containing seven other coffins mouldering in ghastly nearness. The family felt it very bitterly that Michael could not be alone in death, and my mother has always stipulated more dignified obsequies for herself. She says that she is to be cremated. The master-plumber sent a wreath, the cobbler a bunch of white marguerites, and the people in the top floor back expressed themselves in a wealth of violets, for they were flower-sellers. These flowers lived happily in my mother's mind as the redeeming beauty of a bitter day. Helen and George went in the mourning coach with Martha, for the baby Alice was thought too young to be taken. She was left to play in the street, the doors of the house locked against her: she never forgot her feelings of abandonment. I think her melancholy and hysteria had their roots in that awful day as had also her aloneness, the great source of her strength.

My grandmother was too steadfast to keep her family by the easy way of whoring, but she could exploit her beauty by being an artist's model. George Cruikshank gave her introductions to his friends. Middle-Victorian pictures seem full of her head and hands and feet. Often I see her or parts of her in the Tate Gallery, and I am heartened as I think of the hours of patience and tedium that went to make the half-crowns to fill the little stomachs and cover the little bodies.

Martha found a Welsh lover among the artists, Lister by name and a gentleman. He went off to New Zealand and left her pregnant. Even this added burden my grandmother was able to bear. The new baby, Annie, became a successful child model: she is still to be seen smirking out of pictures of the period with a blue sash round her tummy.

When times were bad my grandmother went charring, made chenille hair-nets, did endless miles of tatting, and was caretaker to austere Hampstead families away on holiday. She made her children's clothes, and cooked their food on her return from work. She had always a sense of quality in clothes, so the children's pinafores were of fine diaper, and spotlessly white. From years of strain and self-abnegation she developed a lung disease. She seldom had money for the simplest remedies, but sometimes one of the artists would send the family some article of luxury – a pineapple or an iced cake. These gifts seemed magical manifestations to the children, and there were other glimpses of splendour.

An eccentric old barrister in Hampstead gave them a silver sixpence each when Martha finished caretaking for him at the end of the long vacation. A young lodger on the third floor, assistant in an oil-shop, on Sunday mornings, as if to clear his mind of small change forever, always threw his farthings into the yard below, where the children hunted for them. Delightful pieces of dolls' furniture and odds and ends of confectionery could be bought in Camden Town in those days for a farthing. God bless all these generosities which robbed poverty of the grinding monotony which is the greatest hardship for the children.

Martha sent her children to the Church of England School. The girls showed great proficiency, but George, a rather stupid boy, she sent into the navy. When he sailed away to the Ashanti war her heart died with fear. George, however, took no more harm than from a bag of coal which fell from a winch and hit him on his nose. He carried the blue mark of the grafted coal-dust to his death.

On Saturdays the children helped out by making chenille hair-nets. Martha was able to save a little money, took a house in Henrietta Street, and added to her income by letting lodgings. By this time Helen had left school, and Alice was soon to join her for six wretched weeks at Hart and Weatherby's and the black-bordering. Martha had a natural love of poetry and kept an early copy of the *Ingoldsby Legends*, given to her by George Cruikshank, in her kitchen-table drawer. Alice had a reputation for being a great reciter, and ventured an audition at a suburban musical hall, but this attempt was half-hearted, for Martha feared both the uncertainty of the stage and its doubtful reputation.

The School Board for London was established, and wanted teachers. Martha saw here a possible career for her clever girls. Teaching was a respectable profession, and the board-school teachers were chosen from the cream of the small tradesmen and working class. Helen and Alice crammed together, sacrificing their youth and their nervous health to the demands of competitive examinations. This new generation of teachers became a segregated class. Losing contact with their own class, they became outposts of the governing class in the great marsh of illiterate democracy, yet were not acknowledged by, or admitted freely into, other long estab-lished classes of brainworkers. They developed an inferiority com-plex, accompanied by a cocksureness which was destructive of a creative mind. Compensating aggression for this has often been a crippling handicap even to artists and writers of genius.

A more influential as well as more talented lodger joined the family circle. His father was a judge, opposed to his son making painting his profession, but Frank Potter escaped from their fine house in Hampshire, to paint in Camden Town. Although he even-tually became engaged to Helen, to whom he bequeathed his pictures and what money he had, he was really in love with my grandmother. He painted a very fine portrait of her. One of his pictures, the *Music Lesson* in the Tate Gallery, shows my mother Alice seated at the piano teaching a small girl. To paint her so showed insight, for she was a magnificent teacher. I have never forgotten the English gram-mar she taught me, though her vigorous enunciation made me feel like a tombstone under the chisel of a stone mason.

Martha had a natural taste in painting which had been developed in the studios of the artists for whom she had sat. Later Potter's work

69

received considerable attention. The family opposition had left its mark on him. He stuttered a good deal, avoided society, painted very slowly, and was overcritical of his work. The French bought a number of his pictures, and the portrait of my grandmother is now in the Louvre. The only personal recollection of him I've been able to find is from Aunt Gertrude, the flower painter. She remembers he would air his underclothes by his studio fire until they were scorched brown, and this she told me with scorn.

Aveling, the atheist lecturer, was also an habitué at 401, Camden Road. Aveling took the girls about with him, notably to fine feasts at the Holborn Restaurant, the memory of which lived on into my childhood to allure me in my turn with the names and knowledge of complicated foods. When he set up house with Eleanor Marx, they sent a notice to their wide circle of friends, inviting them to an entertainment which was to be a ratification of their union. This made a great stir at the time when free unions were unusual in spite of the example of George Eliot and George Henry Lewis. Aveling soon tired of Eleanor Marx sexually. Dolly Radford, her best friend, told me that he left her deliberately over the weekend she committed suicide.

My mother, Alice, was for a time Aveling's secretary. One Christmas when the other girls received elegant presents from him she was given a large supply of notepaper which she used afterwards for his correspondence. Neither the youngest nor the eldest nor yet a boy, she seemed always to be having the worst of things. Aveling got Alice a job at the theatre in the Royal Polytechnic in Regent Street, which later became a cinema. They were showing a set of tableaux-vivants of scenes from the life of Mary Queen of Scots. Alice recited verses, very bad verses, illustrative of the tableaux, from the stage. She did this so well that the critic of the *Illustrated London News* wrote an article calling her the new Siddons.

Her talent might have carried her into the professional theatre if it had not been for the young Geoffrey Harper who watched her ardently, every night, from the gallery.

Geoffrey had met Alice Whelan at a dance at the Holborn Town Hall given by the dramatic society of which she was leading lady. Alice, splendid in a brown dress and long kid gloves, came on to the dance from the Polytechnic. He, his waltzing perfected by constant practice in the shop with an Austrian chair for partner, had taken his sister – the flower painter – to the dance. Gertrude wore a home-made white silk dress with a row of irridescent shells. She was a bad dancer and looked undistinguished, while Alice made clothes look better by her manner of wearing them. Alice could have filled her programme several times but Gertrude sat out most of the evening. From this night dated the critical attitude of all the Harper women towards Alice, who was to be, my mother, and my future father's love for her.

The Harpers had friends in the dramatic society who had known the Whelans at their poorest. Martha had actually charred for the Reeders; John Reeder was a sub-editor of a financial newspaper and his brother, James, did ornamented capital letters and drawings for *Punch* and everyone knew that *Punch* was *Punch* and very creditable indeed. John and James Reeder played chess with Edwin in the shop parlour: they were Catholics and acknowledged Edwin's pro-fessional status as organist at their church. Edwin had heard a rumour of Martha's indiscretion with Lister – the gentleman painter who had gone off to New Zealand. With the bitterness of the debauchee robbed of his debauch he was rude about it and so planted everlasting bitterness between the families. George Whelan, home from sea, was so enraged by Edwin's insult that he wanted to fight him. Somehow the fight was prevented. Never a very imposing figure, George, but he was a good son.

Helen and the child model, Annie Whelan, were both beautiful, so that Alice's good looks were rather passed over. She had fine brown eyes with very blue whites, and a magnificent forehead which she covered with a fringe. Later, she dyed her brown hair yellow, and curled her fringe into a serried thicket. Erysipelas had straightened her top lip which she thought entirely spoiled the shape of her mouth. It was, in fact, rather charming and suited her naturally mas-culine character, which she always tried to hide by emphasising femininity in her dress and appearance. Dissatisfied with her small breasts, she filled the pouches of her high stays with yards of cotten wool, which she drew out as she unbuttoned her bodice at night. She had a peculiar charm which was round her like a scent. In her moods of tenderness you could imagine a ray coming out of her, and to be near her was healing and peace: but in her moods of rage she emitted an aura of extreme tragedy which had a universal effect of paralysis.

God gives to plain women a special spiritual virulence for offence

71

or defence. If this were not so there would be few marriages. Alicia had held Edwin against all barmaids, all young women in choirs with promising soprano voices, all superior virgins with a pitying eye for the spoilt genius of the music-master. She was wary, while Alice was overconfident and inexperienced. Alicia decided to prevent the marriage. But my father's infatuation for my mother-to-be was, in part, a direct reaction from Alicia, against her slovenliness, her want of charm, and he was as doomed to fall to my mother's charm as the antelope is to the panther.

Geoffrey called at Camden Road early one morning, partly to see how Alice looked in the morning, thinking that no slut ever looked presentable before eleven o'clock. He found her at breakfast, the very perfection of neatness. Martha's good cooking and orderliness were in happy contrast to the scramble and grubbiness of the shop. While she was at the Board School, Alice had attended a course of lectures on Physiology given by Thomas Henry Huxley: this convinced him of the inevitability of his love, for one of his heroes was Thomas Henry Huxley.

The Whelans intensified their attack. They commented on Geoffrey's choosing such an eccentric hour to present himself and on the meagreness of his excuse in bringing a book for one of the girls. As if any girl really wanted a book! They ridiculed his clothes and his conversation; his clothes for the contrast of their poor quality with his dandified way of wearing them; his conversation for its verbosity and pretentiousness.

In the eighties conversation was a creditable social art. Geoffrey knew this and had no shame in talking. A sympathetic audience might have stimulated him to make a more permanent record of his thought but, though the young women listened with necessary politeness to Geoffrey's flow of words, it aroused in them ridicule and antagonism. With the exception of a few Shropshire provincialisms, Geoffrey used the same sort of words as the lecturers at the Polytechnic. The young women pounced on his defects like herring-gulls on a fish swarm. Their own speech had a Cockney intonation but they were stridently correct about small points of grammar. Geoffrey was an apprentice piano-tuner, with frayed trouser ends and a rather noisy way of eating, who carried his tools in a black bag, and therefore had no right to his professional speech style. The Whelan girls had dissociated themselves from tool-users forever when they had passed the examinations which put them in the class of brain-workers. It did not strike them that they brought to their work the quality of the factory hand, that their textbooks were to them so many tools. Learning by heart could now be, thanks to the 1870 Education Act, exploited as a way of earning a living with more comfort and respect than that of a factory hand. But where was the sense of taxing the mind or overburdening the memory for any less practical use than making a living? Their attitude was very like that of my future father-in-law, James Hepburn, who had given his eldest son a gold sovereign for repeating a chapter of the Book of Job by heart.

The mass of the people were developing a sense of power which was supported by a constantly expanding suffrage. The Hepburn class had an instinct for maintaining the *status quo*, and policed the rising democracy with young Whelans, an efficient police force which has protected the tradition of the Hepburn class for a generation: the ground has been held for the Hepburns by penalising imagination and putting genius under restraint.

They have allowed no hero to rise to save the citadel of democracy, for no hero after his contact with popular education has ever been wholly himself. The Board School castrated the mind of my father as it did later that of D.H. Lawrence.

The sterilisation of my father was begun on the morning of that first breakfast. Geoffrey, in a fine criticism of Marx, had crossed his legs and grown so strenuous in argument that his right foot had firmly embraced his left leg, so that the legs began to resemble the twisted stem of a Venetian wineglass. Admonitory finger raised, he constantly interspersed his talk with the phrase 'D'you see', and, in a crisis of argument, he sniffed. Marx quite annihilated, Geoffrey definitely sniffed. Helen, hiccoughed to hide a hoot of derisive laughter. She had not followed the argument but she knew Geoffrey was ridiculous. Helen knew also that Marx lived in an impressive house in Maitland Park, and that Dr Aveling had been very proud of his connection with Marx's daughter. Who then was Geoffrey with his lanky forefinger and his black bag to be making fun of Karl Marx? Alice noted the hoot of laughter!

Alice had been brought up to respect Helen as the eldest, and the best at examinations, but she wanted to assert herself against this respect. She was jealous of Martha's preference for Helen whom she knew to be selfish and rather dull. Helen in her turn was jealous of

Alice because of her superiority at the Dramatic Society, and her power of attracting people. Many young men had wanted Alice while Helen had only the devotion of Frank Potter, and the not altogether creditable attentions of Dr Aveling. Frank Potter and Dr Aveling were gentlemen at any rate. Helen was not really sure in her heart that Geoffrey was as ridiculous as she wanted to think him. But surely there was something ridiculous in Alice's way of looking at Geoffrey, or rather in her way of not looking at him. A queer stillness seemed to possess Alice in the presence of Geoffrey. Here evidently was a new and intriguing situation, and if Helen was to endure as leader of the Whelans she must leave her mark on it. So Helen hooted with laughter at Geoffrey. She had assayed his amateurishness with the tests of her board-school professionalism, and found the young man spurious.

Geoffrey was eternally an amateur, the Whelans were professionals. No University Extension lecturer had told the young Whelans that the great artist is always an amateur. If they had been told this they would not have been able to apply the truth to their own lives. And yet the truth applied to them: as models, chenille net makers, knitters, teachers, they were professional: in acting only they were amateur, and in acting only were they artists. Helen played Desdemona perfectly in the Dramatic Society's production at the Camden Theatre. Somehow she understood with her heavy blood. Alice, more gifted, understood with her senses and instinct.

Annie Whelan, the child model, had by this time become a pupil teacher. In the elder Whelans the mixture of Irish and Italian bloods had made for sturdiness and resistance with flashes of brilliance, and in Alice something almost approaching genius. But the Lister Welsh admixture with the Italian seemed to neutralise both. Annie had an inherited lethargy, and existed rather by habit than by any particular effort of her own. Her attitude to Geoffrey was vaguely hostile. In this she followed Helen, as she had followed her into the board-school.

George regarded Geoffrey as a young man with a thin neck and very small biceps who had never been to sea.

Martha was kind, not vulgarised by education, her fine quality refined rather than hardened by her struggle for life. She found Alice with her hysteria, epilepsy and black moods, very difficult, and might have been inclined to pity Geoffrey if Helen had not carried on a constant campaign against him. Helen pointed out to Martha that the second time Geoffrey called for tea he had eaten almost all of a two-pound bag of strawberries he had brought for Alice, carried into a state of absentmindedness by his attempt to explain to her exactly what Herbert Spencer meant by 'pangenesis'. To Martha, a great part of whose life had been spent in dividing an insufficient quantity of food equitably, this action of Geoffrey's seemed very damning.

There was some promise in the loves of Geoffrey and Alice, some possibility they would supplement each other, react on one another in such a way that the aspiration towards power and attainment which was in both their families might be realised in them. The Harpers and the Whelans, both fiercely proud, both striving for some visible justification of their pride, might have joined hands to foster the potential strength that lay in the combination of their bloods. The love of Alice and Geoffrey had too firm a physical basis to allow the opposition of their families to be effective against it. But there is no doubt that Helen and Alicia, who were the faction leaders, sowed seeds of dissention and maladjustment. Alice never forgave Geoffrey for not knowing how he exposed himself to the scorn of Helen. The hatred which grew up in her for Geoffrey's intellectual interests was rooted less in any antipathy natural to her, than in the feelings of shame she experienced at the judgement of her sister.

Meanwhile the loves of Geoffrey and Alice went along happily. Geoffrey went every night to the Polytechnic to watch Celia from the gallery, and on Sundays there were excursions to Epping Forest and walks on Hampstead Heath and in the fields around Hendon. Sometimes Alice would cut the fringes off his turnups and so put him beyond Helen's criticism. Alice knitted him socks with the wonderful marching heel, the same heel that Martha had knitted for her brothers when they were away at the Crimean War and she would listen to his reading while she sewed shirts for him, fine shirts with gussets in them, such as she had learnt to cut out and sew for the sewing tests at the Board School. Geoffrey would deny himself a bus home so that he could buy her things, though she was making much more money than he was. He gave her a book, a collection of Victorian poetry, large with fine gold scrolls and in-lay, saying, 'You can give that to the children to tear up', which showed that he had no sense of property whatever. A week later Alice knew that she was going to have a baby. Geoffrey was in a great hurry to marry her.

Edwin had enough fatherly feeling to put up fifty pounds to establish Geoffrey in a music shop in Wimbledon. So Alice had to abandon the theatre and become a shopkeeper's wife.

Alice was, by prejudice, darkly and sensually chaste. She had fits of being religious: when she had attended the Sunday evening meeting of a hot-gospeller, she came home and composed a hymn, crying her repentance into the washing-up water:

> Death is the way to Heaven
> Death is one step from earth,
> It leads us into glory
> It gives us the new birth.

My mother liked death: it was spectacular. She liked diseases: they were a definite departure from the normal. Bored by the straightened conditions of her childhood, and by the ugly and monotonous routine of the Board School, all her life my mother courted dramatic situations. Geoffrey satisfied her sensationalism by the insistence and hurry with which he made an honest woman of her. He was ill in bed the day before the wedding and was pushed to church in a bathchair, much to the anger of the Harper women, who took it that their young man was being sacrificed to Alice's lust.

The wedding breakfast was heavy with the fine manners of Mary and Beatrice. Helen was lovely in an amber silk dress, a gift from Frank Potter. The warring gentilities of the young women seemed to stretch the air. The guests were definitely in two camps. Thus the union of my parents, Alice and Geoffrey, got off to a fidgety start.

There was no money for a honeymoon. In fact, there had only been money for a quarter's rent and a minimum amount of stock. Edwin had lent two or three second-hand pianos on the chance of a sale. The lovers quarrelled in the train. Geoffrey would have bought a ton of coal, but Alice wanted to begin with a hundredweight and keep a larger money reserve. This difference of opinion, which showed an essential difference of temperament, gave rise to angry feelings which spoiled the wedding night.

My parents could never agree on matters of business management, and the shop could never comfortably hold their two systems. Martha, that notable manager, always kept what money she had in a small china basket on the kitchen shelf, and cut her coat according to her cloth. A money shortage was met by automatic economy. My mother wanted to continue by this rule of thumb method, the advantages of which were clear to everybody. But Geoffrey had had a successful shopkeeper in his family, as well as old William Harper the farmer. William had kept books, and Geoffrey wanted to keep books. He bought a large account book in which to keep the tuning account before there were any pianos to tune. How this poor little ship kept afloat was a miracle. But are not all such survivals miracles? They let the best floor above the shop to a curate and his sister. And while my father was canvassing for tunings at the houses of the local superior people he thought of the curate reading Greek in seclusion above the shop, attended by a quiet and serviceable woman, and he became very jealous of the curate, for the ambition of his life was to have empty hours for dreams and a quiet room in which to write about them. My father tried to make my mother agree that they should never talk business on a Sunday, that the day which most people kept empty for God should be kept empty for books. But my mother, pregnant, bored, chafed by a poverty from which her family had worked its freedom, had only one recreation and that was in angry expostulation. For a greater part of Sunday she angrily expostulated. In spite of this, my father read widely, and he began a written controversy with the Christian Apologist, Redmond, which might have established him in the coveted habit of writing regularly, if it had not been for explosive tactics by my mother.

After six months in the shop, a boy was born. People were told that he was premature, a story which could not be challenged for he was born dead. Poor young Geoffrey, for he was then only twenty-one, slept for a week on the sofa in the shop parlour with the little William laid out on what was the family dining table. The baby's namesake, William – the farmer – now a very old man, had retired from the farm and the mill to await his call to paradise. He sent a cheque to tide the young people over the tragic time. They could afford only the simplest of small coffins, and my father had no overcoat to wear at the funeral though it was on the coldest of winter days. The death of this small boy – my brother – decided the direction of my life, for my father made me a substitute for his dead son.

My mother was thrown into an agony of grief by the death of her love child, but it was in her nature to get the utmost dramatic effect

77

out of every situation in her life, and I imagine it was Geoffrey who felt the grief, and Alice who manifested it. She would leave her bed at night, throw a coat over her night-gown, and make her way to the graveyard. In this preoccupation with graves she was probably acting out a poem by Byron! Geoffrey would follow her, and bring her home.

A year later I was born. She had an epileptic fit during her labour with me, and I was helped into the world with forceps while my father sat, crying with terror, on the stairs outside the bedroom door. My mother's condition was so parlous that the midwife had no time for me, and I was actually put by on the chest of drawers for dead. I yelled, and so set out on my difficult way.

My father, very much in need of an intellectual companion, despaired of my ever having any brains as the forceps had left so many bruises on my head. In time, however, I healed and my capable mother made a creditable baby out of me. One evening when I was three months old she was bathing me by the sitting-room fire. Father was reading, his feet on the mantelpiece. Struck by a passage in his book, he brought down his feet upsetting a boiling kettle over me. My mother's hands were scalded and the greater part of my body. For sometime after, I lived in oiled cotton wool. For the second time I escaped death. I take it that God used these means to sensitise a nervous system to his uses! My mother suckled me until, when I was five months old, she contracted brain fever and I was sent to my grandmother Martha.

My mother recovered from her brain fever, and I soon revived under her management. I was sent out on the common daily with a nursemaid, and returned larger and rosier, clamouring for food. My mother's enthusiasm grew. She resented advice on my upbringing from the villa-dwellers who came into the shop to buy waltzes, but looking after me never gave her scope for all her energy. As she grew more and more bored with the shop, she became more and more appalled at the infamies of my father. He irritated her so much that she fell from one attack of hysterio-epilepsy to another. She went to Camden Road and complained about Geoffrey to Martha and Helen. This showed a change of heart in her: she no longer resented her sister's scorn of Geoffrey, though Helen stung my mother to fresh furies by the superiority of her smile.

My father, lonely and aggrieved, would go in his turn with a tale of woe to Mary and Beatrice. Judging everything by Sumner standards, they left confusion worse confounded. At the Wimbledon shop the gap between them widened and widened.

CHAPTER III

After some months of frustration my mother decided to get out. She sold a few trinkets left from her acting Polytechnic days, gathered her clothes together, took me, now eighteen months old, in her arms, and hired a furnished room in London. Somehow, though she hadn't enough money to pay the fare, she arranged a passage on a sailing ship to Australia. The Harper women, delighted that everything had happened which they most feared, said that she was the captain's mistress. My mother always told me that on board she did the sewing, but how there came to be so much sewing on a sailing ship she never attempted to explain. My mother loved the idea of the sea, she wanted to travel, she wanted to go to Australia, and she contrived to do what she wanted. Moreover, she had removed me from the contaminating influence of my father. She knew that my father loved me, and that I had begun to be a compensation to him. By removing me she punished him, though she was not at the time conscious of the motive, and her intentions towards me were fiercely right.

The first day on the sailing ship I burned my hand on the galley getting a hot potato for my mother. I can remember hot nights of sleeplessness in the bunk, and the tropic moon just beyond the porthole which I thought I could touch. I cannot remember a storm when, as my mother recalled, she, with me in her arms, was lashed to the mast. What we were doing on deck at the time heaven only knows, but my mother would have liked to be lashed to the mast. We were four months at sea. I can remember the shanties of the sailors. The night before we got to Sydney my mother went on deck in a rainstorm dressed only in an oilskin, which she opened at the neck to allow the rain to drench her. The day we landed she was taken to the public hospital with pneumonia.

I was put in some charitable institution, and the authorities communicated with my father. For six months he had not had the slightest idea of our whereabouts. There was a great conference of the Harpers. All the Harper women were for my father divorcing my mother, without being quite sure if he had cause. My father went down to Shropshire to consult old William, the farmer. The aged Puritan, who had very strict ideas on the indissolubility of marriage, said: 'Well, Geoffrey, my boy, she's your wife.' In this spirit of Christian forbearance and moral uplift, Father wrote to Mother to come home. William supplied a cheque for the fares. My mother, who had got a job in Sydney, refused the cheque but worked our passages back. We had been away in all a year.

I remember the return to Wimbledon, and the gloomy walk together up the hill from the station. My father had brought me a wicker doll's pram. He had better have brought flowers for my mother. Our absence had done nothing to improve my parents' relationship with one another.

But I was an immediate delight to my father. I wrote my first verses for him when I was four. I was already very sorry for my father and glad to find so easy a means of pleasing him. I felt we had common difficulties with my mother. I loved my mother passionately, how passionately! but this made me all the more vulnerable to her devastating fits of rage. For the offence of some small unrealised lie, or some piece of childish nastiness, she would turn on me the whole force of her great moral energy. Seriously concerned for my education, believing in corporal punishment, she would beat me with a stick. My mother ought not to have been cooped up in a small shop. She was a tragedienne. She wanted scope, a stage, and always a part to play. At four I sensed this, and I played the part with her to the limit of my strength. As she beat me I cried to her, 'Beat me, mother, but love me — O love me'. Enough of our scene and her mood would clear, and I would see again the old fairy mother with her scent and her sweetness. But I found it fatiguing and I attributed a like fatigue to my father.

I must have had a precocious talent for loving which my parents discovered in me, and used to make good the defects in their own relationship. In cycles they quarrelled and the house rocked with the storm, then my mother demanded my tears and my father my pity. I early found I could manage them, and early felt responsible for them. But I began to fear their periods of amity, for they would then become absorbed in each other. At first they would neglect me, but then turn the light of a common criticism on me − with a sincere desire to improve me. And I caught myself wishing that they would quarrel again. My mother detected this and very much resented it. She saw in me a rival to her husband's interest, and she did not like the Harpers well enough to want me to be the means of the fulfilment of any ambition of theirs. She began to attack me on the same grounds as she had attacked Alicia. She pointed out that I was slovenly, lacking in every practical capacity and all those very feminine attributes which went into her own make up. By the time I was six my mother knew that I was useless with my hands and my father knew that I was a poet, that I would be a glory to him, a compensation for the black bag, the small shop and all the ugly thraldoms of his life.

Meanwhile, life at the shop had its pleasant side. My father had attracted a number of the most intelligent men in the suburb. First, there was James Lecky − nephew of the Irish historian. James, born in his father's old age, was a great scholar and an authority on folklore. He seemed unable to play at anything, his lightest recreation being a game of chess. He died before he was thirty of brain depreciation. My father loved him very much and, while James lived, he supplied the sympathy and understanding which my father lacked in his marriage. Another of the circle was Henry Sweet, the philologist, and there was Henry FitzMaurice, a barrister, and lastly, of the intimates, George Riddell, at the time studying law. George afterwards became the newspaper peer, Lord Riddell. The friends would meet in the shop parlour on Sunday evenings to drink whisky and play whist, and to talk, endlessly to talk. My mother avoided these meetings. Jealous of them she made a show of finding so much talk ridiculous: it took my father's mind off his business and a man's duty was to provide for his family. The only one of the circle who really knew my mother was George Riddell and there is some reason to think that he knew her too well. Late in his life, when he was a bitter, parsimonious, very rich old man, he told me that he had learned everything he knew about women from my mother. Maybe the fullness of his suggestion is true and my mother chose him as a means of revenge on my father for the sententious way he had behaved after her return from Australia.

George Riddell at this time was married to an eccentric woman with a chronic skin disease. He was attracted by the great natural force of my mother. But he was too shrewd to form a permanent relationship with her, recognising the dangers of her over-emotional temperament. All the same he was ultimately beaten by her temperament.

My mother, a sensationalist, delighted in tales of crime and loved to read about murders. Murders were a departure from the normal and she longed to leave the normal. In church one Sunday morning the parson related his sermon to the current murder, and she was so overcome with emotion that she had a fit and had to be carried writhing from the church. George got the idea of starting a newspaper which featured crime from my mother, and he made a million out of it, and thereafter his reputation was associated only with his newspaper. He was a respectably minded man, became a millionaire, entertained prime ministers in his beautiful house in Westminster, and passionately desired to make a reputation in politics or in letters. To show that he was alive to modern thought he bought a *Review*, a sort of literary *Tit-Bits*, and printed Elizabethan poems in it every week. But he only ever symbolised one thing to the public mind and that was crime — its odour hung around him. My mother was the only begetter of 'Crime of the Universe' and of the deadlock in the spirit of George Riddell. This was a just retribution, for, whatever his relationship with my mother, he was a profitless friend to my father whose brains he exploited without making him any return.

From the beginning of his career George Riddell was fired with desire to become a public character and took every opportunity to speak at public meetings, though he had a hesitating delivery and could never organise his material. My father wrote his speeches and rehearsed him in them. George's first mark on public affairs was the work of my father. But Riddell did not remember this when he began to succeed. He never turned back to give Geoffrey a hand out of a state which he loathed and which was unsuited to him. But, when my father left England, defeated, Riddell saw him off and, on the boat, gave him a copy of Darwin's *Origin of Species*. In it was written 'Geoffrey with love from George'. Many years later, Riddell went in a semi-official capacity to the Versailles conference. My father, then marooned in a small town in New Zealand, went one evening to the pictures where he saw George on the screen, coming out of the

Palace of Versailles. This was very bitter to my father who knew that he had a better brain than George's.

My father always felt at a disadvantage in life. When I was quite a little girl he communicated the pathos of this dissatisfaction to me. His ambition, together with his feelings of fear and weakness and lack of self-confidence, worked in me and afterwards ruined my life. Though they were in a state of emotional instability and needed to react somehow, I have often thought since that my parents exaggerated the pain of their feelings of inferiority. I was a virgin field for their reaction. But my father had his pleasant circle of Sunday evening cronies who, by their intelligence and status, might have been counted on to cure him of his inferiority feelings. I do not see these people as ridiculous as I do the superiorities of the Harpers with their quite conscious effort of levelling up. My father's friends were attracted to him by the scope of his reading and by the 'Marquis' quality which so irritated Alicia but was real in him. My mother, also, was quite without affectation. But nevertheless, my childhood was full of a special snobbery – the war on the villas.

My young years were darkened with the spirit of vendetta against the upper-middle-classes, the villa-dwellers, the stupid, ugly, arrogant villa-dwellers who scorned my father for tuning their pianos and my mother for selling them their rotten waltzes in a shop. I have since found this so much insisted-on antagonism in my parents to be spurious. Later they were quite capable of reconciliation with this class, even of adopting its standards. And I now realise that they more than half admired the villa-dwellers for using and abusing their privilege, and were more than a little inclined to kiss the hand that struck them. But when I was a child, and too long into my womanhood, I believed in this class war. So much did the child hate the villa-dwellers that the young woman hoped to redeem them: that hope, so vain and so arrogant, was most ruinous to my life. Over and over again I had been told of the parson who refused to suspend choir practice in the Chapel of Ease at the back of the shop when my mother had brain fever, though the doctor thought the disturbance might cost her her life. And I was told how my father had met a major of Horse Artillery at the Mechanics Institute who talked politics with him and, thinking him intelligent, had taken him home to lunch. But when the major found that my father was a piano-tuner he had ordered him out of the house. These stories filled me with anger and shame, and with an emotion which had a most bitter feeling in it: pity for my father.

When I was five the breach between my parents widened and they occupied separate rooms. My father slept in the attic opposite my own. As soon as I woke I used to put my dressing-gown on and go to his room. I put my arms round his head, held his face to my heart and sang to him, making up the words and the music. There was great happiness in this love for my father.

Sometimes the shop would be all horror, with my mother having fits and emitting her dark influence and a queer phosphorous-like smell. I can remember watching my mother in a fit from behind the green baize curtain which divided the basement. A slope of gleaming white tiles went up to a grille let into the pavement. Above the grille one could see the feet of passers-by. While my mother was in the fit I turned my eyes towards the feet of the passers, feeling that perhaps there among them was escape.

But also there was a compensating feeling. There was our love. In spite of my parents' intermittent quarrels, in spite of their need to make me all over again and develop me into a child worthy of their aspiration, during their periods of reconciliation there was always our love. There was a pleasurable and more-or-less superficial emotional reaction between us, rather than any deep flowing together of our wills. But we believed in our love, we talked about it, we demonstrated it, as we demonstrated every sort of emotion. My childhood was spent in a sort of eternal emotional warm bath, and I believed in all the emotions. 'Never let the sun go down on your anger': I was in cold despair if my mother would not kiss me good night. My mother took a great deal of interest in arousing emotions in me which she might not have done had she been able to continue her career in the theatre. She sewed as I sat on a hassock at her feet, singing to me her favourite ballads about death, and I would cry. I can remember that something seemed to click with satisfaction in my mother when I cried. But how lovely the scent of her was and the feel of her body up against me! And how lovely was her generosity and her powers of entertainment when she was in a good mood, and kind! And how well dressed she was, something she managed in spite of the difficulties. She had a red silk Liberty dress when Liberty silk was a new fabric, and it distinguished a little girl to have a mother with a Liberty silk dress. But it was my father who played with me

84

and took me to see the Roman well on the common. He told me the names of the birds and held me up to see the lilac and laburnam coming into bloom. One magic night he took me to see benediction at the Catholic church and I was alone with the beauty of the shining candles. The flashes and fury of the quarrels at the shop had no reality. Reality was only in our happiness together, and the heart of a little girl yearned to poor Geoffrey and Alice. Looking back to this time it seems that our roles were reversed and that I regarded their rages and their cruelties as a mother would regard the black moods of two adored children. I had the feeling of wanting to make up to them for what life had done to them, and for what they did to each other. And that must have made me a rather priggish little girl, and rather a sad one.

The Harpers came down to Wimbledon and gave me educating presents with their special air of superiority. They knew what was what in books and pictures, did the Harpers! They gave me a picture book by Caldecot and a work of Mrs Ewing. They read 'Lob Lie-by-the-Fire' to me, and I could scarcely recognise the beauty of the story in the strain of feeling that I was having my mind improved. Culture was never an easy path to the Harpers. One acquired merit by it, and every step on the way to improvement was a strain. The cultivated presents of the Harpers seemed somehow to contain merit as a consecrated wafer or the relic of a saint might contain holiness. Gertrude brought down to the shop a pair of water-colour drawings she had done at Heatherley's. They were very passable representations of chestnuts, wallflowers and blue china. There was a vase in them of peculiarly the right shade of blue. The pictures struck fear into me and filled me with a feeling of inferiority because of the immense height of refinement they represented. The Harpers always insisted on the unique distinction of their efforts in art: they played right, they sang right, they painted right, and their studies in counterpoint had a virtue that was phenomenal. This was paralysing, because the effect of their art was not wholly pleasant. The Harpers fully intended their attitude to art to be paralysing, for they did not want to extend a region of beauty but to keep a monopoly.

My father, delighted with my early verses, my quick memory and powers of sympathy, began to present me to the Harpers as the genius for whom they had been waiting. With that feeling of clannishness which is the root of all incest, the Harpers held that a

Harper redeemer should be all Harper. Moreover, they had a rival genius in Marcus — Alicia's last child. Marcus was only a year older than me and he had a prodigious talent for drawing. He copied admirably the drawings of Caldecot and the illustrations out of the Ewing books. As my mother had no desire to fulfil any ambition of the Harpers and disliked my verses for their promise of being creditable to them, so the Harpers resented the idea of any good thing coming to them from the union of their blood with the Whelans. The Royal Academy of Music snarled at the Board School, and my young talent was surrounded with an atmosphere of scorn. My aunts descended on me from the Olympian heights of Harper standards, to educate me. They taught me the elements of music, the names of the Pre-Raphaelite painters, and how to eat a boiled egg. No lesson of my aunts but left its trail of fear — with the permanent defect that comes from fear. Beatrice taught me to sing a hymn tune which never after could I sing in time.

But my mother's lovely art was education enough, and more particularly as she did not intend to teach anything. How beautifully she repeated verses, with an instinct for rhythm, and a fine light and shade and emotional change. She had no literary appreciation, as had my father who read Walter Pater and knew about style, but her senses responded to beauty of style and from her I breathed rhythms into my blood. By the time I was four I had learned from her to repeat whole passages from the *Ingoldsby Legends* and there is no school of facile composition better than these verses.

My mother was not as good a listener as Alicia. She soon tired of Herbert Spencer and wished the anthropoid apes in Hades. She threw Aristotle's Ethics at my father's head, reacting against agnosticism, though at the same time she quarrelled with the curate on the first floor on the necessity for infant baptism, refusing to believe that her small son, William, was in Hell. She spent a lot of time on her knees by her bedside, tearfully imploring Heaven to send her a sign; the sort of sign she expected was unspecified. She seldom went to church, but liked better to wrestle alone with the deity, feeling him to be a worthy protagonist.

On Sundays my parents sent me to Sunday School at the chapel in the lane behind the shop and I got a lot of pleasure swinging my legs in time to the hymn tunes:

86

Dare to be a Daniel,
Dare to stand alone,
Dare to have a purpose firm,
And dare to make it known.

One Sunday afternoon, a young man, blond and blue-eyed, came to speak at the Sabbath school. He symbolised the states of the soul by coloured discs of paper. A good child was a white child, a child with peccadilloes was a pink child and a bad child was the blackest of black, see disc. There was something in all this that went to my heart. I felt myself to be a very black child indeed and I set up such a heart-broken howl that the young missionary came down from the platform and took me in his arms. I told him that I was a sinner, and that not only I but my father was a sinner. I repeated the Lord's Prayer after the missionary, and he kissed me on my tears. When the service was over I took the young man by the hand and led him to my father who was told that his remarkable child had experienced conversion and was concerned about her father's soul. He took it very well, and did not let the young missionary see that he was laughing. My father was very much in need of sympathy and he talked to me a great deal. As I absorbed verses from my mother, so I picked up a stock of agnostic arguments from my father. By the time I was six I knew about the paradox of a perfect God and the origin of evil.

The quarrels which caused my father to sleep in the attic were a good deal caused by money difficulties. His reading and agnosticism took too much of his attention from the shop, and his attitude to the villa-dwellers was not useful in trade. My mother went back to teaching in a board-school and lived during the week in London. A woman came to keep house for my father and me. She was a pious old woman, and she used to come with me to Sunday School. Her stay was a blessed respite for I lived the normal life of a little girl and the fits and the fights were fewer. But I missed my mother, and the tradition of our love was strong between us. I used to wait for her in the shop window on Saturday mornings, all among the banjo strings and the two black shiny pianos, feeling them to be enemies. One Saturday my mother came home desolate from the deathbed of Martha. I had known that she was in sorrow and had bought her a large navel orange for threepence, which was an enormous sum to give for an orange. We had a time of rare intimacy and fine affection. My mother sat on a rocking-chair with me on her knee. And I had the pleasure of knowing I was a consolation to her. I can remember the look of the orange against my brown dress. My mother clasped me to her in her grief, and I had my first impression of genuine emotion. Later my mother prayed alone in her room, calling on the spirit of Martha to appear to her, and the old histrionic atmosphere returned. Martha had confessed the paternity of her fourth child on her death-bed, and the one fault of her arduous and faithful life was forgiven her.

My father had always feared a rival in business, that someone would start a music shop in Wimbledon with the dreaded defence of abundant capital. One night he dreamed that he had seen a fine new piano shop near the station. A week later, lo, there it was. My father knew he was beaten; with opposition so near he could not hope to make even a precarious living. It seemed that my mother had had an intuition of this when she went back to the board-school. Now she saw a way out; we would go to Australia. She had always wanted to go back, for she always remembered the exciting dramas of our first departure in the sailing ship.

My father would never have thought of being a colonist if it had not been for my mother. Everything he wanted was in England; the popular concerts at the Queen's Hall where my father sat behind Mrs Browning; the Fabian Lectures where he had caught sight of Herbert Spencer; the chance of sitting in the Stranger's Gallery and listening to some critical debate; the Positivist Society at the Essex Hall; and the possibility of running into old Mr Kinglake, the author of *Eothen*, as he took his morning constitutional on Wimbledon Common. Ellen Terry and Irving were at the Lyceum and, the worse business became at the shop, the more relief Geoffrey found in their great dramatic presentations. But my mother sensed that in Australia the family would have scope for advancement. The failure of the Wimbledon business weakened my father's defences against her.

When the furniture and stock were sold there was not enough money left for the transplantation, and Carrie Griffen lent fifty pounds of her savings. The old housekeeper loved my father who had always been tender and considerate to her. He respected her religion, so that when the cronies came in to talk on Sunday night they hid the whisky and never let her see the whist cards which she called the Devil's playthings.

I remember the uprooting as being unspeakably gloomy. We had an old tabby cat, adored by me. Wicken was to be transplanted to the Harpers. On his arrival he went mad. Once out of his basket he bit and scratched and made his escape down Haverstock Hill towards Gilbey's factory, which was to me a sinister stronghold guarding the way to London. Wicken's attitude to the change filled me with foreboding. My mother was depressed by the Board School, often in a rage, always exuding her black light. My father stayed at the Harpers and my mother and I shared a gloomy room in a small street near Primrose Hill.

My father and mother quarrelled more than ever. There was an increased strain between Alicia and her daughter-in-law. Alicia intimated that my mother had ruined the Wimbledon business, and my mother found the manners of the Harpers disgusting. Old Harper emitted foul noises in full family circle, and Alicia, using what remained of the strength of her arthritic hands to make pastry, allowed the young Marcus to be sick on the dough, of which she cut off only a corner without starting everything over again as would any cook with proper feeling. My mother hesitated to think what the family had eaten from Alicia's insufficient clipping. Mary and Beatrice, together with the ex-stockbroker's clerk Charlie, had all taken mother's hint of Australia without being at all grateful to her for the idea. They had decided to take their Royal Academy of Music Certificates to where they could make better use of them. Alicia was tearful at what might be an eternal parting with four of her children, and in fact she was never to see her son again. Everyone looked sardonically and unsympathetically at me: it was no excuse or advantage to be a child. Charlie, the night before he and my aunts sailed, offered me sixpence for chewing up a Beecham's pill. I, who had few pennies, did this and my uncles and aunts laughed over my grimaces at the nauseating taste. The next morning the first party set off for Australia.

My father alone of this circle showed any manners to a little girl, though at this time he was too preoccupied to play or to read me anything. That November he too sailed from Tilbury. He went steerage. Mother and I saw him off and gave him a leather-covered ink pot, contrived not to spill in the roughest weather. I thought it the most civilised ink pot in the world. George Riddell came to see father off on the boat with his presentation copy of *Origin of Species*.

It was desolate when we returned to the furnished room off Primrose Hill. There had always been shelter for me in my father's tenderness. But my mother, the professional teacher, saw no romance in a child. Her life was certainly arid enough to take the tenderness out of her. She earned eighty pounds a year as an assistant teacher: on this she had to keep us both. Somehow she always managed to dress well, with clothes bought from someone's lady's maid. She had no feeling against second-hand clothes.

We had to get to school by nine o'clock, and my mother used to stop on Primrose Hill and cry with the cold. I remember the feeling I had of utter desolation when I used to chafe my mother's hands, and my terror of the ugly barracks of a school that was waiting for us. The hideous colour and texture of the asphalt of the school-yard, called for sake of euphony the playground, symbolises for me the whole of this miserable time. I sat in my mother's classroom trying to compose stories to send to my father. I felt vaguely sorry for the poorer of the children, but this feeling was not shared by my mother and her colleagues whom I heard talking in the teachers' room. To them a scholar was an enemy, a poor scholar was doubly an enemy. I felt here, as I had felt at the Harpers, that somehow it was an offence to be a child. There was a ray of light on my mother's pay days, when she always bought me a box of sardines. All the romance of luxury was in these little fish.

We stayed at the school well into the spring, when a pleasant thing happened. My mother's birthday was on the twenty-fourth of May – Queen Victoria's birthday. All the scholars brought her flowers, bunches of laburnum and lilac. We had so many flowers that we had to carry them home in a double-handed wash basket and they made a glory in our little room. But the months before this had been grim enough. At this time Jack the Ripper was murdering women in the East End. My mother used to go out at night to add a little to her income by managing a dramatic society. I was left alone in bed with no light but the street lamp peering through the window. The springs of the bed sagged and as I moved I felt the hard ridge of our tin box underneath the bed. I used to imagine this to be a tub, filled with fragments of the Ripper's victims, and screamed often with the horror of it! By the time mother came in, I was usually deep into a terrified sleep.

Meanwhile father had obtained the management of a music shop in Maryborough, South Queensland. He began to send home butter-flies which were lovely again like the flowers. He was making enough to keep us, and mother, her quarrels with him forgotten, was eager to join him. She decided to work her passage again. Through an advertisement in the *Morning Post* she came to an arrangement with the Dawnbushes. Our fare was to be paid to Sydney for our services to the lady and her children. Mr Dawnbush, everybody said, was a gentleman. It was the first time this type had been brought to my notice, and for years after I associated the idea gentleman with the idea weakness. Mr Dawnbush had failed in the straw-hat busi-ness; gossip suggested that he had been ruined by his lackadaisical wife, who was not a lady but the daughter of a coal-merchant with an illiterate old mother who bullied Mr Dawnbush, as did her languid daughter.

We went down to the Dawnbushes' melancholy house in Southend while preparations were made for departure. My mother was ill-adapted to domestic servitude and there were always rows. The Dawnbush children bullied me, accusing me of bringing lice into the family, which was manifestly ridiculous; no child of any board-school teacher would ever have been lousy. The whole man-agement of board-schools is death on head lice, because nothing is so deadly discreditable. The grandmother used to scrub me very hard in the bath on the grounds that I was dirty though, because of my having a little Italian blood, my skin is naturally cream.

The Dawnbushes were liberals and used to talk a great deal about Mr Gladstone, and the grandmother insisted on us chewing our food the same number of times as Mr Gladstone, which made meals a terror. My mother helped with the sewing and, my Whelan aunts having given her the material, she made me no less than twelve dresses. I did not feel the sting of servitude because I had so many clothes. On the day we sailed Mr Dawnbush produced four, very large, splendid, dolls. I and his three children were to receive one of these on the day we arrived in Sydney. The Dawnbush children made me feel it was very good of their father to buy me a doll. It cer-tainly was.

I remember about the journey great waves in the Bay of Biscay, lashings of crude lime-juice in the tropics, and my mother's regular quarrels with Mrs Dawnbush. Sometime before we got to Sydney mother decided to break her contract and pay a proportion of the fares. I never got the fine big doll but I have always remembered how pleasurable was the prospect of receiving it.

We arrived in Sydney as passengers not as servants, and took a small boat to Queensland. I remember my nauseating fear as we stuck on a mud bank in the Mary River. And, oh joy, we found my father on the wharf.

He had taken a one-storied wooden house for us, raised off the ground on wooden piles. This was by local standards a proletarian house as the front door opened into the front room. In houses which approached the fringe of civilised life, there was a wooden groove between the first two rooms: the bedroom opened off on one side of it, and the parlour on the other. Our house was imposing enough to me, because we had at least one unused room, which gave a sense of space. This spaciousness was also due to the fact that there was very little furniture. My father had brought with him the fine oak chest in which for centuries the family had kept their linen on the Shropshire farm. It had been made without nails or screws, all the parts of it dovetailing into one another. He had also brought a few pictures, some water-colours by Gertrude, a photograph of Charles Darwin in a stamped brass frame, an engraving of some Victorian sage, and about two hundred books, including the works of Richard Jeffries, and a translation of Schopenhauer. The chest and the pictures were the ark of our convenant with life. We bought a bed, a couple of chairs, and a few cooking utensils. The dining-room, and we called it the dining-room, was bare of furniture except for a row of books on the mantelshelf. My father had got the house cheap because of the white ants. The dining-room was so devoured by the ants, that, tripping against the wall, I went right through into the kitchen beyond. The ants ate through the walls and fed on the books on the mantelshelf. They chewed out all the margins, mercifully leaving the print so that the books were not altogether useless. We had a bathroom which consisted of a tin shower bath, a contrivance filled by hand. Holes were bored in the floor, so that the water flowed down among the piles beneath the house. Looking back over this time it seems remarkable to me that we did not feel this standard of living at all barbarous. Throughout this part of my childhood I felt I belonged to a civilised family: the bushwhacker who lived in the bush in a log hut seemed to be immeasurably distant from us, though there was little difference between his living standard and ours, except that the bushwhacker lived on salt goat and damper. We had the grocery shop, with kippered herrings and Cross and Blackwell's pickles, to keep us in touch with the old life. And of course we had books. There was a library in the town and my people read as they had read in England. Here I read my first novel, Olive Schreiner's *Story of an African Farm*.

The day after our arrival my father began to show the true spirit of a colonist by starting to build a stable in the yard. We were to have a horse, which was immensely exciting. Poor little girls are sustained by promises of an ultimate prosperity when they will own a pony. The pony turned out to be a disconsolate brown beast, with thick fetlocks and vicious eyes, bought for two pounds fifteen. Five pounds was then quite a good price for a horse.

My father had bought a load of saplings off a black man, and I can still see his graceful young man's body as he worked all day in the midsummer sun. He was then twenty-eight. I remember the sweat on his forehead, and I can feel his frustration as he knew he would fail at the work. He never got very far with the stable. Sacking was stretched over four uprights that had been got into place, and there for a time the horse lived, more-or-less exposed to the elements. My mother quarrelled with my father over the stable, seeing in his failure the ineptitude which a vigorous, passionate woman so loathes in her man. I lay in the one bed, while the battle raged in the parlour beyond the partition. Hope died in me. I had imagined that there would be golden peace in Australia.

All these early days we were at a disadvantage to our neighbours, because we were new chums, people from England. Every sort of weakness was attributed to us. I got this feeling from the children around. They were mostly the families of Irish labourers. I was thrilled to know that these children were often beaten with their father's strap, the piece of leather labourers wore to hold up their trousers. This and the fact that they called the parlour the front room – a vulgarism – and had a chiffonier in it in place of an oak chest, determined the difference between us. My father never beat me. Physical chastisement was left to my mother, who mostly made passionate assaults on my head with her bare hands. Twice in my childhood I suffered from deafness but she still continued to box my ears.

My parents met any criticism from the Queenslanders by

adopting the role of lonely exiles. My mother had longed for Australia, but made no pretence of being contented with it. Driving through the bush she pointed out to me the hideous dark green of the native trees, with their disorderly habit of shedding their bark all the year round, instead of their leaves once in autumn, like the admirable oak and ash. I thought a group of gum trees, flinging wild arms to the sky, was rather lovely; but opinion was against me. Away from England, my parents saw romance in everything English. In a Utopia of cheap meat, with rump steak at sixpence a pound, they wanted kippers; in a paradise of peaches and bananas, nothing would do for them but strawberries. At first father had the management of three music shops; he had branches at Bundaberg and Gympie, both sugar towns. One day he put the old horse in the sulky and drove my mother off to visit the branches, leaving me with half-a-crown to keep myself over the weekend, and instructions to go and spend the night with the shop girl. I bought a dozen pineapples for two shillings, and sixpenn'orth of biscuits. I lived on the biscuits and the pineapples, at night I slept with the shop girl, and all day I had the freedom of the town. I was then under seven.

Floods and famine in Queensland forced my father to close the two branches, leaving him a thin living in Maryborough by piano tuning and piano sales. My mother moved us out of the white ant house to a wooden box across the town, which had a passage, four rooms, a wide verandah and two verandah rooms, a wash-house and a shed for the horse in the garden. The man in the next house had made a lawn. I recognised the social value of living next to a lawn. My mother began teaching elocution to children at the Mechanics' Institute. With the extra money, she bought some bamboo whatnots, some small Japanese vases, and a piece of cretonne to cover the settee. We now had a furnished parlour, which was a considerable step forward. In the elocution class at the Mechanics' Institute, my mother found me a difficult pupil, and made me the butt of the class.

My father missed the Fabian Society, the Positivist Society, the Queen's Hall concerts and his London friends. He had really no kindred spirit in the town. One day, as he was riding through the bush, he came face to face with a remittance man whom he recognised as someone whom he had known in Shropshire as a boy. His name was Carson and he had been kicked in the head by a horse and ever afterwards suffered from fits of mad drinking. My father, seeing he was on the verge of delirium tremens, asked him to come and live with us. My mother was very kind to Carson, so that while he was with us he sobered up. He used to make beautiful illuminated manuscripts. After a time he went north, and later went on the drink and murdered a woman, a barmaid, who mocked him with, 'Do you think I'd really marry a drunken sot like you?' Carson, mad drunk, went into her room and upset an oil lamp over her bed; she burned to death. There was always doubt as to whether the murder was intended, and Carson was drunk at the time, yet he was hanged. My father tried unsuccessfully to get a reprieve. Carson died gallantly, thinking only of the clergyman who had the unpleasant duty of attending him to the scaffold: 'Hearten up, Hewitt', he said, 'Hearten up.'

We were at first very poor in Maryborough. A travelling museum came to the town, which I wanted to go to. I was told to look in my father's trousers for a penny. There wasn't one. There was no money in the house, though I never remember in my childhood being hungry. Somehow my parents always managed to get food.

I went to the convent school in return for my father tuning the nuns' pianos. We dined at a long table and I dropped my fork during a fish course. I have never forgotten the shame I felt. All my childhood was full of feelings of inferiority. I was never comfortable in any environment. The nuns did not like me. They knew I was an odd little girl, with an odd windy father who was an enemy to religion. Discovering that I had a very beautiful voice, they made me sing to them, unaccompanied. Quite a good English musician came to the town, one Seymour Dicker, who wanted to take me on tour as a child singer. There was quite a vogue for child singers in Queensland at that time, and even a juvenile opera company called the Lilliputians. I feel I should have been happy as a Lilliputian.

Singing was a retreat from loneliness and isolation. I used to sit in the hammock on the verandah swinging to and fro in an ecstasy of pleasure at singing. While I was at the convent my mother had nothing to do but her home duties and she was always very difficult when she only did home duties: she had too much energy left to discharge at me. I used to start out for the convent every morning in a starched white pinafore. In the afternoon when I returned there was no evidence of the starch, and the pinafore was dirty. My mother was fired with the desire that I should be the sort of little girl who kept her pinafore clean. God knows I used to try, but a day at the convent always played havoc with my pinafore. On my return my mother would be waiting for me on the verandah to launch her rage against me. I think she broke something in me, for never in my life have I been able to keep my clothes clean. I always spill things, though I have used every discipline to get myself out of it.

My mother's emotions reacted in love for me, but she opposed my existence with her will. In regions below the conscious she desired to destroy me. One example of her cruelty has always remained in my memory. Sent to do the shopping one Saturday night, I honestly believed I had been allowed tuppence for myself, and with it I bought a sawdust doll with a round china head. My mother found it at the bottom of the bag when she turned out the rice and the sugar. She took the doll by the legs, and broke off its head against the mantelshelf.

About this time, my father found a friend to whom he could talk about Herbert Spencer. Miss Naylor was an English graduate and she taught botany at the girls' grammar school. My father took great pleasure in making her beautiful coloured diagrams for her classes. One day I came home to the bedroom and found my mother, in the middle of the day, in a curious kind of sleep. She muttered, and she smelt odd. I went and found my father. She was suffering from laudanum poisoning; she had taken it as a demonstration against Miss Naylor. I don't think my mother wanted to die: she knew I would be coming home.

She was very bored at this time and, what was always hard for her, she had no clothes. Quite characteristically my mother gained sudden energy after the laudanum episode. She always seemed to have to go on a sort of hysterical debauch before she gained energy. Providentially about this time her sister Helen sent her out a parcel from the sales. In it was a pretty piece of lilac cotton material. She made herself a new dress and could meet Miss Naylor on her own ground.

She had begun to teach elocution at the grammar school, and soon gave a lecture at the Mechanics' Institute. The lecture was quite a social event: everyone in the town came to it. She never wrote her lectures, but used to rehearse them aloud, memorising them with a rare concentration. 'Mr Chairman, ladies and gentlemen: elocution is the art of reading and speaking with accuracy and ease', and at that slogan the family fortunes began to rise, never to look back. After the lecture her classes increased.

She taught all the young townspeople to recite 'The Charge of the Light Brigade' and 'The Women of Mumbles Head'. She organised a dramatic society to perform tableaux vivants of the life of Mary Queen of Scots, as at the Royal Polytechnic, London. My father and she talked wistfully of the old Lyceum Theatre, where, in a ship scene, the ship could actually be made to look as if it were moving. Mr Harrap, the town chemist, proved to be a talented amateur actor. He and mother played the 'Happy Pair' together, and Harrap became so enlivened that he left his wrinkled shred of a wife and ran off to West Australia with the shop assistant. They gave father a small part as a clergyman, but he fell down on it. His voice had no carrying power, and so he was proved inept again.

One morning about two o'clock a stranger came in out of the blinding rain, which was beating a hell's tattoo on the corrugated iron roof. He said he had been to see his brother-in-law and had been caught in the storm. My parents hospitably welcomed him in and my mother cooked him some eggs and bacon. My father noticed, as he took off his coat, that his shirt was scarcely at all wet. They put him to sleep on the carpenter's bench in the verandah room with hammers and chisels all around him. Next morning he did not wake early, and when my mother went to ask him how he had slept, he said, 'Oh! very well except for the noise of the circus'. We were next door to the Salvation Army Tabernacle, but no one had been playing the cornet during the night. An hour later two policemen rode out through the flood, and took our guest away with them. He was a homicidal lunatic, who had broken all the furniture at the hotel across the paddock and attempted to kill the barmaid.

The Salvation Army Captain, who lived beside the tabernacle, was very poor and his wife was always pregnant. My mother made puddings for them, and when they had the brokers in, she hid their poor odds and ends of property. In spite of these excitements, and these charities, she tired of Maryborough and felt she wanted to press on. It was always my mother who wanted to press on.

She got a job under the Queensland Education Department as assistant mistress at Hughenden, North Queensland. Father went to Brisbane and got a job as tuner and repairer in a big music shop. We went north to Townsville, and then started the weary all-day journey

97

three hundred miles inland. There was no lavatory accommodation on the train.

Hughenden was a town of nine hundred inhabitants caught in a three-year drought. My mother was paid three pounds a week, and we stayed at the Royal Hotel. In spite of our being well into the tropics, the winter seemed very cold. The Flinders River had run dry, and the town water had to be dug from the river bed. We lived on a heavy meat diet, and dried vegetables. The only green things for countless miles were oranges and lemons and watermelons in the Chinamen's garden. These indefatigable workers used to raise water with a man-driven wheel. I believe the Chinese are now turned out of Queensland.

I was very well taught in the Hughenden school. The master announced to us that Lord Tennyson was dead. Miss Walpole, another assistant at the school, also lived in the Royal Hotel. She was said to be a descendant of the great statesman. The salesman at the local store was named Pitt, but claimed no connection. He fell in love with my mother, and I think she fell in love with him, because I saw them kissing one another. I felt excluded, and was very lonely for my father. I used to tie his photograph to a pillow, and hug the pillow and kiss the photograph. The shearers from the stations around who used to come in at night to knock their cheques down, would sing in the bar parlour and dance sand shuffles, and they gave me a fear of brutal and massed masculinity. There was a good deal of sex talk at the school, and I had two quite innocent, though sentimental, attachments to boys. Mr Green, who was a gentleman and manager of Winton Station, fell so much in love with my mother that he followed her to Townsville when we went back there on the way south after our six months at the school was over. I was belle of the fancy dress ball in Hughenden, but still suffered from inferiority feeling because Lizzie and Charlotte Atkins, the daughters of the people at the Royal Hotel, were so much richer than me. A large bottle of champagne at the Royal Hotel cost a guinea. When we got back to Townsville we had a moment in hand, so we went along the rather beautiful main street, and, at a very nice ice-cream shop, ate an ice-cream. Ice was the greatest of luxuries in Hughenden, because when it was sent up from the coast it nearly always melted before its arrival.

We joined my father in Brisbane and boarded and lodged with a family called Groom. Daddy Groom was a stockbroker who had failed. His wife, who was my first impression of a fine lady, lay on the sofa all day polishing her nails with a chamois leather. Mother scorned her because she was a lazy housekeeper.

The Grooms' was a fine house of wood, two storeys high, and built on piles. This was the year eighteen ninety-three, the year of the great Brisbane flood. The morning of the flood a rider came round sent by Wragg, a certain wizardly meteorologist, to warn people to get out of their houses. About two o'clock the flood water oozed through the wooden fence opposite the house. In two hours our garden was under water and mother and I and Mrs Groom were taken down the main road in the police boat to Mr Fenwick's, a friend of Mrs Groom. He was rich and owned a brass water-heater and a clock with musical chimes. From his house we could see the Brisbane river and the bridge.

The boxes of wooden houses lifted off their piles and floated upright with all their contents. All night long we heard the houses hitting the bridge. One of our party counted two hundred. Next morning, which was Sunday, half the bridge was gone.

My father and Daddy Groom, the servants and the two Groom boys had stayed in the house to save some of the furniture. They tried to float the grand piano on the dining-table but the table upset and let the piano down into the water. All night long the flood water mounted. In the morning the water was nearly to the level of the first floor. My father turned his collar back to front and began to read prayers for the dead in order to stop the two female servants from panicking. He then tied a red cloth to a pole as a signal to the police boat. By now my father was alone with the boys and the servants because Mrs Groom had got hysterical the night before and had sent a man swimming through the flood to fetch her husband.

Next to old Mr Fenwick's house was a large church which was used to house the refugees. Hundreds of homeless people slept on the floor. I saw a man dragged dead from the water within a few yards of our refuge. My strongest impression of all this ruin and death is the memory of the clock with the chimes, the brass hot-water heater, and the fact that, as I lay on my extemporised bed on the sofa in the library, I read for the first time *Alice in Wonderland*.

The Grooms' house was not swept away, but very little of their furniture was salvaged. Three weeks later the Brisbane river flooded again.

All this did not immobilise my mother. She got herself appointed assistant mistress at Woolangabba School and, as my father made three pounds ten a week in the piano shop, this was the most money we had had up to date. My parents took a very small furnished house by the railway line, with a peach-tree in the garden. The house belonged to an old widow, and there was a picture of the defunct on one side of the best bed and a picture of his tombstone on the other. My mother heard his spirit moving along the rail at the end of the bed, evidently oscillating between his portrait and his tombstone. This was her first ghost and afterwards she became much occupied with them. I used to go with her on the bus to the Woolangabba School. There she taught me grammar and I have never forgotten it. If there was anything she did not like in my performance of it, she used to keep me in after school and beat me with a piece of raw hide. I take it, she beat her irritation at the school system into me. She hated everything about the school system, and held a great deal against the Under-Secretary of Education. My parents took very much the same critical view of him as they had taken of the villa-dwellers in Wimbledon.

I had a fine party for my tenth birthday and everybody, including lots of the girls from the school, brought me presents. We had a whole tin of biscuits, and I began to lose a little of my inferiority feeling.

My mother came so much to dislike the Under-Secretary that she left school teaching. We moved to a house rather superior to the one in Maryborough. It had a ghost, cost only ten shillings a week, and its garden was the most beautiful jungle, with an orange tree, a lemon tree, a banana palm and two sorts of guava. Here my parents tried to grow Brussels sprouts, and failed. We bought furniture at auction sales, including some charming and creditable objects. Notable among them, a willow-pattern butter dish with the convenient word 'butter' carved on the oaken container.

I went to the Normal School, which was a state school but a very good one. My teacher, Miss Story, taught English very well and every time she taught me the meaning of a new and intriguing word I came home and put it in a poem. My father was very pleased at this, but my mother started again her propaganda against me that I was unpractical. And just about this time she discovered I could not top-sew. I can remember a sombre conference on my shortcomings on the verandah. There were my mother and father and Jerry Noakes. Jerry was a rich sugar grower from Bundaberg, but he believed in woman and in a woman's proper sphere, so, in spite of his money, his wife and daughter always did the washing. To Jerry my mother brought her grievance about my not being able to top-sew, and my father, never a very strong character, was half talked over. I was in the ghost's bed and heard them talking. I felt utterly abandoned, for my father had deliberately induced a verse-writing mood in me, and I knew that no little girl could be expected to write good verse and learn to top-sew all in the same week. When I came home from the Normal School, having learned the word 'inanimate' I put it into a line about the sea. I knew I was imitating Byron and felt guilty about it.

Father took my verses to Brunton Stephens, the most notable poet in Queensland at the time, and asked him if he thought I would fulfil my promise. Brunton Stephens said, 'She will be a poet on a condition you can hardly wish her since you are her father: she will be a poet if she has pain enough'. My father was very proud of this reply, but my mother did not sympathise with all this pother about a little poetry. In the first place her love took fright at the implied necessity of pain. Then she was jealous of my father's preoccupation with my verses. As my mother had failed my father in not supplying him with the complementary energy to enable him to be a novelist or the tranquillity he needed to make some use of his studies, so my father had been repelled by the great natural dramatic force of my mother. He always wanted to discipline it, to teach it. He gave her Green's *Shorter History of England*, so that she should get a truer angle on Mary Queen of Scots. She was maddened at the implied criticism. She had no faith whatever in books, learning only in the school of experience: she learned everything about her acting from life. If my father had given her the same quality of unquestioning sympathy he gave me, she would have felt in some way liberated. As it was she began to put it into my mind that his interest in my verses was ridiculous. She made fun of his habit of showing my compositions to his workmates and to people he picked up an acquaintance with in bars or in the street. My father said that Mr Pine, the manager of the piano shop, had been so affected by one of my poems that tears had come into his eyes. My mother commented that Mr Pine must have been drunk at the time. She ridiculed as an importunity his habit of submitting my verse to any poet he could persuade to read them. She suggested that he was exploiting my work to get to know poets of reputation. When Mr Banjo Paterson disregarded a letter sent with an enclosure of verses, my mother laughed.

One Sunday night, walking on Wickham Terrace, we came to a point equidistant between the Church of England and the Presbyterian Church. Hymns were blaring out of both. My father put his arms around me, begging me with great tenderness to promise him that I would be a poet when I grew up. I gave him my word, and when my first set of verses was printed in the honourable company of Verhaeren and Maurice Hewlett I signed them 'Wickham' in memory of that curious and very emotional pact. My mother recognised my verses as good compositions in the Board School sense. She was herself too efficient to disregard entirely any adequacy, but there was in the quality of her will and initiative a certain maleness, in spite of her hair and her very feminine way of presenting herself. She desired in me a femininity that was not in her spirit, so that I should be in some way complementary to her, so that I should be a love object rather than another will, another intelligence. My father, on the contrary, asked of me a boyishness. He had my hair cut like a boy's when that was very unusual, and was proud of my inattention to my clothes. He often said to me, 'I hate women, old girl, thank God you're not a woman, darling'. Loving them I wished to adapt myself to both, but found their points of view irreconcilable. In trying to realise their conflicting ideas of me I seemed somehow to lose possession of a self.

This time in the Brisbane house, with the jungle of a fruit garden, was a happy one. I was getting old enough to keep the peace between my parents. When we walked out together I would extemporise verses to make them laugh, and my mother said I could get paid for that sort of thing on the music hall.

I went in for a public essay competition and won the gold medal, which, to her great satisfaction, my mother had made up into a brooch and I wore it always. Also about this time my father had a curious dream. He was chasing a rabbit with a stick in a mad rage. He raised the stick to strike. The rabbit lifted its head in death, and it was my face he saw on the body of the rabbit. He shuddered with horror to find that he had killed his daughter. My father's love for me was very real at this time.

I had too the pleasure of a beautiful girl-friend, the niece of Miss Walpole, the teacher from Hughenden. Mary was so lovely that her face is still, in my memory, associated with the first glimpse of happiness in my desolate life. Also we had a kind and charming servant – Naomi, very religious, a Plymouth Brother. I went with her to her strange services, crude in comparison with her gentleness and charm. She gave me a Bible, which I have kept all my life.

My mother, once again with only her home duties to occupy her, began to show characteristic unrest. Sometimes she would develop a sort of trance condition, a state of half-sleep, in which she would live over again scenes from her childhood. There would be sentences in my mother's voice queerly high in pitch and childish in intonation, a pause for the reply of the memory she was conversing with, and then my mother's voice would resume. She was talking, for the most part, to painters for whom she had been a model when a child. These extemporised dramatic performances, a result of her boredom, were like the manifestations of trance mediums. In these states she developed great acuteness of memory, and determined to exploit the kind of powers in her that had interested W.T. Stead.

With characteristic swiftness and secrecy she opened an office in the main street of Brisbane next to my father's piano shop, advertising herself as Madame Reprah, Physiognomist and character-reader-by-the-face, and charging half-a-crown for a spoken reading, five shillings if she wrote it all down. She began to make money at once, and quickly amassed a supply of elegant clothes. This pained my father greatly, for he always had a great desire to keep his family. But my mother was constantly circumventing him by helping him out, and she had the excuse that he never made enough to keep us comfortably. My father, a serious student of science, had a horror of charlatanism, and considered a character-reader a mountebank. His sisters, Mary and Beatrice, confirmed him in his sense of shame by sending condemnatory letters from New South Wales where they were teaching music, as soon as they heard that Alice had broken out again.

My mother felt very bitterly this belittling attitude to her psychic ability, which she now took seriously. It was typical of her to feel no scruple in using her gifts to make money. She had always worked for her living and she was scrupulously honest about giving value for money. I once saw Lord Northcliffe, interested in a certain lady's reaction on some public matter, call for one of his newspapers, in which he knew her portrait was printed, and look very carefully at her face before making up his mind about her. My mother too believed that she could read the mind's construction in the face. By an intuitional process, which she imagined she got from looking in their eyes, with practice she attained considerable proficiency at thought reading. She could tell her 'clients' how many children they had, or describe some absent friend. Once when she was reading a 'character' her subject, a woman, fell asleep. My mother, who had read about hypnotism, knew the technique of awaking the woman, but called my father to help her to make the necessary suggestions. This they did very successfully. She was very excited about her new gift but my father was grudging in his recognition. He had a strong sense of *comme il faut* towards the objects of his serious attention, and eliminated all subjects not included in or inferred from the *Synthetic Series* of Herbert Spencer, which neglected hypnotism. A few weeks after this, however, his life was saved by this very power of my mother's. He had a very serious attack of typhoid and could not sleep for ten days. His doctor asked my mother to induce an hypnotic sleep, which she did, and achieved what drugs had failed to do.

Even this proof of her powers did not reconcile him to them. With the exception of his appreciation of my talent (which amounted almost to a form of self-belief), my father semed to need to base his judgements on some exterior, some accredited standard. My mother, on the other hand, was fearlessly personal in judgement. She had the spirit of a pioneer. She gave her 'clients' a good half-crown's worth of entertainment, and often, by her intuition and knowledge of people, she functioned as a psychoanalyst. Also, by her nearness, by her method of looking hard at the sitter and taking their hands in hers, she functioned as a contact healer. Her science was probably as sound as Coué's, though she had not, and did not need, the shelter of a medical degree.

By another curious power she could tell the time at all hours of the day to a minute without clock or watch, and what is rarer and less easily explained, she knew to a furlong how far she had come along a road. All this could scarcely be accredited to subconscious memory, as might the time-recording power, nor can there be any parallel in homing birds or savages who, though they might have an instinctive sense of distance, could not give their impression a numerical connotation. This recording function was not a throw back to some older form of consciousness, for mother said she got her time and space judgements from a sensation in the back of her arms: this has also been said by some dowsers and water finders. My mother never understood her powers, nor how quite to control them, but she had a belief in their importance and a wistful desire that someone should interpret them.

My father's preoccupation with what was native to my mind, and his rather unintelligent disregard of my mother's extraordinary powers, caused the jealousy she developed towards me which was to be the most destructive agent in my life. She came later to regard me not only as her rival in the emotional region with my father, but also as an artist who succeeded with a public which had failed her. Her character-reading was really a diversion of her powers as an actress. Somehow the histrionic faculty invades other consciousnesses and other realities to know them and to interpret them. The mystic and the poet are of one blood. But my father was more interested in poetry than in acting or in religion, and his love did not go far enough to carry him to an appreciation beyond his interest. My mother afterwards practised curative hypnotism with very good results.

After some time in Brisbane my mother, always wanting to press on, decided that she would travel, much against my father's wishes. He always wanted a home and a wife at home to raise his prodigy of a daughter. My mother's instinct in not giving too much attention to me was probably a sound one. She carried too high a nervous charge for one small child: always when I was long with her I became ill. Having sold the office furniture, she went off to Toowoomba leaving me in charge of Naomi. At the end of a week, my father received, unregistered in a tin Bryant and May matchbox, twenty gold sovereigns – profit from the first week's takings. She lectured in Toowoomba every evening, as well as reading 'characters' by day in a room in her hotel. She had the knack of going unadvertised to a new town, setting up her tent, and making money at once. She made about forty pounds a week in Toowoomba, which was affluence, her clothes became many and splendid, and she bought herself gold rings, which she wore all over her beautiful hands. A gipsy, my mother! And my father had a loathing of gipsies inherited from his farm folk who had protected their fields from such garish marauders;

so there was no peace between them. My father longed for a home where the best books from the libraries could be read aloud in the evening, and his wife would help educate and observe his remarkable child.

My mother would never again live on his three pounds ten a week from piano tuning while the good gold sovereigns rolled into her hands through exercise of her gifts, so scorned by Mary and Beatrice, and so unregarded by the *Synthetic Series* of Herbert Spencer. She sold up the Brisbane house and the oak butter-dish and the picture of a yacht in full sail by some very creditable artist which my father was so proud of. We went to board and lodge in a large rambling house with a billiard room at what was then a high rent in Brisbane, twenty-five shillings a week. There were two Bunya-Bunya trees in the garden. Our landlord, Mr Taylor, had a chemist shop in the main street, and, though a chemist and a shopkeeper, was here rated as a gentleman. He spent most of his money on himself, and his wife, sad-eyed and blousy, lodged and boarded us to eke out her income. She made lemon curd tarts in rather a charming way, and I felt her to be a superior woman. At this time of my childhood my chief knowledge of superior persons came through our lodging with them.

I was sent as a boarder to All Hallows Convent, the best school in Brisbane, a fine academy for young ladies, made possible by my mother's going off on tour to make the money to pay the school bills. My father, never able to do anything different, kept on piano tuning and lodging with the Taylors. It was there he got typhoid. Mrs Taylor, a motherly woman who panicked at the thought of illness, was quite unable to deal with him. My mother came home, treated my father by hypnotic suggestion as I have related, and then went back on tour to make the money to keep him at a good nursing home.

A fine Lancashire matron got him round with the most careful nursing. There would have been no hope for him in a public hospital. At one time the doctor feared the fatal symptom of perforation. I was called out of the convent to watch my father die. My mother was wired for, and had to leave just as she was going on stage to lecture. I sat up all night in a room off my father's sick chamber reading comics. I had that queer feeling of levity, which is the mind's adjustment to tragedy. I could hear him moaning in his delirium that he feared my mother would be left without money. This was just the sort of situation her courage was designed to meet. She arrived with a bag of sovereigns, the profits of her last week. This she put into my father's hands, so relieving his worry. Although she saved the day by her hypnotism and by her quickly and cleverly earned money, no one seemed to hold her in particularly high esteem. Anything good she did was taken as a matter of course, as a sort of make weight for all her other embarrassing and eccentric behaviour. Mary, up from Sydney to see her brother die, was antagonistic to her sister-in-law even after Alice had saved him. There was nothing in her Harper standards to deal with springing into a breach and saving life. And by no Harper standard was a character-reader-by-the-face acceptable. Mary was quite unfriendly to me, too, though I did my best to amuse her in the way I had been taught to amuse my father and told her, as cleverly as I could, what I remembered of the book I had been reading by Seeley.

Back at the convent, which was a large and impressive building in white stone, I went out into the grounds, knelt down, pressing my knees against the earth, and prayed that the people at school would never know I was not like them. But they did. I was at the same sort of disadvantage that I had been nearly everywhere. I was not rich enough, and my family had no status. The aristocrats of the school were for the most part the daughters of Irish publicans. My clothes were not the right clothes, and presents my parents gave me were the wrong presents. My mother brought me some charming Japanese prints; I remember wishing someone would give me a really impressive box of chocolates, one with several tiers and a picture of pansies on the box lid. This would have been enormously useful in my struggle to save my personality and standards from the assault of the publicans' daughters. The nuns had agreed with my father that I should be allowed to read an hour a day. In the convent library I read daily the lives of the Saints and the works of Sir Walter Scott, and I don't think I took as much good from my reading as I took harm by my segregation from the teachers and scholars.

My father went north for his convalescence to Charters Towers where he tried to go into partnership with my mother in the lecturing and character-reading business. This was a failure: there was nothing for him to do but to see to the advertising and get together material for the lectures. My mother was an impressionist: her object was to be interesting; truth, and fine points of style and accuracy made no matter with her. My father would spend a day verifying a reference, and at the end of the day the public would be bored. My mother wishing him and his books to the devil, proceeded to hold audiences by her uninstructed native genius. Sore at his dispensability, my father tried to settle down in the hotel and write a novel. He never got past the first four pages.

The holidays came and I was then eleven. The fare was sent, and off I travelled to Charters Towers quite alone, without being put in the charge of anyone. On the boat I met Judge Paul, a high court judge aged about fifty, and I talked to him in the way I talked to my father. He was the first person I had met to be amused by me. He told me I was a beautiful little girl, and gave me a copy of Laing's *Modern Science and Modern Thought*, and a volume of the poems of Calverley. Excited at being told I was beautiful, I went down to my cabin to look at my flushed face. The poems by Calverley I have always remembered. I went ashore at Mackay in the middle of the night. The neighbourhood was full of Kanakas who might have raped me, but in spite of all the chances I took in my childhood, nothing ever went amiss. A friend of father's met me in Townsville and took me to a hotel, and the next morning I started for Charters Towers alone in a corridor coach. I travelled most of the way on the step reading a copy of Phil May's *Annual*. There was a fair state of unanimity at Charters Towers; we had fricassee fowl for dinner in the hotel, and I manicured my feet for the first time, which I knew somehow was an effect on me of Judge Paul.

I found the convent dreary and stupid after life with my parents. I was very lonely, and I used to cry a good deal. The nuns made much of their great ideal of modesty. I was bullied into shame at being discovered with my body bare after a very hot night. In my sleep I had thrown the covers off. We were always supposed to wear bathing clothes in the bath. Yet this did not stop a great deal of sex talk. Many of the girls had boys, and an adventurous group used to go, before breakfast every morning, to a certain music room to watch from the window a young man get out of bed. My mother had planted in me a horror of such precocious sexual activity. Sex talk filled me with a too violent feeling of shame. Cheated of my deep, affectionate relationship with my mother, I became attached to a girl older than myself called Tickie Kerr. I was emotionally in love with her, and used to get out of my bed in the junior dormitory and go and kneel beside hers. There she would pour out to me the tale of her piety and of how she had a vocation to be a nun. In Lent we would kiss the five wounds on the crucifix happily together. Because of my good voice I sang in the chapel choir. I became very devout, partly owing to the reaction of my starved emotions to the incense and the music, and partly in order to be on terms of spiritual intimacy with my friend Tickie. Often during this time I would write a poem for my father. This got me little credit with the nuns, who thought it queer. We wrote our home letters on Sunday afternoons in the large classroom, and we always had to show what we wrote to the nun in charge. On one occasion I had written in reply to some sad word of his, a very inspiring poem on the beauties of hope. Sister Mary Aden looked up at me virulently from the verses and said, 'I have read this before in a book.' That was the cruellest thing the nuns ever did to me. I was a favourite of none of them except the wise old reverend mother, Mother Mary Patrick, who often used to talk to me in her room at the nuns' house. My mother would call at the convent entrancingly dressed, exuding her lovely personal scent and I adored her. Somehow, to the other girls she was not in the category of things admirable: by this time she had dyed her hair a bright yellow. Aunt Mary and my father thought this discreditable, but my senses welcomed mother's yellow hair and my impression, as I remember her, was one of charm.

About this time (I was twelve) we had a holiday together at Sand-gate, Brisbane's chief seaside resort, staying in splendour at the best hotel. My father used to go shark-fishing with Captain Pine, who was aide-de-camp to the governor, and I used to go down to the pier with them. Sometimes they would send me scuttling up to the hotel for a grappling hook, or some other piece of apparatus, telling me that they would give me all the gold watches they found in the man-eating sharks. They treated me like a little girl, but I would try and draw Captain Pine into conversation to make him interested in me, for he reminded me of Judge Paul.

On this holiday my parents had one of their bitterest quarrels, with the horrible suggestion of physical violence by my father. I see now that my mother often invited this violence, but I was a shocked audience of such emotional debauches. And she made a great point of the blackguardliness that made him strike her. I never believed he was a blackguard, yet I was torn between my love and the evidence of his unworthiness to my mother.

I believed everything they told me. Once I believed that my mother had left Sandgate with the idea of running away alone to North Queensland. I could not find my father, I had no money, so I started in the blinding heat of midsummer to walk the eighteen miles to Brisbane along the railway track. When I got to Brisbane I found it was a false alarm, so I borrowed the fare from the convent and came back by train. My parents, thoroughly alarmed at my absence, had had a search party out after me. They made up their differences in their emotion at the splendid qualities of faith and devotion of their child. I slept in their room, but I writhed all night on the floor with colic, brought on by physical strain.

During this holiday, one night on the pier, I had a curiously emotional scene with my mother. There was a lack of sentiment in my father that failed her. That night she got what was missing from me, and I never have had an impression of more perfect love. These quite sincere emotional scenes made no difference to the deep antagonism she had for me: they were of a semi-erotic nature, and belong to a region I have never seen touched on by any psychologist.

On my birthday my mother gave me a brooch with three gold swallows on it, an impressive piece of property, that did me quite a lot of good at school. Even better was the news that I was to leave the convent and that we were all to join up in Sydney. In spite of the storminess of our life together I vastly preferred it to the aridity of the convent. Tickie Kerr had put her hair up and gone home to her father's sheep station, by now a young lady. I left the convent regretting nobody and feeling that nobody regretted me. They knew very well I was not like them.

In Sydney my mother and I lived at first in boarding-houses. My father, having found a rather better appointment with the leading piano house in New South Wales, was on the road selling pianos. When he joined us there was the usual alternation of violent, brutal quarrels and a rather beautiful emotionalism. There were always books. My father read everything, and often aloud. About this time he began to despair of my intelligence, and I began to be less amenable to his suggestions. He read to me Emerson's *Essay on Nature*, and I felt a boredom which I did not attempt to disguise.

I went at first to the free school in Sydney, but afterwards got a scholarship to the Sydney High School for Girls. I was only a passably good student; the condition of our life, the quarrels, the boarding-house, did not give me much opportunity for concentrated work, and I was naturally inaccurate. My mother had given up character-reading-by-the-face and was an agent for the Equitable Assurance Company of New York. A pioneer in this branch of work in Australia, she used to go out without introductions, yet somehow always brought in business. She suffered from a gastric ulcer at this time, and our life was made rather horrible by the feeling that she was working at a physical disadvantage. She loved to make money and loved to work, but she always exploited the fact, suggesting to me that my father was lacking in manhood to let her work. This was particularly unjust as my father longed to have his wife at home. But my mother always made the point that if my father was a man he would keep her.

For a grim time we lived in the same boarding-house with Aunt Mary, who had a little box of a room which looked on to brick walls. She brought with her a Broadwood cottage piano, some distinction-conferring pieces of china, and odds and ends of pictures. She taught the piano at superior schools; and in the Harper manner did what she could to teach me to scorn my mother.

Mary was friendly with the government astronomer and his family, and also with the Archbishop. My mother on the other hand was content to live solitary, and still would not have called the Queen her aunt. Beatrice, who was in an equally distinguished way of music teaching in an inland town, used to come to Sydney for the holidays, and wishing to embarrass me, attempted to stir me to shame because my father was a piano-tuner.

My mother and I had a fine front room where we lived with a parrot, which my mother trained in a remarkable way, by encouraging it to climb round the room gnawing the woodwork. It must have been quite a remarkable boarding-house keeper to stand for this. Business for the assurance company slacked off, and she became specially convinced of the inadequacy of my father, so we had another suicide scare. This time she drank two bottles of Chlorodyne, hid the empty bottles in the tea canister she toured with, and waited the death that did not come to her, perhaps because she was curiously immune from poison.

I was now fourteen, and for the first time a man fell in love with me. He was a bank clerk called Alexander MacKnight who also lived in the boarding-house. My life became elaborate with the flowers

111

and chocolates of this Alexander MacKnight. I took not the least interest in him, though one night, riding with him on a bus, I became aware of something stirring in me. It had no relationship whatever to the gentleman, but was rather suggested by the idea of love which my mother poured into the air. Having no love affairs of her own at this time, she lived a vicarious love life through my lovers. We went on holiday to the Blue Mountains. Alexander followed us, bringing with him a pound's worth of pennies in a leather bag. With them as counters he taught me to play poker at the bottom of a mountain valley. I let him kiss me, but entirely because of the things mother was saying about love. I was by this time beautiful. I think my mother fostered my love affairs to annoy my father, who had a horror of my being diverted from my destiny of artistic attainment. She it was though who brought things to the final quarrel, and when Alexander wrote me a farewell letter she steamed it open, read it, fastened it up again, and returned it to him unopened! This exploitation of my love affairs by my own mother gave me a false attitude to love, which afterwards served me in bad stead.

We moved into another boarding-house where there was a young dentist, Mr Eardley Swift, the son of a Wesleyan minister, struggling along with a makeshift chair, whom I remember with nausea. He was stupid, sensual, addicted to books on sex, and used to write me bad poems adapted from birthday books. My mother took a fancy to him, and there was a scene in which she told father that if only I would marry dear Eardley she would die happy. Once she left us alone in the boarding-house for the night. Swift said, 'I am surprised at your mother doing that. I might have come into your room.' I, dimly sex-curious, told this to my mother who said casually, 'Well, did he come into your room?' I became engaged to him, and went down to stay at the parsonage. My father suffered very much: he loathed Wesleyans. Mercifully, the daughters of the parson intervened, telling their brother that I had no principles. My next lover I found for myself.

At sixteen, when I left the high school, I was horribly over-strained and dyspeptic. By this time my parents had saved twenty pounds in gold, a very respectable sum. We moved to a charming old wooden house at Double Bay with a pink carnation bush on one side of the front door and a white on the other. By the carriage gate were fir trees, against which I used to rub my face in the loneliness of my

112

adolescence. We bought furniture at auctions, notably an oil paint-ing by Sir James Lynton, whose reputation my father had known when he was in England, of which we were very proud. My mother bought a double bed with a horsehair mattress on which an old Jew had died. I thought this rather horrible but it did not worry my mother. I used to sleep with her in this bed when my father was travelling.

While my mother went out after life assurance, I stayed at home. I was supposed to do the housework which I did with great nervous strain, and horribly, always convinced of my extreme incapacity. But I practised the piano four hours a day. Although I made quick progress, I always played with a sort of stutter because my Aunt Mary, who taught me, did not associate pleasure with art; and her lessons were somehow always a criticism of my character, which was *a priori* defective since I was my mother's daughter. My beautiful voice began to develop, to gain in power. I used to sing by myself, longing for someone to know how beautiful it was. My aunts always chastened me for faults of technique, lest pride should grow in me. I know now that they knew nothing whatever about technique. But they awoke fear in me, so that not till much later could I sing accu-rately. They brought their creditable friend Milly Russell, the daughter of the government astronomer, to hear me. Millie was her-self a singer, a graduate of Sydney University. She sang atrociously with a curious grimacings of the mouth. She said I sang a great deal too loud, so the fine organ in my altogether too suggestible body was doomed to a paralysis on account of her.

My mother grew tired of the life assurance business, and under-went a nervous crisis, as always in periods of boredom. She felt dis-tinguished by illness, and, when she was in funds, went to doctors, and to very good doctors. She could always diagnose her symptoms because she read them up in the *Encyclopaedia Britannica*. She was under treatment from Doctor Jarvie Hood, a very shrewd Scotsman who practised in MacQuarie Street which is the Harley Street of Sydney. Doctor Jarvie Hood had given my mother a sleeping draught containing one hundred and twenty grains of chloral. One night she went over to the wash-hand stand in the room with the bed in it on which the old Jew had died, poured the whole bottle into a glass and drank it off. I toiled up the hill to the chemists and found that forty grains was a poisonous dose. All night I kept my mother alive by rubbing the skin on her ribs, which gave her enough pain to keep her slightly conscious. I got our maid-of-all-work out of bed and made her make emetics of strong coffee and mustard and water. Next day my mother was very vigorous: she drank a bottle full of a strong solution of bromide of potassium, and a bottle of Stephens ink: she chased the fox terrier round the room with a carving knife, and then her rage abated.

Two days after this she bought a new hat and went without any introduction to interview the minister of education. She left his office with permission to teach elocution in the state schools and technical institutions of Sydney, with the laudable purpose of combatting the Australian accent. Whenever my mother was about to change her job she had to clear her mind with some melodramatic scene, after which her energy was restored.

I was at this time delicate, and Doctor Jarvie Hood said that if I remained with my mother I would suffer a nervous breakdown. I did remain with her as I, more than anyone, could manage her. At first I was not included in the elocution business as she thought I, like my father, had no talent. But on one occasion my mother was ill and I had to deputise, and made quite a good thing of it. After that I was allowed to teach the children under ten. The Duchess of York, later Queen Mary, came out to Sydney: there was an exhibition and all sorts of educational competitions. Out of a class of seven, six of my pupils won medals, so I was well set in the elocution business. I could make a small child act anything. My star pupil aged ten played Juliet, and I, without in the least realising the assault I was making on childhood, trained a child of three to sing before three thousand people. Although my mother was the organiser and had thought the idea up, it was I who really had the teaching talent. She went on teaching adolescents to recite 'The Women of Mumbles Head', and I developed more spectacular work with the young children. The schools paid five shillings per head for ten lessons, and with classes of over forty we often made two pounds ten an hour between us. Our life became a sea of half-crowns, and we used to bring the takings home wrapped in a handkerchief. The work was so tiring I would sometimes leave some of the half-crowns in a teaching room and not trouble to go back for them, a far cry from the thin days in Maryborough when I searched my father's pocket for a penny and found nothing. And this was my triumphant justification with my Aunts

114

May and Beatrice who had tried to apprentice me to a smart drapers.

My mother began to organise concerts in a vast mission hall in Sydney to raise funds for orphan children. We split the takings with the mission. The concerts were given by children from our elocution classes, for whom I wrote plays in verse with lots of speaking parts so that the families would buy tickets to see their children perform. We used to make about eighty pounds from each concert, and bought a carriage and two horses so we could drive round to our classes; we also kept a groom. My children used to say their lines beautifully, and my father would come to rehearsals and cry with the satisfaction of it all. For recreation I used to go to the Technical College and study geology, and I had a happy time playing with fossils and rock sections.

About this time I went to stay with my Aunt Beatrice, who was in small-town society and went out to dinner a good deal. Led out, in my best dress, to the nicest houses to play bridge, I began to see that we had not enough table linen in our house at Double Bay, and, to impress my aunt with my social seaworthiness, I got engaged to Leslie Parker, the best tennis player at the club and M.C. at the dances. He was a clean young man of twenty-eight with a fine collection of books. I used to sit out on the balcony with Mr Parker's arms round me, but my emotions had suffered a sort of dry rot from the kisses of Alexander and the dentist. I was never at all serious with Leslie Parker about love, but I found his tidiness and well-organised ordinariness a pleasant contrast and a rest from the eternal *sturm und drang* of our family life. He wore the right kind of tennis shoes, carried the best brand of racket, and, at the dances he organised, there was always a splendid kind of oyster pâté. I had a sort of pride in being able to approximate myself to anything so entirely unlike me or my people. Leslie Parker had points of similarity with Aunt Beatrice, whose coats were made of eternal tweed, cut and braided with a correctness altogether meritorious. Always victim to inferiority feeling, and always over-suggestible, I was very sensitive to niceties of equipment. My mother dressed imaginatively and opulently, but Mary and beatrice were always there to suggest that she dressed unsuitably. My aunts, forced into adaptability by their hostesses and their pupils, impressed themselves, with the savage pride of mediocrity, on what they could find malleable in their environment. This was a reflex from their enforced social adjustments and I, undisciplined and unoriented, was supremely malleable. They sowed in me that social fear which is the spirit of all snobbery. They dominated me until I could have believed the vaunted rightness of Aunt Beatrice's umbrella to be holy.

I returned to my mother with trepidation, for I had found a respite in the low intensity and emotional stability of small town society. To an extent I had adopted its standards as an escape from those I had inherited, and I had put in the first stone or two on which I would begin to build a self. My mother scouted my suggestions for new domestic arrangements, little elegancies, and attempts to conform to the norm of people from whom we were so different. My returns always led to scenes, discharges of a black emotionalism. So the new will growing in me was cut back, and my adolescent but quite reasonable attempts to establish my difference from the family group were frustrated.

Leslie Parker's father had been a chemist in a small town, and one of the pillars of the Wesleyan chapel. But he had made some sort of default of chapel funds, and had had to leave the town. There had been no prosecution because of his wife's sound family connections. Undeterred, he started a larger and better chemist's shop in Sydney. There were ten children, all orderly and ordinary, in offices and banks; the women, neat, frugal and without charm. Leslie Parker gave me a sapphire-and-diamond engagement ring which I prized very much because of its entire normality. At this time I had an instinct to imitate and cultivate all ordinariness. I was received into the Parker family, and liked the placid ordinariness of Mrs Parker, and her concentration on the mere business of living, which had brought her family safely over the shoals of their father's default. I also found the old sinner himself sympathetic. He seemed to be reacting against his destiny as chemist, his preoccupation with drugs and boluses, for he recommended, as a universal panacea, black pepper; pepper with the soup, the fish and the entrée, almost pepper in the tea. In his opinion enough pepper would make him and all chemists unnecessary. He would gladly have died of pepper.

The Parkers came to see us at our charming wooden house in Double Bay with the camelia trees, and my father wept because of them. Their ordinariness, which was such a relief to me, appalled him. Was this where I was to end, where he had begun, with

116

Wesleyans? Wesleyans now depreciated, vulgarised, lacking the spirit and spunk of his forebears. I, who was to be his justification, who was to represent him, and establish his powers and his spirit among the people and in the world to which he belonged, here I was, imitating the Parker women, trying to keep my shoes on trees, to wear only fashionable and feminine clothing. I read the women's papers and made for myself complicated little undergarments, and articles for the toilet. If my father had accepted these imitations, he would have added considerably to the chances of my survival. But he insisted on his and my difference, recalling old glories with tales of James Lecky and George Riddell and pointing forward to the spacious regions in which lay the victories of mind. I was not to marry the neat foolishness of any Wesleyan; I was to make a reputation, and my father was to experience the satisfaction felt by Nellie Melba's father in Melbourne. It was this Parker business that put the ambition in him for me to go back to England, back to the territory of George Riddell, who had made a fortune and a great place for himself, although he had less brains than my father.

This attitude of my father's proved merciful to Leslie Parker for whom nothing could have been more disastrous than to marry me. As it turned out, energised by losing me, he somehow raised money to become a doctor, and made a success in the profession his father the chemist would have chosen for him. He had, as a matter of fact, fallen on a technique of his own to escape from me. Because I was attempting to be ordinary, I said nothing to Leslie about my poetry, but Leslie wrote sentimental verses to me:

> A maiden so rare,
> With brown wavy hair, and eyes,
> Who ever has seen such a pair?

In his verses he had defects of wit in spite of his inexpensive chic: unable to speak French, he would ask, '*Vouley-vous pompdenciey madame*?' with an ineffable waggishness. This and his verses released me. Moreover one of my aunts wrote tentatively, from the small town, hinting at his infidelities: he had been seen sitting out on a balcony with a rich Jewess, Oravida Bensusan. I sent him back his diamond-and-sapphire engagement ring, advised by my mother who knew the etiquette of such disembarrassments.

117

To the house at Double Bay with the camelia bushes came another bad poet — Oswald Phillips, a solicitor. He wrote:

> If thou wilt give thy love to me
> I then indeed will worship thee,
> For woman's love is better far
> Than all the pride of King or Czar.

This clear statement had no personal application because Oswald, a Catholic with a natural instinct for self-preservation, never made love to me. We felt rather distinguished for having him as a guest. We had begun to buy elegant china and articles of silver, and my mother prepared special dishes for Oswald. Our attitude to the professional classes at that time was one of appreciation to such of them as would come to visit us, and of general antagonism to the majority which did not. From Oswald I got the impression that my parents considered solicitors to be a creditable class.

My mother and I were making about twelve hundred a year in the elocution business, and my father was not doing so badly with his pianos, so I, who at this time had certain instincts for thrift, began to persuade them to buy houses. They bought two. One, in Lower Moss Bay, was built on the sudden hill-slope from the harbour; it had a garden which rose sheer from the back of the house, and it was damp. They let this and bought another at Balmoral Bay, which was my choice and was surely the most beautiful little house in the world, with roses and waratahs in the garden, and the most lovely view of the harbour and the coastline — lovely as the curves of a woman.

The house was well furnished, there was elegant food and a capable housekeeper, but hardly any visitors. My mother exhausted by her classes, would come home and go to bed by eight o'clock. We belonged nowhere. I continued at the Technical College and was zealous and ambitious about geology, but, most important of all, I went to the best singing teacher in Sydney who told me I had a great voice. If we had touched Sydney society anywhere, I would have been promoted throughout Australia as a singer, and probably sent home by subscription to study.

My father decided that I should return to England to make a success in one or more of the arts, and my mother, although she had no real interest in my talents, fell in with his wishes. I was anxious enough to go to England, first because of youth's universal desire for change, and then because I had met May Mukle. She had come to Sydney playing the cello in the company of Edwin Floyd – the great tenor. She had every scope, every cachet that I lacked; and sometimes, when I was toiling round from one mechanics' institute to another teaching our dull recitations, I used almost to cry with envy at the idea of May, elegantly dressed, in European concert rooms, in the society of persons whose names were prominent in the newspapers. May, with her English prestige, said that I was a great deal more brilliant than she, that our dramatic teaching was not equalled in England. She was ten years older than me, and I found her so strong and lovely that I wanted to join my life with hers.

May and I went to the Jenolan caves together, and I called the first book of verse I published *The Songs of John Oland*. May was, early, a rabid feminist; she had had the devil of a time establishing herself against male prejudice, while making her way with an instrument considered unfeminine. She had no opinion of marriage, an attitude I did not share with her. She said that men would destroy and betray me. When she went back to England I spent most of my leisure writing to her.

May gave me an object in going to England more definite than any vague ambition. Anyway, I had no ambition for myself, being only the medium of my father's. Arrangements began for my journey with full sentimental honours. My mother bought everything. I was rather uneasy about my equipment; I found my crocodile dressing-case splendid but too heavy, and I felt that my clothes were wrong. I probably exaggerated this, but I had not the least idea how to buy clothes as my mother had always done this for me, and I had no faith in my mother's taste because of the criticism of Mary and Beatrice.

My father and I went for a farewell tour outside Tumut, up to the gold-washing country on the roof of Australia, and we were very happy and lover-like; he glowed with enthusiasm for the destiny that lay before me. He said that superior people of intelligence would adopt me because of my talents and fine voice. His general instructions to me were to sing to the great heart of the people, and he told me over and over again that there was plenty of room at the top. He had, however, no explicit instructions as to how to get to the top. My mother was more definite. She wanted from me a set of love relations that would interest her, as she had been interested in my love affairs with Alexander and the young dentist. Her comment was, 'Don't marry for money, but go where money is'. My father's instructions were careless, but my mother's were insincere. It was not in her character to be a marriage broker and there is no reason to think that she seriously thought marriage the right career for me.

They bought several pieces of electroplate and some ebony walking sticks for me to take to the Harpers and the Whelans, and had them inscribed with emotional messages, 'To the dear Home people from Geoffrey and Alice'. I remembered with wonder that there had not been much flow of love and soul when Geoffrey and Alice had last been in contact with the Harpers and Whelans, but they both needed to say something poignant and exciting.

My parents had little capital, but the elocution classes and the piano business were going well, so they made me an allowance of four pounds a week out of income, and, with the most indefinite of objectives, I set out. I knew that somehow I had to get my parents into the news, fortify their self-respect with grand contacts and successful exploits. I had a general commission to know people so that my father, through me, could come near to the famous society that delighted him. I was his only child, and the only object with whom he had had a satisfactory love relationship. And his ambition to make an impression on the country that had ignored him was so strong, that as the ship moved out from the Wharf, he called up to me, '*Punch*, Anne, *Punch*', meaning that he wished me to write for that monumentally humorous paper.

CHAPTER IV

I travelled second-class and regretted it. I carried twenty pounds in gold in a belt round my waist, and I considered paying the difference between my fare and the first-class, but decided not to. There was a young man who had been to Eton in the first-class, and this was important to me because I knew that that school was in the news. There was also an actress from the Sign of the Cross company which had been playing in Sydney. These were the sort of contacts I needed. I followed the actress round when we went ashore at Melbourne, but was too shy to talk to her. I thought instead of all the love songs I would write. I was a bad steward of my talents and responsibilities because I began a flirtation with Mr Layton the first officer, very impressive to me in his gold braid.

After Melbourne, the first-class people used to come over to our saloon in the evening to hear me sing, and a very nasty gentleman tried to make love to me in a manner that could have meant me no good. He quarrelled with the first officer with whom my relations grew more and more affectionate.

At Colombo, I shook myself free from all emotional entanglements, the first officer being engaged with the management of the ship; I went ashore and spent three of my twenty pounds presenting to myself an interpretation of the rich and intelligent traveller. At Gibraltar, a gentleman took me and the actress to lunch at a luxury hotel and I began to feel that my career had begun.

I was met at Tilbury by my Harper aunt, Matilda, she who had hoped to marry a naval surgeon and had married instead a merchant who was half German. They were stolid and bourgeois and did not impress the first officer when I introduced him. My aunt, who disliked me because I was my mother's daughter, because I was very good-looking and because she wanted to keep the attention of her half-German, declared war on me at once. She said that my manner made her feel like the niece. They gave me ham and coffee in an A.B.C. shop with the air of showing me the town. My aunt would scarcely let me out of her sight for some days for fear of my being molested in London, I, who had travelled all up the coast of Queensland alone when I was eleven. Mr Layton never called on my family, and I never heard from him again.

I was driven in a four-wheeler to my grandfather's house which was in a dingy part of South Hampstead. The family were met to receive me. They were all rather laconic. So this was the prodigy, the genius about whom Geoffrey had written so enthusiastically, the champion bred by the regrettable Alice. Alicia, a very old woman now, was crippled but powerful in her horsehair chair. The house was rather dirty and without any elegance. Old Edwin, in leather leggings and a soiled and frayed tweed coat, had a humorous glint in his eyes which was partly hatred of his puritanical and superior family. He remarked that the lodger on the first floor had started a bow window, by which he meant that she was pregnant. My aunts Matilda and Muriel sang a Goddard duet together in cracked voices that had never recovered from their training. Muriel also played the viola and said she was learning the bassoon. I sang 'O Divine Redeemer' with great feeling and a song by Meyerbeer. The Harpers knew a good voice when they heard one, but in those days I had an affected habit of letting down my hair while I was singing, and Alicia cast a severe old eye over me, suspecting my mother's inchastity in me. The redeeming thing about my reception was the piano playing of old Edwin who played Mozart like an artist. An understanding and affection sprang up between us. This was the place from which I was to start my conquest of the world: my heart failed in me.

I slept that night with my aunt Muriel, but went to supper with my aunt Matilda. She had had three children in three-and-a-half years, and lived heavily with her German in an atmosphere of Mellin's Food, trying not to think of the naval doctor. Her husband was kind but quite unintellectual. He read William le Queux and looked after his business. Matilda had inherited a turn for Ruskin and the Greek vases at the British Museum. She quite saw the point of her Fritz' attention to his business, but a dream was dead in her, and her relief from the pain of it was to kill the dreams in others.

I decided to go down to see the shop in Wimbledon where my parents had striven and suffered, and, with the rather false emotionalism that had been planted in me, I over-dramatised the pilgrimage. 'What,' said Aunt Matilda, 'going to see where the tablet will be put up?' in an ineffable accent of scorn. I found one of my rhymed plays, that I had written for our dramatic classes and which my father had sent home with such pride, torn in pieces in Matilda's lavatory.

Fritz now made the sensible suggestion that I study at the Royal Academy of Music, but this was rejected by my aunts Muriel and Matilda. Their friends the Sumners had a protégé named George Dukes, the son of a Cornish labourer, who had a great bass voice which the Sumners had helped to have trained. He had studied in Paris with Bouhy, and everyone knew what a teacher was Bouhy! By sending me to Dukes my aunts would be obliging the Sumners.

Dukes was rough, but a good voice producer. He put me on to operatic arias, and bored me about them until I came near to nervous prostration. One day he bullied me so much I ran from the room in tears, and I found he'd brought in friends to hear me sing. He said I had a great voice, but added, 'I suppose you'll marry and have a lot of dirty kids'. Aunts Muriel and Matilda talked so much about the necessity of hard work that I sang more than ever out of time. I could never work at an art: I could either do it or refrain from doing it.

I went over to Maida Vale to see May Mukle in a dream of pleasure and anticipation; with my over-emotionalism and affectation, I took off my shoes before going in to her room. May really loved me and had faith in me. I found her surrounded by a number of sisters, all unimaginative but efficient instrumentalists who had engagements in such theatre bands as would take women in those days. They had the technical background which I lacked. Their family and the Harpers had always been rivals, with May's people in a slight ascendancy because of their greater technical proficiency. The father was a mechanical instrument maker who had forgotten how to speak German and never learned English, so that he was almost speechless and spent his time reading Swedenbourg in the original. The whole family were immensely proud of May who had got into the news, and had made quite a reputation in London. The sisters felt that I – a Harper – could in no way enhance that reputation. They began to ridicule my affection for May who had a new friend in a young ballad singer – Carmen Hill: she had a small but true talent, and had already had the success of singing small parts with Seymour Hicks. All my dreams of forming a life with May fell to the ground as I found when I left my grandfather's house and went to lodge with the Mukles in a gloomy house by the Regent's Park Canal to be near her. She and Carmen were always together, and the female oboe and double-bass players laughed and made me feel like a rejected lover.

Tree's Academy of Acting had recently been founded. I recited to Pinero and Tree and Bancroft a poem that I remembered from my childhood, and made a little speech to the examiners, telling them that I had come all the way from Australia for the benefit of their school and asking them to give me a scholarship, which they did.

At the audition was Betty Kalisch from a rich Dutch-Jewish family, who said, 'My mother says I'm to know you because you're the only girl here with a decent face.' The Kalisch's were friends of Sarah Bernhardt, and I felt I was getting near to people in the news. But by this time, I had got my nerve back and my natural arrogance and I did not take advantage of this chance to know Miss Kalisch. I, who had been too timorous to speak to the small-part actress from the Sign of the Cross company, now decided that Betty was a bad actress, and rejected her. I was in the advanced class and arrogant enough to think that they taught no better than we had taught in Australia. In this atmosphere of freedom I began to lose my feelings of inferiority.

While I was at the Mukles' I had influenza, but they, to whom life had often been hard, had no time for students who were ill. One night, lying gloomy and uncared for in my room, I remembered Bernard Shaw was to talk on 'The Economics of Art' in the dome room of His Majesty's Theatre. I got up and drove to the theatre. As I was getting out of the cab a young man bowed and spoke to me. He really thought I was a girl he knew. (I met her afterwards and she was quite like me.) As we climbed the staircase to the dome room he said he was William Ray, a freelance reporter, who had written for the *Daily Mail*. I had not forgotten that I had been sent home to make connections interesting to my father, and he considered London newspapers interesting. He had known journalists in the great times with James Lecky and George Riddell. After Mr Shaw's speech in the dome room I asked Mr Ray to come to tea. He wrote me a number of felicitous letters in bad journalese, and he came again.

I was at this time very lonely. My relations didn't like me, and I didn't like them. I had been rejected by May and her friends had treated me with scorn. At home in Australia we were demonstrative, we kissed each other, we showed our emotions. I never wanted passion when I was a young girl, but I felt it, somehow, *de rigueur* — I felt it was in the part. With me passion was always a dramatic performance. Now I wanted companionship, and William Ray was there to give it. He was a year older than me, and pretended at first to be in society. He also told me that his sister was one of the best dancers in London. In fact, she was the jaded wife of a barber in a back street in Finsbury Park. I scorned him for this pretence. He lost ground too when it came out that he knew my Whelan aunts. He had been a clerk in the Education Department, and he had the scornful attitude that ambitious officialdom has for board-school teachers. Ambitious clerks may climb into the professional classes through journalism or other means, but a board-school teacher is always a board-school teacher, always socially in no man's land.

He might not have been so scornful if it had not been for his friendship with old Hamilton who was high in the Education

Department, and watched over his career with interest. Hamilton was a pompous old dilettante, who knew and scorned my Whelan aunts. I did not love them but I resented this scorn of my family, so my relationship with William Ray started all wrong.

A board-school boy, he had won a scholarship to a minor public school where they had taught him his snobbery, but not enough sense to talk civilly of a young woman's aunts. I went to the Ray's home in Finsbury Park and met William's father, who was a builder in a small way, a strong evangelical, whose only reading was a philosophical paper called *Great Thoughts*. His mother was admirable, a keen-eyed, thrifty woman of the upper working class. His sisters were deplorable, talking in Cockney accents without intelligence or distinction, or half the general knowledge of my Whelan aunts.

I became engaged to William, more or less out of a habit of becoming engaged to people, and he gave me another sapphire-and-diamond engagement ring very like Leslie Parker's. William was clever, but he was a lowbrow, taking no interest in Ruskin, the *Synthetic Series*, the Pre-Raphaelites, Henry James, or in any of my father's holy things. Only through his connection with the daily newspapers would he be acceptable to my father. As he took me with him on his assignments I got quite close to things in the news, and wrote long letters about them to my father. William made acquaintances with an eye to his career. One day he said to me, 'If you want to marry a rich man I'll introduce you to one': I took this as wanting in sentiment and delicacy, in a fiancé.

My mother began writing hysterical letters about my father, saying he was drinking. I was very attached to my father and fears about him took the strength out of me. Then my mother sent me a silk blouse. I decided to leave Dukes, whose brutal approach to singing had become too much. I put on the silk blouse as a mascot, and pulled on new gloves and went to call on Randaegger, carrying a sheaf of white irises. I sang very ineffectually – I was nervous; but Randaegger said something about my personality, and told me with many chuckles how he had refused to teach another Australian, Nellie Melba, and how when he dined with her much later she had said, 'Randaegger, were not you an old fool?' He started me on singing technique with his wife, and one day he came to me with a delighted expression and said, 'Madame says you'll set the Thames

125

on fire in eight months', and as an earnest of the sincerity of his opinion he reduced my fees considerably.

By this time I had helped William to get his first regular job in journalism. We had gone one night to Wonderland, the boxing ring in Whitechapel. William was reporting for an American news agency on a month's trial, and the occasion was the indignation meeting of the Russians in London for the brutalities of 'Black Friday' in St Petersburg. The meeting was crowded and extremely exciting. Revolutionists harangued in many tongues. A Russian girl in a nurse's uniform, with the red ribbon of the Revolutionists, was in a high state of agitation, tears pouring down her cheeks: she threw herself into my arms in a paroxysm of emotion. William, who had gathered that she was an important figure in the revolutionary movement, told me to get her address. She was in charge of the Rothschild crèche off the Commercial Road, and close to the leaders of the movement. Through her I met Karski and persuaded him to pass on to us the Russian news he received from a revolutionary press in Paris. I used to go to the Polish Club in Whitechapel, or to Karski's lodgings in Walthamstow, while William waited for me outside. The agency cabled the news to the *New York Sun* who were able to print it before it appeared in European newspapers. This scoop turned William's month's trial into a permanent job.

In small rooms in Whitechapel I came to know prominent revolutionary Russians, including Tsaikowsky and Sasha Kropotkin, then about sixteen and the darling of the revolutionists. With her and the nurse, at the Whitechapel Theatre, I saw the best acting I have ever seen. The play was in Yiddish and, although I did not understand a word, the acting was so good that it did not matter: the leading actress was Nazimova.

One day William said to me, in a fretted sort of way, 'I want you to come and see a man.' We went to an unbelievably dirty and untidy room in Great Ormond Street, and there was Patrick Hepburn making lantern slides with feverish concentration. Patrick was a partner in his father's solicitor's practice, and William cultivated solicitors because his ambition was to become a barrister. Patrick said that what he himself most feared to be was an eminent solicitor. Soon after our meeting his father died and Patrick inherited the business, one of the oldest in the City of London. Old James Hepburn, a successful company lawyer, left sixty thousand pounds.

Patrick told me that no funeral had ever been organised better than his father's, and I felt that this was the first thing Patrick had ever been allowed to organise. He was thirty-two and, although a partner, had worked as a sort of superior clerk in the office. A brilliant student, he had taken the Lincoln's Inn Prize, but he loathed life in the City. Every moment of free time he spent on his push-bicycle, performing prodigies of endurance; riding to York in a day, through heavy storms of wind and rain. It was his pleasure to take physical risks and to exhaust his body. As a boy of ten he had swum across the dangerous tidal river at Littlehampton: he had been stranded on a rock ledge in Norway: he broke the ice to swim on Christmas Day.

Patrick had a passion for scenery, but he also had a purpose which he carried out with high efficiency. He photographed churches – chiefly Romanesque churches, all over England and France, and even a part of Spain which he went to in August, bicycling through the heat of the day. He had made a unique collection of photographs of Romanesque churches. And he relieved the tedium of his life in the City by making up his photographs into lantern slides. Occasionally he gathered his slides together and lectured on them, giving a lot of attention to measurements and points of exact detail. But he had no plan to publish or gain wider recognition. I was immediately attracted by this activity of Patrick's. In the first place because architecture was a good subject in my father's eyes. I detected in Charles the 'painful man of science' so approved at home, and his entire preoccupation with his intellectual interests was exactly what my father had always desired for himself. Indeed, in many ways Patrick reminded me of him. My father's love for me was a refuge from the passion of men of my own generation, against which I always reacted. I felt in Patrick a simplicity, and I imagined a chastity. William was, by this time, pressing me hard. We went only to places that interested him, never to a concert or the opera. One night in an angry scene by the gates of Finsbury Park, William told me that I would do better to give up my ambitions and marry him. And this when Randaegger had expressed his very high opinion of my prospects.

My father had a pathetic pride in my plays for children, seeing a delicacy in the versification. I gave the plays to William to show to people in Fleet Street who might publish them. He returned them with, 'I can't do anything with this rubbish'. His scornful tone had the antagonism of the professional writer for the amateur, and I loathed him. I expected from Patrick, in contrast to William, the sympathy I received from my father. Nonetheless something in the appearance, the youth, the affection of William attracted me, and I felt at least a superficial emotion for him. But his depreciation of my mind and my natural disposition to create weighed heavier with me than his appreciation of my sex attraction.

I saw in William a disposition to exploit Patrick for I understood the lower middle class! William was of my class; Patrick, with his preoccupation with things of the mind, was of my kind. William had for Patrick the subconscious hatred of the exploiter for the victim. He thought Patrick − the man − a fool, though Patrick Hepburn, the social personality, son of a rich solicitor and descendant of Stuarts and Tudors, was altogether desirable to him. My sympathy was at once with Patrick because, feeling him the weaker, I sensed that I could protect him against this enemy. I dramatised the situation. I did this because Patrick came pre-eminently from the class − 'villa-dweller' − the people who had insulted my father. I knew that I, as well as Patrick, had 'gentleman' manners, that I was going to have no difficulty with the sort of people that were in the news, and that, by aiding and protecting this supreme type of villa-dweller, I would doubly establish my father's dignity. I felt this more than ever when we all went down to Harrow School to hear Patrick lecture on his Romanesque churches. Harrow School was a place most impressive to me.

Patrick lectured weakly, his back to the audience, his pointer wandering without precision over his diagram. He emphasised the points that did not seem to me dramatically essential. The strongest impression I carried away was of the slack of his badly fitting trousers. The lecture started late and the showmanship was abominable. A part of my mind knew this, and pride stirred in me for the beautiful promptness and management of our performances in Sydney; but another part of my mind was charmed by this very inefficiency, by the appealing inadequacy, by the scholarship, the pains that had been taken, the effort that had been made.

I travelled down in the train with a fat woman whose large black arms, in a coat too tight for her, gave me a feeling of physical revulsion. She was Patrick's sister, Ellen Hepburn. She read a magazine which contained a poem with a border of cupids, and made no pretence of being interested in Patrick's archaeology. She always went to hear him out of family solidarity, but she was as depressing about his performance as she could be. William was also at the lecture at Harrow, dreaming of the triumphant speeches he would make at the bar. He scouted the lecture to me as intolerably dull.

Patrick and I and William had supper together a night or two after the Harrow lecture, in Soho. Patrick's face was very high-bred and beautiful, but he was prematurely bald. As he told us with passionate enthusiasm about one of his Homeric bicycle cruises, William jockeyed him along with his calculated cordiality. I spent most of the time looking at myself in the restaurant mirror and noticing that I was beautiful. I said to William afterwards, 'I like that man, though he will never know the first thing about me.' Patrick had fallen in love with me and spent hours of that night walking up and down outside my boarding-house in his slippers.

Later I gave him one of my children's plays to read. Though civiller than William, I got no sympathy out of him. Yet at his apathy, I felt none of the hatred I had felt for William. Respecting Patrick's judgement because of his status as a scholar and his association with Harrow, I became ashamed of my father's belief in me, and remembered what my mother thought. William had aroused in me self assertion: Patrick, by the weight of his authority, caused me to deny myself. Not for years did I let Patrick know of my pretensions to be a poet, or of my father's ambition for me.

Patrick knew Shakespeare's sonnets by heart and had read all Tennyson. The eldest of a large family, generally top of his form at school, he had a high opinion of himself which was reinforced by the Hepburn women, who kept up a purr of intellectual admiration and an attitude of obeisance, and so were able to dominate him morally. When Patrick joined the Royal Naval Air Service during the Great War, his cousin Emma said the navy ought to be honoured to have him, and she meant it. Patrick knew himself to be first in his own circle, but he knew there were other circles and other authorities, and he took a sort of sensuous pleasure in thinking of the fine societies in which his knowledge and attainment were as insignificant as a mustard seed on a mountain.

Patrick was definitely attracted to me because I had a mind. Lonely in his hobbies and preoccupations, he needed an audience, and I, with my pliability, my suggestibility, my sense of *métier de femme*, was a supremely good audience. (I was, of course, working hard on my voice.)

He started to educate me by pointing out to me charming architectural details in the houses in Bloomsbury, and then took me out to dinner and explained the mechanics of the eye. For years I listened, until my mind became full to irritation with his general knowledge, and I began to want to say something myself. I enjoyed Patrick's lecturettes which I knew were altogether admirable from my father's point of view, and though at this time Patrick's science was no more modern than my father's, I delighted to think it more accurate. I began to see myself as an influence, and to have a consciously stimulating effect. Going over in my mind what I had learned at school, I asked Patrick if he could bisect a triangle by a line drawn parallel to its base. For some days Patrick could not, and I had forgotten the secret of it.

I went down to the country to rest my voice. Patrick followed me and we sat about the fields in an idyllic springtime, he glowing with love for me, and attempting to bisect a triangle with a line drawn parallel to its base. There was something about this combination of interest which appealed to my imagination. Remembering my duty of making a reputation to satisfy my father, I was afraid of love without an admixture of triangles. The geometry of William's love concerned itself only with the curves of my person. His embraces became more and more intimate: coldly interested in his proximities, I began my erotic apprenticeship.

Patrick did a very clever thing, by playing charmingly with me and some children at the top of a church tower. This made me think that Patrick liked children, which was not the case. As the male bird develops a blue wing-feather in the mating season, so he developed this technique of attracting my attention and touching my heart.

William, with a fretted desire to hold Patrick and dominate him, lent me to Patrick, even asking me to influence him. One day at the rooms in Great Ormond Street, William said, 'You can do anything with that man: go upstairs and make him give away some of his mouldy old clothes.' Patrick was a hoarder, though at the same time he scorned property for property's sake. He had thrown away his diamond studs because of their association with some boredom, some banality, but had kept every pair of trousers he had worn since he was breeched, every theatre programme of every performance he had ever witnessed, every piece of string that had come to him round a parcel, and every envelope with every letter. He never allowed sweeping or dusting so the agglomeration was unbelievable. In this confusion, Patrick carried on his meticulous work. Flattered that I could make my influence felt, I persuaded him to clear out his wardrobes, which he did with anguish. I was entirely unpractical and untidy, but my disorder was rather a sickness of the nerves than a lust of the spirit. I loathed disorder while Patrick loved it. His accumulations were as native to him as the bower is to the bower-bird.

So, with my priggishness, with my desire to be a light and an example, I began to set Patrick's house in order. I made him some cretonne covers for his chairs and, delighted with the womanliness of this, he took a photograph of me sewing, which was entirely misleading as, at this time, I sewed very badly.

I began to feel myself caught between the two men, involved with them, somehow held between them. Neither man was really interested in me, but rather in my effect on them. Meanwhile Randaegger was more and more insistent on the brightness of my prospects. I got frightened. I could never sing to William, who found Gluck boring but knew a man at the Savage Club who could play ragtime like an archangel. Patrick pretended to marvel at the beauty of my voice but I knew this to be a pretence. He would far rather sing himself in his weak baritone for me to admire, than listen to the most finished of my performances. He practised one of Mendelssohn's *Songs without Words* on the piano, over and over again, always with the same endearing error. I decided to get away from both of them. If I was as good as Randaegger said, I could get the best instruction in the world by going to Paris. I left my boarding house one morning with three pounds in gold; I knew only the French I had learned at school, I had no introductions and only a vague plan of going, like Bernhardt, to the Conservatoire.

I found a little hotel off the rue St Honoré and somehow gathered enough French to ask the garçon de café the way to the Conservatoire. My idea was to contact Monsieur Masson who taught the advanced singing class. He said that I could attend his class and listen to the singing, though I could not of course join it fully until I had been admitted to the Conservatoire. It would take some time to arrange an audition, and in the meantime he would give me private lessons.

I wrote to William, proud to have justified myself in Paris, asking him to arrange for my allowance from my parents to be transferred, and saying that I felt lonely. He came over for the weekend, Patrick having lent him the fare.

William stayed in my hotel off the rue St Honoré and we became lovers. It was not sincere in me to become his mistress. I wanted to devote myself to the Conservatoire and make a career like Bernhardt. I did not know that she had been a negligible actress till she had a bastard child. I was interested in sex, feeling that love was somehow in my part in *la vie de bohême*, and my role as expatriate student. Next morning I was tearfully sure I was pregnant. William was a vigorous young man: I was his woman, so he took me off for a honeymoon at Montmorency. There, strolling in the woods, I gave a charming imitation of being in love from the sheer pleasure of acting. But I was really quite bored, and William made me despise him by showing fear of a wolfhound we met in the forest. He went back to London with his insufferable male air of disregarding me as soon as our love-making was over.

I moved to a pension in the Clichy Quarter where I paid five francs a day. There were bugs in the room so I used to sleep outside the bed. I hired a piano and practised hard. William came over to see me at intervals, on Patrick's money; he insisted on his rights as a lover. Erotically our love went well enough, but it meant little more to me than the pleasure of giving a perfect dramatic performance. Suffering agony of conscience at what I felt was my infidelity to my parents, I used to take a tearful farewell of my mother's portrait before William joined me or I joined William: Patrick in his remoteness, with his churches and his triangles, became enhanced in my regard. Always, when I came back to Paris from our love trips, I used to go into a church and, at the Shrine of the Virgin, ask forgiveness for having risked being the mother of a bastard. William and I talked tenderly together about children, for he was genuinely fond of children, the sort of young man who might have made a good scout-master. He was a competent journalist too, and, later, was among the best reporters in London.

Once William, invited to a literary party at the house of a woman novelist in Paris, scornfully left me behind, suggesting that this was not my sort of world. I never forgave him.

I had moved away from the Clichy district to the Latin Quarter and was living in a boarding-house in Notre Dame des Champs, when Patrick wrote very civilly that his sister Ellen was bored at home since their father's death, and would like to come and stay with me. Now Ellen was the woman with the fat black arms, when I had travelled down to the lecture at Harrow, who had been reading a poem on a page with a border of cupids. I must have been in love with Patrick at the time to have agreed to have her. It was the most disastrous decision of my life. I have lately read letters from her to Patrick, written while we were together in Paris. In them were the seeds of the vile crop of weeds of misunderstanding which choked Patrick's and my life together. She refers to me scornfully as the 'Prima Donna', tells him that my health is weak, that I am eccentric, and most damaging of all, that I am extravagant.

I was keeping myself on four pounds a week, and studying in the most distinguished school in the world; so I could not have been extravagant. But small straws showed Ellen how the wind blew: I took fiacres, and, when she had gone with me to the fair at St Cloud, I had spent two francs in throwing darts from which I had, as reward, only two small vases worth perhaps sixty centimes. A sheer loss of one franc-forty on the afternoon. When we were first married I had every reason to believe that Patrick condoned a few fiacres and a little dart throwing, but later our life became a hell because of money. I never felt as grateful as I should, in those early days, for Patrick's readiness to share his money with me because it was his idea in the first place, and he was making twelve hundred pounds a year from his practice and had four hundred a year private income. Later, Patrick suggested scornfully that I had failed in my career; but, when we married, I really had the makings of a Prima Donna, apart from my success with the elocution classes. I did not feel that I would fail if left to my own devices.

Ellen, fat, unintelligent and self-satisfied, had the enormous resistance of her type, the long patience and huge reserves of force. I never had a chance against her and she beat me, though in beating me she destroyed her brother. I gave her battle, though I was fighting her, in my arrogance, for the salvation of her own soul. She was pre-eminently the villa-dweller – the old enemy. By this time I had lost my inferiority feeling and I decided to do good to Ellen. She had not the remotest idea of doing any job, spending her time like any Croydon young lady, darning her stockings and writing letters beginning 'Very many thanks' on notepaper which she kept in a neat receptacle of her own contriving. Ellen so dominated me that I alarmed my parents by writing to them utterly colourless letters beginning with the words 'Very many thanks'.

We moved to a flat together opposite the cemetery in the rue Edgar Quinet, and I began to teach Ellen to do housework. I made her wash the paint and, under my instruction, she made her first dish of stewed chicken and rice. Ellen had been sent to Paris to safeguard her brother's interests, a kind of team-work well in the tradition of the Hepburns. She did it very capably, getting the hang of me by the light of her instincts which were far more powerful than my intelligence. She filled me with her virus as a spider does a fly.

My mother had always bought my clothes for me. She used to call me her baby or her doll and proceed accordingly. When I came to Paris I had no underclothes and used to wear three blouses one on top of the other, alternating them when I wanted to change my appearance. This worked well, as the small boys in the street called me *la Belle Anglaise*. I had, at any rate, character and distinction, and in the world of the high theatre there are so many clothes that one excels as much by divergence as by conformity. But Ellen had her Croydon standards, and she took me to the Bon Marché to buy woollen combinations. I thought in the back of my mind that I might develop a wifeliness for Patrick Hepburn, though the texture of the combinations irritated my skin and interfered with my voice production. For my audition at the Conservatoire, Ellen dressed me in a blue dress and a blue velvet hat, and I looked respectable enough for a Church of England bazaar. I failed at the Conservatoire: in France it is very hard for a foreigner to get in anyway. But in my large old brown felt hat and three blouses I looked international, and I believe I would have made it if my performance had been as free as it had been before Tree, Pinero and old Bancroft.

I left Masson, and went to Jean de Reszke, who had a private theatre near the Bois de Boulogne, and was then the most sought-after teacher in the world. He said I had the best voice he had ever had from England. All I wanted now was social freedom, and that I had not with Ellen. We lived in Paris by the light of Croydon. We never went to the cafés, but to the American Mission and the crémeries, meeting women who did arts and crafts and leather work. Ellen bought several small black hats for ten francs each, and when she came with me to the great voice doctor − Poyot − he thought she was my maid, for which she never forgave me because she knew very well I was not a lady. She called me Martha Jane, and found fault with my manners, particularly that I ate the rind of a camembert cheese. I learned later that it is permissible to eat most of the rind of a camembert cheese.

Every Thursday night, while I was singing with de Reszke's master-class, Ellen used to long for the Croydon Choral Society. This was not only because she wished to raise her mezzo-soprano voice, a voice which quite reasonably was the most important voice in the world to her because it was her voice, but because she had formed a sentimental attachment for Edgar Turner who also sang with the Choral Society. Now Turner suffered from tuberculosis. The Hepburns objected to him not only on account of the tuberculosis and the fact that he was always breaking out in spots, but because his family and his job as a bank clerk were not good enough for them. Ellen told me tearfully that all his uncles were C.ofE. clergymen. But the Hepburns, remembering the Stuarts, the Tudors and Charlemagne, demanded of the Turners at least a rural dean. If the Turners were not good enough for the Hepburns, how about me and the slime of my lower middle classness? The point was that Patrick was a man and free to make a misalliance. I saw this at once in defence of Ellen, and my feminism writhed at the injustice.

After our marriage, I determined to use my very strong influence with Patrick who *was* the Hepburn family. He objected to Edgar on account of his poor health rather than for the Turners' shortage of rural deans. I persuaded him that, as Ellen was thirty-three and in my opinion quite without charm, she would never get another chance of marriage; nor, with the fidelity and tenacity of her character, would she ever want to marry another man. I said that it was scandalous to spoil her happiness for mere social prejudice. I had my way. When Ellen and Edgar had exchanged engagement tokens, she took the trouble to tell me how great a success she had been at the Croydon dances and how the young men had swarmed around her. She wrote of me to her brother: 'She fascinates everyone but me.'

Ellen made Edgar an admirable wife for twelve peaceful and unruffled years, nursing him with the utmost kindness until his inevitable early death. She kept her bond to him better than I have kept any human bond. The housework I had prompted her to was her salvation, for it gave her pride and an interest, but she never forgave me for having so much influence on her brother. Edgar's tuberculosis threw the support of both of them on Ellen's not very large private income. She managed admirably, indeed, her life was a miracle of good management. But she was naturally independent, and, at the back of her mind, I think she associated the pain of all this effort with the influence I had had on her, without giving me any credit for her emotional satisfaction. She always knew I was no lady.

There is in women of Ellen's inbred type a sort of spiritually incestuous relationship with the men of their family. They are bound to them by every tie but the physical. Hepburn wives are never more than mistresses and domestic officials. The genetic strain is too thin for there to be those vigorous reachings out into difference which are essential to true marriages. Although Patrick's generation had an instinctive feeling that it must renew itself from stocks unlike its own, the Hepburns – mass-hardened, amorphous, inflexible to the new influences – neutralised the influence of these co-opted strange women and for the most part destroyed them, allowing them to have no regenerating effect. My instinct of revulsion against Ellen Hepburn in the train to Harrow was a just one, for in my relationship with Patrick she was the arch-enemy.

This cohesion of Ellen to Patrick did not imply any deep sympathy, or any of the qualities of love except a feeling of possession. Ellen had no intellectual sympathy with the true Patrick. She was proud of his successes at school and in his law examinations, but his preoccupation with science and architecture, because they had no money value or even social value in the world she understood, she considered ridiculous. She had gone with him to Spain to see an eclipse of the sun. Scornful of all the trouble taken, she complained that Patrick had entirely disregarded her comfort, that he had got her out of bed at an unearthly hour in the morning to witness a spectacle which was interesting only to specialists, and that he had made her follow him round a smelly Spanish town with no consideration for her fatigue. Here was my mother again in her relationship with my father: here again was the shadow of my childhood. Ellen afterwards invented a sentence which is a masterpiece: 'Eclipses are all very well, but business should come first.' Now, I knew that Patrick had

136

an altogether lovely interest in eclipses, that his passion for them was akin to the passion of the religious for his God. Mixed up with my antagonism for Ellen was a determination that somehow he should be honoured for the qualities that she despised in him, and I became ambitious for Patrick as a mother is ambitious for her son.

Patrick himself loved things which interested him for their own sake, and he loved only things that interested him. I interested him, and he loved me very much. He told me that he had given up reading *The Times* while going up to the City, in order to think of me on the top of the bus. Ellen thought this madness, and on a par with his fervour about an eclipse of the sun. But faithful and efficient she continued as procuress to her brother. She told me that there was among the Hepburns, a bishop, a law lord and a certain speechless member of Parliament. I was not impressed. I felt, like Hernani, that my race could begin with me. I could make some mark in the world of Bernhardt, and my father was right in thinking that the board-school and the little music shop could triumph in me.

I had no conscious idea of marrying Patrick Hepburn when Ellen and I left Paris to spend Christmas in England. I went to the Foundling Church on Christmas day and wept because I might have given birth to a foundling. William would not be easy with me if I gave birth to a bastard. I knew that there was a deep sex jealousy between us which would make it a pleasure to him to let me down. I think my feeling about children was the one sincere thing in me, the one thing I did not act about even to myself. My parents were always sentimental about children. My mother used to take me out at night to look for my dead brother's eyes among the stars. And she told me often about her birth pangs with me, urging me to continence on account of them. When I was thirteen I read Shakespeare's sonnets and, at the one where the poet tells his friend to be a father, I burned with a passion which seems now more real than any transport I have ever experienced in love.

Two days after Christmas, William lent me to Patrick and we went down to Oxford to see the colleges. I had a queer fit of trembling in Oxford, and back in town, by the iron gates in Mecklenburg Square, Patrick kissed me, giving me the impression that he was not experienced in kissing young women. He told me he loved me and that he had been giving William money to spend on my behalf, and that he had been interesting himself in my career to the extent of financing it. William had only assisted me in a way that was pleasant to himself, and I burned with indignation against him. I believed implicitly in Patrick's chastity. I remembered how kindly he had read to us from his favourite novel, Stevenson's *Wrecker*, William seated at my feet, his hands approaching me more and more intimately. And my soul revolted from William.

Every one of my conclusions was wrong. Patrick had had two women before he met me, one – a whore, the other – a maidservant. And his giving money to William was a very characteristic plant. However, I decided to throw William over and marry Patrick, for whom I developed a sort of religious faith and love. He was to be my rock of ages, my refuge from the destructive passion of men. Had he not been like a father to me in his willingness to endow me? Next day I told Patrick that I had been William's mistress. In a high state of exhaltation I sang him the story of my loves with William in a sort of lyrical hysteria, and went back to my lodgings to return to William his letters, and the blue-and-grey coat and skirt he had given me for a Christmas present.

That night Patrick took me back to Paris. Patrick was eccentric in appearance, in an old tweed knickerbocker suit with the clean starched wing-collar which he invariably wore to support the dignity of the Englishman on the continent. He had brought a pair of his own bicycle stockings for me to wear on the train, making an atmosphere of 'O were ye in the Cold Blast on Lindenlee' romanticism which for the moment struck me as ridiculous. Patrick had reserved judgement as to whether he would marry me. In Paris he made a point of not staying in my hotel. But next night he told me that he had decided to marry me, and added, curiously, 'You'll never leave me will you? It would be such a shock to my family.' I thought that I would rather he asked for my faithfulness on behalf of himself. He went back to London, and I continued my studies. Without conscious affectation I was a mirror of chastity, and shivered with fright at the sight of the French comic papers. I had no thought that Patrick would ever be my lover when I married him.

After a time, Patrick returned to Paris to take me back to England to meet his relations. We went down to Watford to visit his ugly, middle-aged cousins, all maiden ladies, one of whom had been in love with him. As the train drew in he said, 'You won't show me too much affection before Eleanor, will you?' I nearly got out of the train

138

and went home. I found the cousins civil, but there was no common interest between us. Each had her hobby, and each cousin was cold and critical about the other's hobbies. They were Baptists and Kate, the eldest, with the coarse, almost male face of a secondary syphilitic, did art photography, and had a considerable reputation in it. She took young friends out into the fields, with only a mackintosh over their nudity, and photographed them as nymphs and other mythological characters. About this time, Maud Allen was dancing her Salomé at the Palace Theatre and Kate was asked to photograph her, but Maud could only go to Watford on a Sunday, and Kate, the Baptist, would photograph no one on a Sunday.

Margaret's hobby was jewellery. She mounted moonstones in delicate bands of silver, and was much disregarded by the rest of the hobbyists. I gave her all the sympathy I had and she offered me the glad hand of the undesired woman to the desired. It was evident that they held Patrick against me. There had been a great deal of bickering between them. I gave eternal offence by suggesting that it would benefit one of their young nephews, who had a slight stammer, to study elocution. They resented this suggestion from an incoming woman not yet admitted to the Hepburn clan. I had no right to a self, as a co-opted Hepburn, and no right to assert myself.

A day or two later we went up to Scotland to a most impressive family house at Bridge of Allan. James Duncan had married Patrick's aunt Florrie. His grandfather had been a weaver, and he was proud of his connection with the Hepburns, and had written the first of their family histories, bravely including in it a few pages about his own folk who were descended from the Duncan clan. Moreover, James wrote verses and 'taught' what was a good rhyme and what was a bad one. They had a kitchen maid who was a descendant of the poet Burns, whom they seemed to think rightly placed in the kitchen because Burns had been a peasant. James Duncan had a large kauri-pine library with two small rows of books in it. The house was of the miniature country-house type with crenellations. They gave a party for me, to which the sons of important Glasgow merchants turned out in kilts. I was not asked to sing: nobody took the faintest notice of me as myself, I was of concern only because I was to marry Patrick Hepburn. My evening gown which I had brought with me from Australia was inadequate, and my beauty did not console them in the least.

Aunt Florrie had adopted the youngest of Patrick's full sisters whose birth had been the occasion of the death of his mother. Dorothy Hepburn's life was so perfect from the point of view of domestic comfort, and so barren in any other respect, that she spent three-quarters of it in nursing-homes. A great authority on manners, she had no discernible intelligence. Her character was all eaten up by the domination of her aunt. I afterwards came to fear having a child like Dorothy Hepburn. Aunt Florrie dominated all her nephews and nieces by giving them presents of complicated electro-plate contrivances for warming the breakfast dishes, and dinner gongs of a standard pattern. Wherever she planted a dinner gong she seemed to eliminate personality.

In the train I took pleasure in being very loving to Patrick. I draped violets in his drooping brown moustache. He slept in my arms, and, on waking, he said ceremoniously that he had learned to sleep in a sweet school. Very occasionally my mind would register something like derision at him. I had expected to be engaged to him about a year, a decent period because of William. My impression now is that Patrick did not really resent my relations with William. At any rate, he kept moving the date of our marriage forward and forward, so in the end we were married in the autumn. We had been down to Worthing to see Ellen Hepburn, Patrick's stepmother, not long widowed. Chilled as effectively as a piece of Canterbury lamb, she was somehow sympathetic. I wrote the first poem I ever wrote in England to Ellen Hepburn: she was puzzled when she read it. The house was ugly, orderly and without taste except that in the dining-room were a number of Dutch pictures − minor works by good painters: but these were no index of anyone's taste as James Hepburn had taken them in satisfaction of a bad debt. Out of this house came gloom that could have been cut with a knife.

Ellen Hepburn dressed like a charwoman, and, indeed, her chief pleasure was in helping the two servants with the housework. She was relieved at her freedom from the staff of seven which had been kept in the large Croydon house. One morning she sat on my bed and exuded a sort of silent sympathy. I wondered if this was quite sincere, or part of her propaganda against Patrick, whom she plainly hated. One of the two servants had been in the household a long time, and it was evident that she was laughing laconically at Patrick, taking it as a joke that he should be lovering. Clearly she was echoing some derisive emotion of her mistress.

Ellen was tied to the bedside of her eldest daughter who was dying of a disease of the spinalcolumn. Patrick's half-brother – George Hepburn – was home for the holidays: he was in his last year at Westminster. George was the first public school boy I had known intimately, and I liked him very much. Home bored him to tears and he had diverged so far from the norm as to own a copy of Karl Marx's *Das Capital*, given him by a friend at school. I was struck by the narrow range of the Hepburn family. Their habits were set and their circle limited. They would as soon have asked the baker to dinner as get to know the peerage. And this was odd because, in recommending the public school system, they always said that a boy went to school to make friends. If any Hepburn had made a friend a degree out of their orbit, God knows what they could have done with him. Everything I was or might be lay entirely outside their horizon, but they were very civil to me, so I set about imitating them. Ellen had a very neat contrivance for keeping her needles and thread, and for years I coveted the spirit of it; and I set myself, because of my strength of character and native courtesy, to become a creditable Hepburn woman. This was stupid, for Patrick had sickened of Ellen and her contrivances, and was marrying me because I was not a Hepburn type woman.

Patrick, a freeman of the City of London and romantic about the City, decided that we were to be married in St Margaret's Church opposite the Bank of England. He loathed big weddings, as he did every practice and habit of his family. I had not given my parents time to send me money and it was a great pleasure for Patrick to provide my wedding clothes. His sister, Ellen, and I set out together from Worthing and bought more combinations, a plain white dress and a hat with pink roses on it. Patrick did not like the law, but he enjoyed spending the income from his practice on hats and combinations. But Ellen saw in this expenditure a menace to the family's resources, and so within the family a spendthrift reputation was built up for me, though in Australia it was I who had been provident and prudently persuaded my parents to buy houses.

I was married from the Kingsley Hotel, Ellen my bridesmaid. There was, as far as I can remember, no best man, but present in the church were a one-eyed man, representing the great public, and the pew opener. During the ceremony I was seized with a fit of levity which Patrick sensed and controlled by putting his hand on my arm. He had made no special change in his dress for the occasion except for a new pair of gloves. The night before, Patrick had taken me into the offices of Hepburn, Son and Cutcliffe to show me his will, and what provision he had made for me. This did not interest me. Ellen was wrong in suggesting that I married Patrick for his money. I married him because he was creditable according to the standards of my father, because I felt that somehow we might make a career together, and I married him to have children. We returned to the Kingsley Hotel for a sober tea with Ellen and William Hepburn and his new wife who had joined us. We were to spend our wedding night in Oxford. Just as we drove off, William Ray appeared and tried to get into the cab. I was pitiless and would not speak to him. I did not feel that I treated him badly. I believed utterly in my marriage with Patrick.

In the train going down to Oxford, I read the first chapter of Herbert Spencer's *First Principles* in honour of my father. We took twenty-two books with us on our honeymoon which set the key of my serious intentions towards Patrick. I controlled the etiquettes of our wedding night, although I was still surprised that Patrick wanted to be my lover. He said, 'Why should I not be expected to behave like any other man?'

Patrick had mapped out a tour for us in France during which we were to visit twenty-two towns and see twenty-two Romanesque churches. Before we crossed to France we went again to the office, and I was bold enough to suggest that the clerks should be given a glass of wine. This surprised everybody, but Patrick, very much my slave, sent out to Simpsons for a bottle of champagne. George Cutcliffe, Patrick's partner, son of a distinguished actuary, saw danger in this. James Hepburn had taken him as a junior partner because he had good business connections in the City, and not enough brains or character to exert independence in the practice. He owned a property in Devonshire and spent all his enthusiasm in fly-fishing. He had a large, placid, amiable wife who had given birth to a daughter after many miscarriages. Now, Cutcliffe had wanted a son and he was jealous of Patrick, and this jealousy had been fed by old James' boasting about his son's success in his law examinations. He thought Patrick an impractical dreamer, and resented the fact that he, Cutcliffe, was still the junior partner. If there had been any hope

142

that Patrick would become interested in the practice of law, he would have spoiled it. He suspected opposition from my suggestion about the wine, and he leant over his desk and said to me, 'Now the less you have to do with your husband's business the better.' Sensible of Cutcliffe's status as a gentleman in the City, I believed him and for years never showed any interest in this aspect of Patrick's activities. Indeed, I was rather afraid of the business, as were all the younger generation of Hepburns who associated it with the severities and vast energies of their father. Twenty years later, however, I introduced the biggest piece of business that had come to Hepburn, Son and Cutcliffe since the death of old James.

Our honeymoon was happy enough. I was still interested in Romanesque churches. It was strenuous in its way, with me always following Patrick's legs in search of the next church. I felt that the churches were objects of veneration and that they took the guilt out of our love relationship. Winter came early in the Pyrenees that year; we were alone in the hotel surrounded by acres of unoccupied space; we walked in the snow, sometimes falling into drifts up to our hips. I was determined to show fortitude, in contrast to Ellen. One night I saw signs of a second personality in Patrick, his melancholy, his bitterness. He said, 'This is all very well, but how are we to meet the ordinariness of life?': and there was a queerness in him, and a cruelty which made me doubt the permanence of his tenderness for me. At Pau I found waiting bitter letters from William.

We returned to England, to the Kingsley Hotel. We had the sweetest pleasure making our first home. I knew that a glorified bachelor flat would suit Patrick and I found one in Tavistock Square in the house of a drunken old woman named Gringer, married to a retired sergeant of the Guards much younger than herself. I was for taking two floors at a rent of sixty pounds a year, but Patrick was for three floors at a hundred. I went to Liberty's and bought the newest fabrics. I had the walls covered with plain papers of a low tone of green. It satisfied my pride to organise Patrick, to put him in a condition of elegance so that no Hepburn could ever again see eccentricity in him.

Patrick suffered an infinity of torture tearing out his roots from the rooms in Great Ormond Street. I threw away as much as he would allow of the dusty accumulation. Very deeply Patrick and I loved each other those last days at Great Ormond Street. In his aspiration towards a new life he bought a great filing cabinet and put all his scientific papers in order, and I was all zeal to catalogue them. But I had become pregnant which was premature and lacking in judgement. I suffered so much from pregnancy sickness that the doctor thought he would have to induce a miscarriage, and there was poor Patrick, who had been so loving and so wanting a companion, all encumbered with a sick woman. But he was very tender about it, and these first months were the happiest of my life.

I was a bad housekeeper, always trying experiments. We had a Dutch cook and then a Chinese cook and, in a lust for cleanliness, I engaged a pensioned seaman who even scrubbed out the coal-hole. My desire was entirely subservient to Patrick, and there was not a single crumpled rose leaf in our marriage. Then, suddenly we heard that my mother was coming home to see her dear daughter. I cried all through the night before the day she was to arrive. With Patrick I had had peace, and there had never been any peace with my mother. We went down to Tilbury to meet her, I so weak with my pregnancy that I had to lie down on the floor of the carriage. My mother greeted us in full tragedienne: 'Anne, O Anne,' she called from the rail of the steamer, straining towards me, her eyes full of the most devastating emotion. It had all begun again, and peace had gone for ever. Six little months of happiness with Patrick. How kind he was to me, how utterly devoted to my happiness.

Into this paradise my mother broke like an avenger. She told me that when she was six months pregnant with me, my father had knocked her down. I was torn between my desire to be filial and my wistful longing for the old peace with Patrick. There was I trying to be a creditable Hepburn woman and there was she with her yellow hair, blaring theatrical emotions. I loved my mother; but I felt somehow that after the use she had made of my childhood, I had a right to respite from her. She pretended to me that she was ill and old at the age of forty-eight, and went through the motions of collapsing on Patrick. She suggested that he should repay the three or four hundred pounds she had spent on my journey to England and my musical education. This was deliberately mischievous as she was naturally independent about money and nothing ever stopped her making it. She sensed my feeling of duty towards Patrick's family, so she tried to get their names and addresses out of me with the idea of becoming a book canvasser and selling books to them. In short, she raised all the hell she could. Feeling that all this was damaging to my relationship with my husband, one night I became hysterical. Patrick asked my mother to leave the house, and she went to stay with an old schoolteacher friend in Hampstead. But the damage had been done, and there was the first rift between me and Patrick. The Watford sisters were giving their annual garden party and, knowing my mother was in England, they asked her to it, and Patrick said, 'I'm sure I don't want her to go', and there was in his tone evident scorn of my mother.

With my mother safely in Hampstead, Patrick took me sailing on the Norfolk Broads in a small yacht with a cabin in which I could not stand upright. This was very uncomfortable for a person in my condition, and we had a small quarrel. But he wanted a companion, and we walked from the river bank to churches in the neighbourhood — two miles there and two miles back — and then the dinghy capsized throwing me into the River Bure. I was picked up by a wherry, my wet clothes clinging sadly to my pregnant young body. We returned to our flat in Bloomsbury and I gave birth to a premature child. When I was in labour, I asked him for some brandy and he said to me severely, 'I'd rather see you dead than drunk.' At this I registered a sort of laconic amusement: that he should think it fitting for me to lie dead at his preference. My little girl lived for a few moments and I heard her cry; but they did not let me see her and the fact that I never set eyes on this child has been a sorrow to me all my life. A month later I went back to Patrick's bed and in due course conceived again.

I went to see my mother as soon as I was able to go out. She seemed not to forgive me for being a lady, although she had brought me up to the idea of marriage outside my class. To her, with her energy and originality, I was probably not lady enough, and she refused to accept that I was physically weak. My mother had no feeling for solicitors' wives: she was making fun of me and my little social eminence. Why, my god, did I not laugh? I had lost the desire and habit of laughter. She took one look at me and said, 'My girl, you're hypnotised.'

She had settled happily with her friend in Hampstead, had bought lots of elegant clothes, and her peroxided hair was dressed beautifully with a great barrage of curled fringe in what was called the 'princess' manner because, I think, it was first worn by Queen Alexandra when she was Princess of Wales. She opened a physiognomy parlour at the bottom of Regent Street. My mother's physiognomy activities had been a great excuse for scorn to my father's exemplary sisters, but I was not at all embarrassed by the physiognomy parlour. Even in the worst days of my subjection, I had a respect for genius. And mother with her yellow fringe and her flow of words had more than a touch of genius.

Patrick showed great tenderness and devotion during my convalescence. Woman was new and intriguing to him, even her morning sickness. When I was strong enough to walk he took me away again: he wanted a companion for his cathedrals, someone with whom he could share their beauty and romance. We were very much in love with one another. We went to Holland and I wearily followed his legs round Amsterdam and Rotterdam. Patrick was immensely physically strenuous, and I had to be interested in what interested him. We walked miles through foreign towns with Baedaeker. He had a vanity which would not allow him to ask the way, so we lost hours of time and walked leagues of distance in pursuit of his topographical discoveries. At this time I did not allow myself a personal individual interest. It was a sort of spiritual game with me to follow Patrick. I listened without absorbing anything but the spirit of his talk, until the serious business of maternity put me out of conceit with compliance.

Mercifully my mother had decided to return to Australia. When she came to say goodbye I was in bed with a miscarriage. From Marseilles she sent me a sporting cable 'Luck in thirds'. She was right in her prognostication for when I conceived again I determined to protect myself from the excursions and cathedrals. Early in my pregnancy came Easter, and I persuaded Patrick to spend it alone. He sailed round England in a steamer, and I went by myself to Margate. I experienced a sort of glorification at my condition; 'Blessed art thou among Women'. I took my harmony exercises to the beach and worked as far as 'suspensions' as preparation for the songs I would write, but the child in my womb came between me and my music. I went my full time and a beautiful eleven-pound boy was born. My husband, whose fatherly feelings had been aroused by the sight of the little dead girl, loved him and was proud of him. Our happiness I have never forgotten, and all the years of tragic misunderstanding have never taken it from me. The day of this son's birth was the happiest of my life. This was the self-expression which

I believed in, and which gave me delight. As I lay after my labour, clean, completed, with the child on my arm, I felt something that was like physical passion for the first time since my marriage.

CHAPTER V

The baby was very well formed and, the nurse said, intelligent. She was from the London Hospital, and instructed me in the etiquette of upper-class babies: such and such a viscountess had six dozen lawn napkins. I was grateful for this, partly out of sheer suggestibility, and partly out of a desire to act creditably as Patrick's wife. The mother of his articled clerk, an old family friend, said, 'Well, Patrick, I suppose there never was such a baby', and Patrick delighted me by saying, 'Well, there are not many to beat him'. This was the tenderest fidelity to me, for he had no interest in fatherhood, no individual desire for it. My interest in the child excluded every other subject. I adopted the nursery system because of the Hepburns' prejudices, but I trained my own nurse after reading all the books I could on baby culture, and examining every baby I could find. For a year, at least, no other subject entered my mind. I still entertained Patrick as well as I could at dinner, but our son lay beside us on a chair. My husband, bored at the transference of my interest from himself to the child, showed signs of abstraction, and a settling into himself.

I had trained my cook as a nurse. She became efficient, but was of a waspish and aggressive character. Presuming on my youth and inexperience she bullied me about the food, which was excellent. On one occasion she objected to her midday meal of hot boiled beans and bacon, and I threw her dinner out of the window to assert my authority. My method of domestic management, though unusual, was indeed quite successful, for the servant later was head nurse to the Sultan of Turkey; and she retained an affection for me all her life. At the same time I was aware that I ought to be imitating the domestic management of the Hepburns, who impressed on me the necessity of conforming, insisting that I should have in my house just this and not that quality of white paint. My natural humanity and lack of

147

discipline sometimes asserted themselves, and one Sunday afternoon we carried our son, without an attendant nursemaid, to Mary Hepburn's house in Well Walk. This was the best ordered of the Hepburn houses. Mary had never in all her history run out of her special brand of champagne.

I joined the School for Mothers movement with religious enthusiasm. Because I was a solicitor's wife, it was assumed that I knew how to instruct the working classes. But, remembering my own grandmother, I thought that there might well be something that I could learn from poor working-class mothers. I soon mastered the techniques of caring for the bodies of children, of keeping hale babies in health, and restoring sick babies to what health was possible to them. By helping other mothers, I began to work out my own salvation. I began to use my hands, and became skilful with feed-bottles and utensils. I apprenticed myself to the social workers, but did not succumb to the contagion of their point of view. I did not believe that working-class mothers had less intelligence and goodwill than middle-class mothers, and since they produced a great many children with little house room and a minimum of money, I thought they must have at least as much goodwill, and more than ordinary tenacity. Without looking very deeply into sociology, I saw that working-class conditions could be improved by clean saucepans and more milk. I supplied more milk, and lost caste forever with the social workers by filling a cab with new saucepans to deliver them at the tenements, for the marasmus cases. My idea was that the sight of a new saucepan would be stimulating to an over-tired, working mother. Most of the committee of the 'School for Mothers' thought my action subversive, in that I was attacking the economic system by giving things away. My reply was, 'What about the undertakers? By lowering the infant mortality rate you are putting them out of business.' This they thought was pushing the argument too far.

I took delicate slum children into my nursery, thrusting my infant son into the company of the offspring of scavengers and coal-heavers. There was no more real virtue in this than in the easy good nature of a whore. It was easy for me to give milk and saucepans: I had money enough, and to entertain sick babies in my nursery was silly and spectacular. I should have devoted all my energies to my family, but like my mother I had more energy than my family could absorb. As it was, I developed the fine baby strength of my young

148

James too rigorously, so that I overtaxed him and induced a nervous stammer that will inconvenience him all his life.

My proper function as a woman was to accumulate energy, hold it still in me, and transmit it to my husband by the techniques of love so that he could shape our family's future with the welded power of the two of us. But I was not suitably mated, and only nominally a wife. I was a mistress, and a substitute for a life-starved man's dead mother. Utterly impatient of being a mistress, I also did not want to be a man's mother. When a woman assumes the mother attitude to her man she ultimately devours him. For such a feast I had only distaste.

My husband had no concern with the future but only with the past. He lived on the past; on interest from investments, and on energy that his father and grandfather had put into the family business. He did nothing to re-invigorate the family practice, and so ultimately it died. His imagination lived in the past, on the beauty of the Romanesque. His physical reflexes helped the future in that he planted a seed in me vigorous enough to induce a new organism. As this physical act was not supported by his lust or his will, his fatherliness at the birth of our son James was his supreme compliment to me. He was kind about James because he saw the child as a completion of myself: he should have been willing to immolate me for the child. We had no common intellectual or artistic interest and, although he showed a polite sympathy with my feelings about James, he found the nursery on the whole a nuisance. My preoccupation with fecundity bored him profoundly, and he began to develop moods of abstraction, to draw into himself.

In spite of my interest in the child, I began to want to follow my own devices. I needed to talk to Patrick as well as have him talk to me. He became disturbed and disoriented by the rapacity of my call on his intellectual cooperation. He liked to instruct me and tell me what he knew, but when my curiosity passed the bounds of his knowledge he was discountenanced and at a loss. Our life was easy, but without ambition or plan. I felt like an eternal pensionnaire at a creditably equipped seaside boarding house.

My contract with my father to get into the news began to haunt me. I scented the danger of my own activity, desiring to give all my energy to James, but I began to be ambitious for Patrick. I wanted public activity for him; I would have been glad to see him on the

149

local council. Patrick scorned politics, local or imperial: it was a dirty business, and unworthy of a gentleman. I argued that politics would continue to be a dirty business so long as all the clean men kept out of affairs.

I had not the least idea that I was attacking his liberty. I acted on instinct; and my instinct seems to have been almost invariably wrong. I took my right to pregnancy as unquestioned. I was a passionate, puritanical and energetic girl, but with a bitter distrust of passion. All my life, I have never forgiven the objects of my passion, and never had the least respect for them. I was entirely submissive in my love relation with my husband. I considered it my duty that coition should be pleasureless. I found later that my husband considered it *his* duty that it should be frequent. I shall never forget my horror when I discovered that he had been embracing me from a sense of responsibility. I had pleasure in tenderness with my husband, from the heart-and-hands mode of Victorian sentimentality, the pleasure I had had as a child from my father. My relationship with my husband was spoiled and confused by my relationship with my father. I wanted to be petted and fondled, to have my birthday remembered, flowers on my wedding anniversary, and a good time at Christmas. From Patrick, with whom I was entirely serious, I did not want erotic callisthenics at all. The only aspect of physical love that interested me was impregnation, and constantly and conscientiously I became impregnated. I then had no doubt whatever of my right to it. I now doubt very much my right to it. It never occurred to me to consult my husband as to whether he wanted to be a father. I knew I wanted to be a mother. Patrick did not in the least want to be a father; he wanted me. He wanted love experience, the companionship of a woman civil enough to listen to him, and even a woman clever enough to understand.

Patrick continued with his little lantern slide lectures on the Romanesque. He was a passionate photographer. He photographed barges on the Thames, oaks in Epping Forest. Romanesque doorways he photographed and made enlargements of them. He belonged to a photographic club, the members of which submitted their works for criticism by the other members; one of them dealt unsparingly with Patrick's work, and this induced a curious hate in him. He was apparently very modest about his performances until they were challenged, when a passion of self-approval blew up in

150

him. Nevertheless, he had no desire to excel, only a disposition to be himself, to pursue his activities with a freedom that was pleasurable to him. I began vigorously to attack Patrick's liberty to be himself. I arranged the lantern slides in such order that they could be found and used. I sorted his scientific periodicals, and, in a bullying way, insisted that they should be bound. Patrick loathed any change at all. I wanted change at all costs. I said to him, 'Let us have the journals bound', and he resisted me. 'If you don't have the journals bound in ten days, I will take them to the binders myself.' I did this and Patrick was angry for three weeks, after which he relented saying he really wanted them bound from the beginning. Being young, and in many ways unwomanish, and not realising that such inconsistency is a common quality of husbands, I experienced a sense of injustice. I had wanted the credit of my initiative, and wanted him to feel that I had made a contribution.

My peace was further disturbed by Emily Colles – the superintendent of the School for Mothers. She had the same sort of interest in modern poetry as the fans of the Poetry Bookshop. She knew all about G.K. Chesterton, thought it creditable to have a poem in the *Dublin Review*. She put it into my head that there were folks about the town writing verses. My old feeling that I had in me the capacity for writing verses began to stir. New creation had a sort of licence from Emily, but Patrick thought, while things might be observed, nothing could be created.

I was still singing at places like the Lyceum Club. Patrick would take me, usually smoking shag, in a closed hansom cab. He was never at all enthusiastic about my performances, which were good enough. I felt a sort of envelope of repression closing on me from Patrick; Emily and her interests were a method of escape. I wrote verses to her capably enough. I was quite unhumorously pleased that she was the cousin of a peer. I had grown tired of the old ancestral glories recited whenever the Hepburns met, at dinner, at weddings and I believe even at funerals. It came into my mind that there were distinguished people still alive. This thought was somehow a support to my individuality at risk of being drowned in the flood of Hepburn history. The existing peer near to my own acquaintance was a support to me.

From time to time members of the family would come to stay with us. The house was then clean, and the food was good, but I became strained with the feeling that I was never quite dustless enough for the Hepburns, who endured their sojourns with me rather than enjoyed them. My housekeeping suited Patrick well enough, but I became uneasy about it, lacking courage to maintain my own way of life. I became terrorised by an ideal order I could not accomplish, and disproportionately rabid about clean paint. Young George, who had by this time left Westminister, came to stay with us bringing with him the works of Karl Marx. He was altogether delighted by the contrast with other Hepburn houses, but I remembered our old Wimbledon war with the villa-dwellers, and I was still afraid of them. So my sense of myself became fretted and unharmonious.

One of Patrick's sisters had married a solicitor, grandson of the founder of a world-famous vinegar business. Hugh Squire was a rival of Patrick's, for he had gone into practice and made a success of it with a capital of five pounds, while Patrick, with the support of two generations of his capable family behind him, was known to be lax and eccentric. Ethel Squire, Patrick's sister, a mighty housekeeper, had miraculously clean paint and bought her clothes from Bradleys. With a feeling of acquiring merit, we went to tea at Bromley one Sunday afternoon, I in clothes far below the Bradley standard. There we met Josiah Squire, inheritor of the riches from the vinegar business. He painted in water-colours and lived in Florence, a very superior man indeed. An amateur of all the arts, he played the piano while I sang to him. Looking at Patrick with distaste, made permissible by all those shares in the vinegar business, he turned to me and said, 'So you're married. O what a pity, what a terrible pity.' My husband had really a sort of King Cophetua attitude to me, quite liking being married to me, but feeling he had done well by me in establishing the relationship. Old Josiah rather shook him. He told me in the hansom going home that I had talked too much during the evening, which was discouraging. For it was the first time since my marriage that one of the family had been at all aware of my singing, and old Josiah really had been quite interested.

Patrick in the gentlest manner had contrived that I should no longer be in contact with any of my own family, and took great pleasure in correcting my manners. At a hotel in Brighton, with a great air of solemnity, his hands folded on his widespread table napkin the way his governess had taught him, he told me never to rest my elbow on the dinner table. I took this indoctrination docilely at first, but soon I began to see Patrick's manners as a little too good to be perfect. He never looked really happy in God's world and in his care to be correct at dinner, he looked almost as if he were suppressing a hiccough. But this was only what education had done to him: a great deal of the natural Patrick was beautiful. His urge to instruct me in table manners was the expression of his faithfulness to his people. I began to develop a faithfulness to *my* people, and realised that the table manners of my aunts Mary and Beatrice, who dined so often with the bishop, were good enough for anyone. I had been carefully instructed in deportment by my aunts; I had even been told when to leave a P.P.C. card. However Patrick and his table napkin frightened me as Mary Hepburn and her saddles of mutton and her hares baked whole frightened me. I have always been frightened by vigorous signs of self-belief in other people. I have never had enough sense of myself.

In this first year of James' life, I taught my husband to sing and we read aloud to one another: Eothen, Erewhon, and the works of George Borrow. But intellectual and emotional and erotic frustrations were beginning to make me ill. Suffering from bronchitis and dyspepsia I looked round for a tertium quid. Perhaps it would be truer to say I instinctively co-opted a tertium quid: I took Emily Colles — the Superintendent of the School for Mothers — right into my home. She ate with us, she read with us and she mingled her mezzo-soprano with my husband's light baritone voice nearly every evening. Neither of them seemed to want to hear me sing. I never expected desire or any particular interest to develop between Patrick and Emily, considering them only in relation to myself. She was ten years older than me, not beautiful and with no chic, and I was constantly rude to her about her badly shaped blouses. But she had breeding, and a toxin came out of her that poisoned my relationship with Patrick. I wrote verses to Emily: my love relationship with my husband died as I wrote the verses, which were a confession of the entirely bogus quality of that relationship.

There was no immediate conscious lessening of our love, but came August and I wanted to go, like a good bourgeoise, to the seaside with my man and my baby — to show our son the sea — while Patrick wanted to forget all about babies and take his woman to Scotland. So he hired a nurse and settled her with the child near Epping

Forest – all at great expense. This, a dawning thrift in me resented. We read Ibsen together in a dirty and uncomfortable Edinburgh hotel. Afterwards we travelled round the west coast where I heard salmon fishers laughing. My heart went out to them, to their tweeds and their laughter, but I hated Patrick and I hated his tailor, though I would have been content enough with both if he had let me take my baby to the sea.

I returned from the holiday uninvigorated and almost sullen. My mind felt debauched by having its attention constantly directed, and its powers unused but absorbed. At the wall which had divided the Picts from the Scots, I became irretrievably and finally bored: mildew began to contaminate my soul, and even to invade my relationship with James. It somehow lessened my pride in him, that he had survived six weeks motherless, growing satisfactorily in my absence from the attention of the nurse and the servants. I was rude again to Emily Colles about her blouses. In a fit of inspiration I invented a scheme for co-ordinating all the Infant Health Movements in the country, combining the national maternity services in an overall efficiency. I proposed to found the Church of God in Life. Emily looked at me over the lunch table laconically. She worked in the School for Mothers movement for the two hundred and ten pounds a year she got out of it, but her heart was in her bed-sitting room, her peasant pottery, the Botticelli photogravures, her anemones, and in the *Dublin Review*. It was also a little in the duets with my husband. As she and Patrick sang together after the luxuriance of my inspiration they smiled at one another.

I began to consult doctors about my health, supplementing what was deficient in my intimacy with my husband with these consultations. I tried various systems of diet, living sometimes on raw beef and coffee, sometimes on lettuce and beans. I began to read economics and to rule my life with Spartan regularity. I grew more and more conscious of my untidiness and suffered continuously with my lungs: but it never occurred to me to take a lover.

Patrick proposed that I take a trip to Madeira. He loved to travel himself and saw this as a pleasure for me. It was not. I had travelled in my youth past saturation point. My husband was doubtless as weary of our position as was I, and looked forward to a lunch table that was not a spiritual vortex, but a clear plain surface, reflecting Emily's smiles and amenities. I bought a lot of paraphernalia for my journey, and, in spite of my white hot mood of religious and social invention, I vaunted myself to Emily as a loved and generously endowed wife. At this time I had a spot on my lungs and thought I was pregnant again.

The ship for Madeira was to start from France. Patrick proposed to come over with me, to visit Caen and photograph the cathedral. Since our marriage he had not photographed churches, contenting himself with showing them to me. This dawning activity indicated a change of heart. He always carried very little luggage, and that crushed into so small a space that all the shape was taken out of it. Charmingly, he took a supply of starched collars which, appearing over eccentric tweeds, were enough to prove him an Englishman. He also carried a great many photographic plates. We caught the night train from Victoria.

I was not yet conscious of my emotional unrest, for I had my mind's surfaces arranged in the pattern of a devoted wife. But seeing on the station a coffin being carried away, my eyes followed it with terror: I thought, 'Our love is in that coffin, our love is dead.' Immediately my mind was playing with cruel amusement with the idea that my love was dead.

In the train Patrick thought he had lost his camera; a look of passionate fear and frustration came into his face which altogether excluded me. His true love object was the camera. In our golden days he had said to me, 'I gave up photography for love.' But we were ritually lovers in Caen. We slept in each other's arms. He went out and bought stockings and, dressing me, kissed my feet. Just beyond our hotel was the cathedral – *victrix*! It was February and very cold and I, suspecting the new life in me, had to follow Patrick round the town, with the hole in my lungs, watching the seat of his trousers strain with anxiety as he lined up the view of the cathedral through the lens of his camera. Again I hated him and I hated his tailor. But there was no stability in these moods of loathing and by night-time I was back to charm and endearments, all thrilled with photography for my love's sake. The night before the ship sailed for Madeira I was genuinely full of tears at the thought of our separation.

On board ship, malevolent destiny drove the tenderness out of me. It had been the reinforcement of his hereditary characteristics by his sisters from Tonbridge and Bromley and Worthing that had spoiled my relationship with him. In some way they closed him to me, so that the exchange that was so necessary to me was impossible between us. They created an atmosphere in which my spirit could not keep alive; and I was avid to keep my spirit alive. If I could have got the clean but nauseating smell of these good women out of my nostrils, if I could have washed my nervous tissue clear of their obtrusions, my sense of humour, which was soon to revive, might have healed my relationship with my husband. But on the ship was the daughter of one of Patrick's solicitor friends, the only woman before me that Patrick had thought of marrying. As Patrick wished me goodbye she hailed him, and after a glance, excluded me. Here again was territory immune from me, an area that I could not conquer by my wit, my beauty, my fine singing, my ingenuity of spirit, or my goodwill. With the solicitor's daughter were the solicitor and the solicitor's wife. They were not going to Madeira but to Portugal, and it was decided that I should change my destination and accompany them. Nothing could have been more unfortunate.

Patrick had booked me into the most uncomfortable cabin in the ship, and had left his bowler hat in it. At sea, I held the hat to my bosom and cried over it. But in the morning I met on deck a fine, witty, horse-racing Irishman and at once fell in love with him. I desired the Irishman. This was not at all like the rococo of sentimentality and pseudo-childishness over my husband's hat. I allowed myself the release of this desire alone in my uncomfortable cabin. I imagined just what lovely gesture of invitation would win me my new love. Desire for me was only a solitary game, because I suppressed it to the ruling of duty. I joined the Irishman and his party at lunch, scandalising the solicitor and his family by excluding them as they had excluded me. All the way to Portugal I laughed. God how I laughed! The solicitor and his family could not have understood what the Irishman and I said to one another, but rocks and stones must have understood my laughter. I was glad to leave the ship at Lisbon, for I might have fallen into sin with the Irishman if I had gone on to Madeira. We stayed in a hotel in Mount Estoril, full of superior people, an admiral, and the kind of people who have country houses. They accepted me but excluded my party, so my soul screamed in triumph at Bromley and Tonbridge. One very elegant old lady took it for granted that I had been presented at court: 'My dear, why are you travelling with such abominable people?' My spiritual seduction was complete.

156

At Mount Estoril I lay on the beach reading the works of Mr Wells, and was intrigued with the phrase 'that labour red inane, which this mad world calls Ornament'. My lungs recovered, and I wrote more verses to Emily Colles. On the return cruise the Irishman was on the ship and we laughed together again. He was not in the least physically attracted to me, and would have found my erotics amateurish. I coveted the professionalism of a woman of the streets and longed to travel on with him for some wildness and emancipation in Dublin. Ruefully, I took the train to London. My husband, restored by his respite, met me with passion and love, which I killed with my coldness. Afterwards, in secret, I knitted a pair of socks for the Irishman, tied them round with green ribbon, and posted them to his address in Cork. This was the first quite accurate piece of work I had ever done with my hands, and on finishing it I quite forgot the Irishman. With lust and tenderness banished at the same time from my heart, I set myself to my duty as wife and mother.

My reunion with James was altogether charming. He knew me, he had missed me and held out his arms to me. I bought him a great black doll. He always sustained my imagination and my craving for tenderness and beauty, and I had always the pre-occupation of my dream for him. It was through him that I could support the almost unbroken frustration and boredom that my life became.

As I look back over this long and melancholy road, I am ashamed. I try to think why I endured so much futile pain, and the truth is that I believed in pain. I believed that by suffering and endurance I was working out some salvation. Nearly all the relationships of my life had been tawdry, insincere and unsatisfactory. Many people were attracted to me, but I was intimate with nobody. I was not sufficiently like anyone to invite that self-identification which is the essence of true friendship and love.

POEMS

❖

PUBLISHED POEMS

From 'SONGS OF JOHN OLAND'
(This privately printed volume (1911) contained many
poems that were reissued in later volumes.)

Illusion

I who am great stalk above trees,
And come upon the world from heights.
I kick aside the little boxes of straight built towns,
Those great coveted houses!
Extend my arms to touch the round horizon,
And find the zenith just beyond my fingers.

I am tired of the rounded sky:
The everlasting dome has held me in.
I have looked for change in all lands
And I have found Myself beneath the half-sphere.

Illusion! Illusion! what wonder men
Fight for false hope and die for Gods that are
    not,
Beneath the rounded falsity.
But when I sleep, I leave eternal circles
And where the great stars march
Find Truth in Change.

The Artist's Life
Interpretation

The dreamer found his house
Narrow and stained with years.
The wise man said 'How can this stand!
The tinder walls will fall,
The old roof crush that fool.'

But the garden of the house
Was full of kindly trees,
And brave birds built low nests on little shrubs,
And all small beasts were friends.
At night the marching stars stooped to the house,
And in blue brittle light Truth spoke.
A wanton and an old poor man
Strayed to the garden.
And in the charmed shadows, sang
A clear, clean song.
The dreamer laughed, 'Let the house fall!'

The Call for Faith

Where in this wildness shall I find my path?
When in this whirling night, know one thing
    true?
From the ruins of temples shall I take a dead
    saint,
Prop him in some new shrine,
And cry that God still lives?
This is the faith of fools.

Good Chance, eternal friend,
Who from the mud made apes,
From apes made men,
Stand with us still!
Let me find in you, solace,
Such as a tired man
Finds in a warm sea.
I am so weary, knowing neither wrong nor right.
I have no hope: I am too mad to die.

The Song of the Child

Receive me again, Father God,
There is no room.
There is war upon earth, men fight,
They have no time, no food, no pity for babes.

The women staunch men's wounds and forget us.
Mothers with child are starved.
The new-born dies at the empty breast;
So I died who was your messenger.
I have made no beauty, I have spoke no truth,
I have failed, I was rejected, born too soon,
Receive me again, Father God, receive me.

The Song of the Mother

I who was dumb open my lips in death.
I call to the world across great spaces.
Women, you who would be singers, take heed.
Here are they who have made great songs,
Silent in grief,
Each rocks herself in mute grief,
Seeing the vision of the unborn;
While I who was dumb sing a great song,
For my children come out to meet me.

The Sinner

Why should I sail to new coasts?
Why seek strange lands?
What is there in cliffs that amazes me,
Or in sand that I do not know!

I find no charm in this blue coral sea,
Nor in the coloured sky at nightfall,
All these things I have seen and I remember;
My memories are part of my contaminated self,
The world's beauty rots for me.

God strike me deaf and blind.
Let my flesh close me in as with a wall.
Then cleanse me neither with light nor fire,
But with intimate music, which I cannot hear.

Song of the Low-Caste Wife

What have you given me for my strong sons?
O scion of kings!
In new veins the blood of old kings runs cold.
Your people thinking of old victories, lose the
    lust of conquest,
Your men guard what they have,
Your women nurse their silver pots,
Dead beauty mocks hot blood!
What shall these women conceive of their chill
    loves
But still more pots?

But I have conceived of you new men;
Boys brave from the breast,
Running and striving like no children of your
    house
And with their brave new brains
Making new myths.

My people were without while yours were kings,
They sang the song of exile in low places
And in the stress of growth knew pain.
The unprepared world pressed hard upon them,
Women bent beneath burdens, while cold struck
    babes,
But they arose strong from the fight,
Hungry from their oppression.

And I am full of lust,
Which is not stayed with your old glories.
Give me for all old things that greatest glory,
A little growth.

Am I your mate because I share your bed?
Go then, find each day a new mate outside your
    house.
I am your mate if I can share your vision.
Have you no vision king-descended?
Come share mine!
Will you give me this, for your sons?
O scion of kings!

Surrender

When you kiss me I am blind,
My senses are filled with ecstasy,
I only feel how strong my life is
And so know myself.
From love I understand all things that live,
And even the dead.
I am like a tree shaken in wind,
And like water that is drawn into the air
Through the strong loving of the sun.
When you are gone
I am myself earthquake and eclipse
And all thick darkness and rending grief.
When you kiss me I am blind,
    I am blind.

Divorce

A voice from the dark is calling me.
In the close house I nurse a fire.
Out in the dark cold winds rush free
To the rock heights of my desire.
I smother in the house in the valley below,
Let me out to the night, let me go, let me go.

Spirits that ride the sweeping blast,
Frozen in rigid tenderness,
Wait! for I leave the fire at last
My little-love's warm loneliness.
I smother in the house in the valley below,
Let me out to the night, let me go, let me go.

High on the hills are beating drums.
Clear from a line of marching men
To the rock's edge the hero comes
He calls me and he calls again.
On the hill there is fighting, victory or quick
  death,
In the house is the fire, which I fan with sick
  breath.
I smother in the house in the valley below,
Let me out to the dark, let me go, let me go.

The Town Dirge

A child was dead in the town,
Son of a sick woman and a poor man.
The woman being sick gave only her love,
And what can the poor man give!
A child was dead in the town.

In the house of our pity
The woman wept for her child.
But we, being wise, whispered apart,
'Seeing that the man is poor, and the woman sick,
It is well that the child is dead.'

She, of her courtesy asked us to look at her child,
But I could not enter the poor room,
I could not face its dead:
My heart accused my lips and cried,
'No child should die.'

O you who are strong in the town,
Mighty to build, mighty to shield the weak,
Join with us that we may say,
Under God's grace, and of our good care,
No child shall die.

Why should we weep, who pass so soon?
The old dead wept in a new world.
Is not the tale of man's sorrow told?
Is not that harvest gathered in?
What have we left for all our tears?
What knowledge and what solace?

Now, while I, being old in grief,
Still weep for unfulfilled desire,
In this old town is a new cry,
The first breath of a wanton, new-born,
Doomed to old sins.

There is nothing new in grief.
Why should we weep who pass so soon?

Outline

Man I shall beget tomorrow,
Where is he?
Life a load, the load a sorrow,
Better not to be.
Man I shall beget tomorrow,
Non-existent? Where is he?

He is spread in fields of wheat,
Low in grass that cows shall eat.
There are fragments of himself
High upon some warehouse shelf.
Any atom he may be,
Any atom may be he.

She the focus, will control
The new body, but the soul?
That is free.
The husk is made of any meat,
Any grass or any wheat,
But man has personality,
He alone is he,
The man *is* I get tomorrow
Whole in destiny.

Can I then be free?

Inspiration

I tried to build perfection with my hands
  And failed.
Then with my will's most strict commands
  And naught availed.
What shall he gain but some poor miser's pelf,
Who thinks for ever of his silly self?
Then to the stars I flung my trust,
Scorning the menace of my coward dust;
Freed from my little will's control
To a good purpose marched my soul;
In nameless, shapeless God found I my rest,
Tho' for my solace I built God a breast.

Song to the Young John

The apple-blossomy king
Is lord of this new spring,
He is the spirit of young joy,
My little yellow-headed boy.

His eyes are a bluebell wood, set in a boy's head.
His hair the white-gold, ghost of sunlight, from
    springs dead.
The pink of apple-blossom is in his bonnie
    cheeks,
I hear bird-song in sleepy glades, when the king
    speaks.

He moves like a young larch in a light wind,
His body brings slim budding trees to mind.
How all my senses thrill to the dear treasure,
Till I must weep for sweet excess of pleasure.

    The apple-blossomy king
    Is lord of this new spring,
    He is the spirit of young joy,
    My little yellow-headed boy.

All Men to Women

You have taken our life in your hands, like a
    small sick bird;
As you might feed him with your lips, so with
    your word
Have you sustained us; remembering your kind
    eyes
We have forgot our pitiless ways, and have grown
    wise.

With brittle strength to fight and to desire,
What do we but bring fuel to your fire?
For our best labour, your fine powers control,
O maker of man's body and his soul.

The flower of all our winning we would give
To mightier men, the race that is to live.
On your good courage must our victory rest,
You bear all future days beneath your breast.

There are those among you who scorn their trust,
Who have betrayed us being weak to lust.
Cursed be our weakness, cursed be that deceit
For that black sin is no good thing complete.

O pitiful heart from whom we draw our strength,
Would you have wisdom? know your power at
    length,
From your frail might grant us the thing we seek.
We who are born so small, and live so weak.

From 'THE CONTEMPLATIVE QUARRY'
(Poetry Bookshop, 1915)

I Amourette
(The Woman and the Philosopher)

She: What shall I do most pleasing man?
       I will delight you if I can.
       Shall I be silent? Shall I speak?
       Since I love quick I'll show that I am weak:
       I'll say the wisest strangest thing I know
       That you may smile at vanity, and love me
          so.

He: How can her wisdom flourish and endure
       When her philosophy is but a lure,
       And to the arsenal of charm is brought
       The ammunition of her thought?
       I count her breathing as I sit;
       I love her mouth, but disregard her wit.

171

She: More than love, and more than other
          pleasure
    I desire thrilling combat of the wit.
    As far as I can measure
    This man is rare, and therefore fit
    To be a combatant, let me say one thing
          new
    That I may gage him so, to prove my
          judgment true.

(*Here follows an argument*)

She: Sir it is just I own
    That I am overthrown,
    And I take strange delight
    That I am beaten so to-night.

He: Madam you are a sensualist,
    And, being such, you shall be kissed.

She: What husbandry is this?
    What thrift, that we should kiss
    On the first night we meet?
    What is your need to eat the seed,
    When growth might be so sweet?
    From this first pleasure that you sow in me
    It is my power to raise a gracious tree.
    And, maybe, I will give you a kind grove
    Where you may sit through sunny days,
          and love.

He: This answer, which is rare,
    Is luring as your hair.
    I go from you this night in pain,
    But Madam, I will come again.

She: Dreams, dreams, stay with me till I sleep,
    Then let oblivion steep
    My senses in forgetfulness,
    That when I wake, I may forget my
          loneliness.

II *The Singer*

If I had peace to sit and sing,
Then I could make a lovely thing;
But I am stung with goads and whips,
So I build songs like iron ships.

Let it be something for my song,
If it is sometimes swift and strong.

III *New Waters*

Only a starveling singer seeks
The stuff of songs among the Greeks.
Juno is old,
Jove's loves are cold,
Tales over-told.
By a new risen Attic stream
A mortal singer dreamed a dream
Fixed he not Fancy's habitation,
Nor set in bonds Imagination.
There are new waters, and a new Humanity.
For all old myths give us the dream to be,
We are outwearied with Persephone,
Rather than her, we'll sing Reality.

IV *The Egoist*

Shall I write pretty poetry
Controlled by ordered sense in me
With an old choice of figure and of word,
So call my soul a nesting bird?

Of the dead poets I can make a synthesis,
And learn poetic form that in them is;
But I will use the figure that is real
For me, the figure that I feel.

And now of this matter of ear-perfect rhyme,
My clerk can list all language in his leisure time;
A faulty rhyme may be a well-placed microtone,
And hold a perfect imperfection of its own.

A poet rediscovers all creation;
His instinct gives him beauty, which is sensed
    relation.
It was as fit for one man's thoughts to trot in
    iambs, as it is for me,
Who live not in the horse-age, but in the day of
    aeroplanes, to write my rhythms free.

V Need to Rest

I have no physical need of a chair;
I can double my body anywhere:
A suitable rest is found
Upon a stone or on the ground.
But it is needful that I feed my wit,
With beauty and complexity, even when I sit.
Had I a splendid broad philosophy
I were high man without complexity.
I'd fling myself on any natural sod
To scan the zenith and remember God.
But it is needful man shall strive
With tortured matter, so to keep alive.
Idle man would never live to age:
He would run mad and die in rage.
When fat accumulations cloy,
War brings her sword to ravage and destroy,
That through the smoke of the consuming real
Man sees a clearer and more sure ideal.

VI The Hermit

Fools drove him with goads and whips
Down to the sea where there were ships.
And he was forced at the risk of his neck
To find a refuge on a stranger's deck.
Then that ship sailed away
Far from the land that day,
He watched the sky, and mourned to be
In such a dread captivity.

But from a rift of flying cloud
Burst a tempest quick and loud,
A burning bolt struck the strange deck
Bringing the ship to sudden wreck.
So the poor slave swam free
Over a quick calmed sea:
On a new coast-line he was thrown,
And claimed a virgin island for his own.

In the quiet island was such pleasure,
In solitude he found such treasure,
He took rude tools
And carved a splendid monument to fools.

IX Soul's Liberty

He who has lost soul's liberty
Concerns himself for ever with his property,
As, when the folk have lost the dance and song,
Women clean useless pots the whole day long.

Thank God for war and fire
To burn the silly objects of desire,
That from the ruin of a church thrown down
We see God clear and high above the town.

XII The Affinity

I have to thank God I'm a woman,
For in these ordered days a woman only
Is free to be very hungry, very lonely.

It is sad for Feminism, but still clear
That man, more often than woman, is a pioneer.
If I would confide a new thought,
First to a man must it be brought.

Now, for our sins, it is my bitter fate
That such a man wills soon to be my mate,
And so of friendship is quick end:
When I have gained a love I lose a friend.

It is well within the order of things
That man should listen when his mate sings;
But the true male never yet walked
Who liked to listen when his mate talked.

I would be married to a full man,
As would all women since the world began,
But from a wealth of living I have proved
I must be silent, if I would be loved.

Now of my silence I have much wealth.
I have to do my thinking all by stealth.
My thought may never see the day.
My mind is like a catacomb where early
     Christians pray.

And of my silence I have much pain,
But of these pangs I have great gain,
For I must take to drugs or drink,
Or I must write the things I think.

If my sex would let me speak,
I would be very lazy and most weak;
I should speak only, and the things I spoke
Would fill the air a while, and clear like smoke.

The things I think now I write down,
And some day I will show them to the Town.
When I am sad I make thought clear;
I can re-read it all next year.

I have to thank God I'm a woman,
For in these ordered days a woman only
Is free to be very hungry, very lonely.

XIII The Contemplative Quarry

My love is male and proper-man
And what he'd have he'd get by chase,
So I must cheat as women can
And keep my love from off my face.
'Tis folly to my dawning thrifty thought
That I must run, who in the end am caught.

XIV Spoken to Adonis

Have you observed that one can measure
Poetic worth of words in terms of pleasure?
Honey and milk have been sweet food so long,
These words are naturalised in Song.
And from my joy in you the time is ripe
That I find lyric value for your pipe.
What tender pleasure do your lips invoke
Moving in gracious meditation as you smoke!

XV The Mummer

Strict I walk my ordered way
Through the strait and duteous day;
The hours are nuns that summon me
To offices of huswifry.
Cups and cupboards, flagons, food
Are things of my solicitude.
No elfin Folly haply strays
Down my precise and well-swept ways.

When that compassionate lady Night
Shuts out a prison from my sight,
With other thrift I turn a key
Of the old chest of Memory.
And in my spacious dreams unfold
A flimsy stuff of green and gold,
And walk and wander in the dress
Of old delights, and tenderness.

XVI The Marriage

What a great battle you and I have fought!
A fight of sticks and whips and swords,
A one-armed combat,
For each held the left hand pressed close to the
        heart,
To save the caskets from assault.

How tenderly we guarded them;
I would keep mine and still have yours,
And you held fast to yours and coveted mine.
Could we have dropt the caskets
We would have thrown down weapons
And been at each other like apes,
Scratching, biting, hugging
In exasperation.

What a fight!
Thank God that I was strong as you,
And you, though not my master, were my match.
How we panted; we grew dizzy with rage.
We forgot everything but the fight and the love of
    the caskets.

These we called by great names —
Personality, Liberty, Individuality.

Each fought for right to keep himself a slave
And to redeem his fellow.
How can this be done?

But the fight ended.
For both was victory
For both there was defeat.
Through blood we saw the caskets on the floor.
Our jewels were revealed;
An ugly toad in mine,
While yours was filled with most contemptible
    small snakes:
One held my vanity, the other held your sloth.

The fight is over, and our eyes are clear. —
Good friend, shake hands.

XVII Artificiality

Poor body that was crushed in stays
Through many real-seeming days,
You are free in the grave.
You held a ghost 'neath roof and law
Well by contrivance and by wit and saw.
All storms that rage now strike your mould,
Now dead, now low, now cold;
And air, turned foe, your ready breath forgot,
Shall wanton with you till you rot.

Poor bodies crushed in stays,
Think of the rotting days!

XVIII Ship Near Shoals

I have been so misused by chaste men with one
        wife
That I would live with satyrs all my life.
Virtue has bound me with such infamy
That I must fly where Love himself is free,
And know all vice but that small vice of dignity.

Come Rags and Jades! so long as you have
        laughter,
Blow your shrill pipes, and I will follow after.

XIX The Revolt of Wives

I will be neither man nor woman,
I will be just a human.
When the time comes for me to bear a son
With concentration shall the work be done.
My medium then is flesh and blood,
And by God's mercy shall the work be good.

If all of women's life were spent with child,
How were Earth's people and her area reconciled?
Nor for my very pleasure will I vex
My whole long life away in things of sex,
As in those good Victorian days
When teeming women lived in stays.

We often find the moralist forgetting
Relation betwixt bearing and begetting.
What increase if all women should be chaste?
But it is good all women keep a natural waist,
For a strong people's love of child
With narrow hips can not be reconciled.

Show us the contract plain, that we may prove
If we are loved for children, or are loved for love.
Your children all our services compel,
But from love's charter do we now rebel.
If in our love you find such pleasure,
Pay us in freedom love's full measure.

We, vital women, are no more content
Bound, first to passion, then to sentiment.
Of you, the masters, slaves in our poor eyes
Who most are moved by women's tricks and lies,
We ask our freedom. In good sooth,
We only ask to know and speak the truth!

XX The Free Woman

What was not done on earth by incapacity
Of old, was promised for the life to be.
But I will build a heaven which shall prove
A lovelier paradise
To your brave mortal eyes
Than the eternal tranquil promise of the Good.
For freedom I will give perfected love,
For which you shall not pay in shelter or in food.
For the work of my head and hands I will be
    paid,
But I take no fee to be wedded, or to remain a
    maid.

XXI From Poets, Workmen, Women, and Children in Orphanages

With wine or with faith, with love or with song,
Let me be drunken all my life long.
On hills of ecstasy, in troughs of pain,
Never more sober, never more sane.
For I lived too long in a den
Of sane and solemn men,
Each merciless as a beast,
And my spirit was their feast.
They sucked my soul from me
All for the sake of holy Uniformity.

XXII *The Faithful Amorist*

Am I not the lover of Beauty
To follow her where I know she is hid
By the aroma of her pleasure?
Yesterday I had pleasure of Helen,
Of white, of yellow hair,
But to-day a negress is my delight,
And Beauty is black.

There are some that are as small tradesmen,
To sell beauty in a shop,
Noting what has been desired, and acclaiming it
      eternally good.
So poets fill verses
For ever with the owl, the oak, and the
      nightingale,
I say the crow is a better bird than the
      nightingale,
Since to-day Beauty is black.

The lark sings flat
Of wearisome trees and spiritless fields.
But there is great music in the hyaena,
For there is pleasure in deserts.

XXIII *To a Young Boy*

Poor son of strife −
Child of inequality and growth −
You will never learn: you have only to live.
You will never know the peace of order.
Routine will crush you.
Safe toil has always thought of time,
But you will work in utter concentration
Fierce as fire.

You will find no steady excellence:
You will spend your life in a ditch, grubbing for
    grains of gold.
Remember, my dear son,
That gold is gold.

You will find no steady virtue:
You will live sometimes with holy ecstasy,
    sometimes with shoddy sin.

You will keep no constant faith,
But with an agony of faithful longing you will
    hate a lie.

Life will give you no annuity,
You will always be at risk.
There is one technique, one hope and one excuse
    for such as you,
And that is courage.

XXIV *Eugenics*

In this woman, whose business it is to prepare my
    dinner,
I find the most surprising sensitiveness to works
    of art,
With splendid qualities of sympathy and heart,
And now I learn her father was a sinner.

His lines were laid in unadventurous places,
He was a tradesman in a little town,
But whiles, he laid the yardstick down,
And went and lost his money at the races.

The draper had his quiver very full:
At the thought of his thriftlessness my heart
    should harden.
But had he lived and died like a churchwarden,
I know my housekeeper had been dull.

XXV Sehnsucht

Because of body's hunger are we born,
And by contriving hunger are we fed;
Because of hunger is our work well done,
As so are songs well sung, and things well said.
Desire and longing are the whips of God —
God save us all from death when we are fed.

XXVI Genuflection

I most offend my Deity when I kneel;
I have no profit from repeated prayers.
I know the law too perfect and too real
To swerve or falter for my small affairs.
Not till my ruinous fears begin
Do I ask God for freedom from my sin.
Self-fear is chiefest ally of the Devil,
And I fall straight from praying into evil.

XXVII Comment

The spirit of Mediocrity
Is, as the ant, conservative,
And this is as it well must be,
Else were the creature not alive.

The weakling clings to the paps of the Past,
Draws that assurèd necessary food.
Young Power is strong to make a fast
Within a sparsely-berried wood.

Wherein, as Time and clearances allow,
He'll tether a most fruitful milky cow,
From which all following Mediocrity
Will draw its strength to praise Rigidity.

XXVIII *The Dull Entertainment*

Here is too much food
For the talk to be good,
And too much hurrying of menial feet,
And too kind proffering of things to eat.

XXIX *Weak Will*

No sleepy poison is more strong to kill
Than jaded, weak, and vacillating will.
God send us power to make decision
With muscular, clean, fierce precision.
In life and song
Give us the might
To dare to be wrong
Who feared we were not right.
Regenerating days begin
When I, who made no choice, choose even sin.

XXX *The Religious Instinct*

When I love most – I am turned psalmist.
I have expression from my wrong.
I bay like a ghost-scenting hound,
'Where is God hid? for I would smite him with a
    song.'
Come back Jehovah,
Give me cover.
Come back old god,
For I have lost my lover.

XXXI *Mother Sin*

Out of the womb of Mother Sin,
With stained and sensitive skin,
Is born the strong solitary soul
Who is master of power and of control.
Fearlessness did him beget;
Nor let the moralist forget,
The child of Sin and Courage well may be
Nobler than any child of timid Purity.

XXXII *The Slighted Lady*

There was a man who won a beautiful woman.
Not only was she lovely, and shaped like a
    woman,
But she had a beautiful mind.
She understood everything the man said to her,
She listened and smiled,
And the man possessed her and grew in ecstasy,
And he talked while the woman listened and
    smiled.

But there came a day when the woman
    understood even more than the man had said;
Then *she* spoke, and the man, sated with
    possession, and weary with words, slept.
He slept on the threshold of his house.
The woman was within, in a small room.

Then to the window of her room
Came a young lover with his lute,
And thus he sang:

'O, beautiful woman, who can perfect my dreams,
Take my soul into your hands
Like a clear crystal ball.
Warm it to softness at your breast,
And shape it as you will.
We two shall sing together living songs,
And walk our Paradise, in an eternal noon –
Come, my Desire, I wait.'

But the woman, remembering the sleeper and her
    faith,
Shook her good head, to keep the longing from
    her eyes,
At which the lover sang again, and with such
    lusty rapture
That the sleeper waked,
And, listening to the song, he said:
'My woman has bewitched this man –
He is seduced.
What folly does he sing?
This woman is no goddess, but my wife;
And no perfection, but the keeper of my house.'

Whereat the woman said within her heart;
'My husband has not looked at me for many
        days –
He has forgot that flesh is warm,
And that the spirit hungers.
I have waited long within the house,
I freeze with dumbness, and I go.'

Then she stept down from her high window
And walked with her young lover, singing to his
        lute.

XXXIII *Gift to a Jade*

For love he offered me his perfect world.
This world was so constricted, and so small,
It had no sort of loveliness at all,
And I flung back the little silly ball.
At that cold moralist I hotly hurled,
His perfect pure symmetrical small world.

XXXIV *Song*

I was so chill, and overworn, and sad,
To be a lady was the only joy I had.
I walked the street as silent as a mouse,
Buying fine clothes, and fittings for the house.

But since I saw my love
I wear a simple dress,
And happily I move
Forgetting weariness.

XXXV Magnetism

The little king
Came preening to the presence of the great,
Who wore no jewelled thing
To show imperial state.
Had the small king been wise,
He'd read dominion in a mummer's eyes.

The peacock princeling spoke his will,
While the great lord sat still.
But steady eyes had filched a soul away:
A braggart withered in his husk that day.
Had the great king been wise,
He'd read dominion in a mummer's eyes.

XXXVI Friend Cato

When the master sits at ease
He joys in generalities;
In aphorisms concerning all things human,
But most of all concerning woman.
Saying, 'Women are this or that.'
'Woman is round, or high, or square, or flat.'

Sir, a shepherd knows his sheep apart,
And mothers know young babes by heart.
To taste no little shade of difference
Is sign of undiscerning sense.
Cato, in pity, hear our just demur,
Man, to be critic, must be connoisseur.

XXXVII Susannah in the Morning

When first I saw him I was chaste and good,
And he, how ruthless, pardoned not the mood.
From one quick look I knew him dear,
And gave the highest tribute of my fear.
So I played woman to his male:
How better could his power prevail!
But his hot sense showed quick surprise
At the slow challenge of my shaded eyes.
In a closed room what fires may burn!
O my cold lover will you not return?
To the high night I fling my prayer:
Master of chariots drive me in the air!

XXXVIII Dedication

I walked when the wood was full of minstrelry.
A pretty prince came down to talk with me.
He spoke so kindly, and quite loud:
Then he was gone, quick as high cloud.
That he came here is such a happy thing,
I sit quite still in the wood and sing.

XXXIX The Tired Man

I am a quiet gentleman,
    And I would sit and dream;
But my wife is on the hillside,
    Wild as a hill-stream.

I am a quiet gentleman,
    And I would sit and think;
But my wife is walking the whirlwind
    Through night as black as ink.

O, give me a woman of my race
  As well controlled as I,
And let us sit by the fire,
  Patient till we die!

XL Self Analysis

The tumult of my fretted mind
Gives me expression of a kind;
But it is faulty, harsh, not plain –
My work has the incompetence of pain.

I am consumed with slow fire,
For righteousness is my desire;
Towards that good goal I cannot whip my will,
I am a tired horse that jibs upon a hill.

I desire Virtue, though I love her not –
I have no faith in her when she is got:
I fear that she will bind and make me slave,
And send me songless to the sullen grave.

I am like a man who fears to take a wife,
And frets his soul with wantons all his life.
With rich unholy foods I stuff my maw;
When I am sick, then I believe in law.

I fear the whiteness of straight ways –
I think there is no colour in unsullied days.
My silly sins I take for my heart's ease,
And know my beauty in the end disease.

Of old there were great heroes, strong in fight,
Who, tense and sinless, kept a fire alight:
God of our hope, in their great name,
Give me the straight and ordered flame.

XLI To D.M.

I with fine words wear all my life away,
And lose good purpose with the things I say,
Guide me, kind silent woman, that I give
One deed for twice ten thousand words, and so I
    live.

From 'THE MAN WITH A HAMMER'
(Grant Richards Ltd, 1916)

Examination

If my work is to be good,
I must transcend skill, I must master mood.
For the expression of the rare thing in me,
Is not in *do*, but deeper, in *to be*.
Something of this kind was meant,
When piety was likened to a scent.
A smell is not in movement, not in power,
It is a function of a perfect flower.

I only compass something rare,
By the high form of willing which is prayer.
A ship transcendent and a sword of fire,
For me, the traveller, is in desire.
I write my thought in this most raggèd way,
That being baulked of beauty, I am stung to pray.

Return of Pleasure

I thought there was no pleasure in the world
Because of my fears.
Then I remembered life and all the words in my
    language.
And I had courage even to despise form.
I thought, 'I have skill to make words dance,
To clap hands and to shake feet,
But I will put myself, and everything I see, upon
    the page.
Why should I reject words because of their
    genealogy?
Or things, because of their association?
Why should I scorn a bus rather than a ship?'

Fecundity

Fret and strain,
And ugly signs of pain,
Never yet had part
In birth of Art.
Men are brought forth in grief:
Labour for Beauty is a soul's relief.
Expression is conceived, and has its shape,
Of Sloth's most painful violent rape.
A spirit big with Beauty shall be discontent:
She knows all rapture when her time is spent.
Go! my sick striving spirit, seek
A simple, swift, victorious technique!

Resolution

I will not draw only a house or a tree,
I will draw very Me;
Everything I think, everything I see!

I will have no shame,
No hope of praise or fear of blame!
These things are mean things, and the same.

I am the product of old laws,
Old effect of old cause.
The thing that is, may make the blind gods
      pause.

Formalist

As men whose bones are wind-blown dust have
      sung,
Let me sing now!
I'll sing of gourds, and goads, of honey, and the
      plough.
I am a raw uneasy parvenu,
I am uncertain of my time.
How can I pour the liquor of new days
In the old pipes of Rhyme?

Comment

Tone
Is utterly my own.
Far less exterior than skill,
It comes from the deep centre of the will.
For nobler qualities of Song,
Not singing, but the singer must be strong.

The Poet in the House

A small oak grew in an elder-hedge,
Rustling with growth, he said,
'I am an oak, an oak!'
The elders bent to him with heavy scent,
Taunting, 'O, little weed!'

The oak shrank into himself, and made ready to
    die.
But a wave of courage swept over him
Deep from the heart of his mother-oak.
He drew himself up with passion, crying still,
'I am an oak.'

He pressed himself against the coward leaves,
Up against the heavy scent,
And he prevailed!
In future days, there will be no elder-hedge,
Only an oak.

Fear of the Supreme

I dreamed that I was hungry all day long,
Until at night I ate a song.
It was as if I dined upon the Host, and so was
    satisfied,
But of ecstatic surfeit quick I died.

O! Love, come to me now, and hold me fast,
Lest I should eat that deadly food at last.

A Woman in Bed

Sometimes when I go to rest
I lie and struggle for expression,
And failing, fall to sick depression,
And beat my breast.

By blows, I cannot 'scape
The utter irritation
Of my poor soul's frustration,
For so I know my shape.

And often have I found
An added sadness,
Bringing me to madness,
Because my breast is round.

How can I, being woman,
Dedicate nights
Which should be sacred to delights,
To this lust of words, which is so broadly human!

But through the well-clothed days
I can forget my skirt,
I hide my breast beneath a workman's shirt,
And hunt the perfect phrase.

The Recluse

I'm tired of living in the town,
Of trailing up, and trailing down.
My very heart feels like a street,
Sullied with busy living and with dusty feet.

Nor is there any peace for me in fields,
There I remember crops and market-yields.
In the quiet cow I have no gain,
For she recalls loud milk-cans on a train.

I dream that there is harbourage for me,
In the blue breath of some remoter sea,
On a brown rock weed-tipt to malachite,
Where sea-gulls wheeling from their track, alight.

There I would live, with gulls' eggs for my food,
My only recreation, to be good,
With only passing Time for fate,
Free of my friends, and cool without a mate.

The Tired Woman

O My Lover blind me,
Take your cords and bind me,
Then drive me through a silent land,
With the compelling of your open hand!

There is too much of sound, too much for sight,
In thunderous lightnings of this night:
There is too much of freedom for my feet,
Bruised by the stones of this disordered street.

I know that there is sweetest rest for me,
In silent fields, and in captivity.
O Lover! drive me through a stilly land,
With the compelling of your open hand.

The Unremitting Weariness

I am so tired I cannot move,
I would sit still and love.
I carried souls so long in pain,
I too would be a child again.

Anna with her parents and
Aunt Beat (on left), 1900
Left: Anna aged 17

Patrick Hepburn at the
Observatory of the Hampstead
Scientific Society
Left: Geoffrey Harper, Anna's
father, *c.* 1904

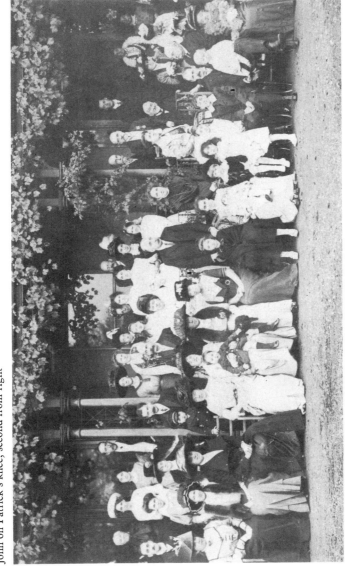

Hepburn family garden party, 1910. Anna seated third from left, James on Aunt Nell's knee, fifth from left. John on Patrick's knee, second from right

Top: Anna with James, 1908
Below: Anna with James and John, 1915

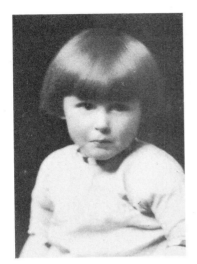

Top left: Richard aged 3.
Top right: George aged 12 *Below:* Anna, 1923

Anna in Paris, 1926.
Photograph by Berenice
Abbott

Patrick in Royal Naval
Air Service tropical
uniform, 1915

A page from Anna's *Where Is It?* book:
'Every pin, rag, tot and tittle in its place.'

Top: Anna at work. *Below:* Anna by the cherry tree in her Hampstead garden. Both photographs courtesy of BBC Hulton Picture Library, 1946

Man who is not child to woman
Is either rogue or more than human.
I rested once upon my father's strength:
O to find peace in love at length!

Man, are you strong to take my proffered hand,
And to be kind when you command?
There was a saint who carried children up a
    steep,
Make me *your child*, and let me sleep.

The Wife

I have no rest,
I am a guest at best,
I can be driven from the house,
Like bat or mouse,
If I please not the house's lord,
For bed and board.

I spend my days
In dull sequestered ways,
Without right to praise.
My brain dies
For want of exercise,
I dare not speak,
For I am weak.

'Twere better for my man and me,
If I were free,
Not to be done by, but to be.
But I am tied,
Free movement is denied.
I am a man's wife,
For all my life!

The Defiance

My enemy!
If you would work the ruin of my mind,
You must not hit me with this ignominy,
You must be kind.

I am soothed and drugged by kindness,
Till I sleep,
But I find a tongue in blindness
When I weep!

Woman Determines to Take Her Own Advice

This is too rare a festival for joy,
As was that joy too rare for my worn kisses,
When first I put a babe to my good breast.
Then was my body justified, with love,
And all such enterprise.

When I conceivèd that good plan
I made no feudal compact with my man,
For in my body's service is not found
A warrant that my will be always bound.

Now, being mother, this I see
I am thrice woman, and the soul of me
Is herded to an end I never sought
Like cow or sheep, and my desire is naught.

Who can my fuller need divine,
From the curved symbol of my body's line?
So for a simple accident of shape,
To work all ruin with my soul's rape.
This is too rare a festival for joy,
For a new thing is born of other labours.
I will break an heirloom, shout and stamp for this
    new victory.

I will fling my freedom at the stars,
And with a good conceit think so to shake the
    spheres.
And when shall Heaven tremble,
But when tired eyes,
Scanning long empty spaces,
So see God.

Definition

What is a wife?
Is it she who stays in a man's house for all her
    life? —
If wife were nothing more than that
Then she were equalled by a homing cat.

What is a wife? Shall it be said
She who by contract shares a bed? —
Go find a thousand wives complete
In girls that flaunt along the street!

Nor is it she, content with sequence from a cause,
Who, like a field increases by just laws,
And from a habit and with no end clear,
Brings forth a child for every wedded year.

Wives are the dreaming mothers come again
Who of blest fertile love bear souls of men!
Sometimes, with decorous silence, sometimes
    with stinging speech
Put a man's high attainment well within his
    reach.

There is a Virgin-Mother, shrined in
    Christianity,
There is a virgin wife in faiths to be,
For the constructive form-inducing principle for
    life,

Is she unknown, unnamed God's wife,
Who out of crystal bearing water drew the higher
    ape: —
She might give even Socialism shape!

The Angry Woman

I am a woman, with a woman's parts,
And of love I bear children.
In the days of bearing is my body weak,
But why because I do you service, should you call
    me slave?

I am a woman in my speech and gait,
I have no beard, (I'll take no blame for that!)
In many things are you and I apart,
But there are regions where we coincide,
Where law for one is law for both.

There is the sexless part of me that is my mind.

You calculate the distance of a star,
I, thanks to this free age can count as well,
And by the very processes you use.
When we think differently of two times two,
I'll own a universal mastery in you! —

Now of marriage, —
In marriage there are many mansions,
(This has been said of Heaven).
Shall you rule all the houses of your choice
Because of manhood or because of strength?
If I must own your manhood synonym for every
    strength,
Then must I lie.
If sex is a criterion for power, and never strength,
What do we gain by union?

I lose all, while nothing worthy is so gained by
    you,
O most blessed bond!

Because of marriage, I have motherhood.
That is much, and yet not all!

By the same miracle that makes me mother
Are you a father.

It is a double honour!
Are you content to be from henceforth only
    father,
And in no other way a man?
A fantastic creature like a thing of dreams
That has so great an eye it has no head.
I am not mother to abstract Childhood, but to my
    son,
And how can I serve my son, but to be much
    myself.

My motherhood must boast some qualities,
For as motherhood is diverse
So shall men be many charactered
And show variety, as this world needs.

Shall I for ever brush my infant's hair?
Cumber his body in conceited needle-work?
Or shall I save some pains till he is grown?
Show him the consolation of mathematics
And let him laugh with me when I am old?

If he is my true son,
He will find more joy in number and in laughter
Than in all these other things.

Why should dull custom make my son my enemy
So that the privilege of his manhood is to leave
    my house?

You would hold knowledge from me because I
    am a mother,
Rather for this reason let me be wise, and very
    strong, –
Power should be added to power. –

And now of love! –
There are many loves.
There is love, which is physiology,
And love, which has no more matter in it than is
    in the mind.
There is spiritual love, and there is good
    affection.
All these loves women need and most of all the
    last.

Kiss me sometimes in the light,
Women have body's pain of body's love.
Let me have flowers sometimes, and always joy.
And sometimes let me take your hand and kiss
    you honestly
Losing nothing in dignity by frank love.
If I must fly in love and follow in life,
Doing both things falsely,
Then am I a *mime*,
I have no free soul.

Man! For your sake and for mine, and for the
    sake of future men,
Let me speak my mind in life and love.
Be strong for love of a strong mate,
Do not ask my weakness as a sacrifice to power.
When you deny me justice
I feel as if my body were in grip of a cold
    octopus,
While my heart is crushed to stone.

This rapture have I of pretence!

To the Silent Man

That you should love is not enough for me,
Come tell your love with pleasing courtesy.
I keep no faith in silence, I am wild and weak;
Now by the beauty of all wandering fires, I beg
    you speak.
Here is a rout of whispered loves and laughter,
And I must turn about and follow after.

To hymn Love, to live because of Beauty,
That is Love's life, that is a lover's duty.
Can you not see I weep because I go,
Speak, dumb Man! speak! Say, shall I stay or no?

Supplication

I stretch starved hands through the night,
Praying for tenderness.
Mary! From your calm height,
Pity my loneliness!
Incline a heart to loving-kindness,
Which strikes me dead of cold, because of
    blindness.

Creatrix

Let us thank Almighty God
For the woman with the rod,
Who was ever and is now
Strong essential as the plough.
She shall goad and she shall drive,
So to keep man's soul alive.
Amoris with her scented dress
Beckons, in pretty wantonness,
But the wife drives, nor can man tell
What hands so urge, what powers compel.

The Shrew

You wish, O master of my destiny,
That I control myself!
'Twere better you ruled me.
For if I rule myself, I smile at you, and hate.
If you rule me, I love you though I curse, O
     mate!

Reward

There is great gain,
Of pride and pain:
Let me be proud to claim the highest for my own:
Let me bear pain, to fight my claim alone.

The Artificer

I feel that your neglect has flayed my soul
And left it a sore, bleeding, pulsing whole!
I feel there is hot fire in pain,
To boil the iron-pot that is my brain!

All my experience, all my thoughts and dreams,
Bubble together, and the mixture steams;
In lovely shapes the bluey vapours rise:
Angels and kindly goddesses console my eyes.

Into the boiling pot I plunge my spoon,
And of hot misery receive my boon,
For from the viscid liquor make I shapes,
Fairies and goblins, little goats and apes.

Many-hued jewels, gem-like flowers,
Bright beads to count kind prayers and happy
  hours.
Once from the pot a crystal sphere I wrought,
It was a new, clear, and quite splendid thought.

Necromancy

If she could take two types of man,
Man that she loves, and man that she desires,
And fuse them in a magic pan,
Over the holy fires,
She might by Sorcery discover
A perfect Lover.

But she must build her Paradise above her,
Inherit Heaven after she is old,
For she can find no pleasant Love to love her,
The world is void of pleasure, and death-cold.

The Recompense

Of every step I took in pain
I had some gain.
Of every night of blind excess
I had reward of half-dead idleness.
Back to the lone road
With the old load!
But rest at night is sweet
To wounded feet,
And when the day is long,
There is miraculous reward of song.

Flagellant

Happiness is like a kind wife,
Within her rounded arms, she carries Sleep.
But I who am mad for Ecstacy, would keep
The favour of my mistress, Sorrow, all my life.

For Sorrow's sake,
Through the dark hours I lie awake.
So that my songs shall greet a day,
Which has forgot the pleasures of my clay.

Words

There came a lazy Celt,
Sunny and gay,
And he caused black ice to melt
With the things that he did say.

He said, 'O! My Desire,
Behold your Lover stands,
His heart a cage of fire;
Come! Warm cold hands.'

He said, 'O! My Delight,
Be happy and be brave,
Weep no more for fright,
For I am a cave.

And I am kind and warm
And shut from icy air,
Where you shall find no harm
But live like a small brown bear.

O! Shelter in me, Sweet,
And let me give you rest,
For I love your hair and your feet,
And your pleasant moving breast.'

Abdication

O judgment sleep!
I love an unkind thief.
Let me be friend of Frailty
For my sick heart's relief.

I would be as the shore's sand
Subject to an advancing sea,
I would be as sunken land
Swept by a tide's strong mastery.

But my contemning mind is as a lighthouse
    tower,
And I am sore for strength, and lashed because of
    power.

Aseptic

To live on a sterile hill
Suits not my mood,
I'll walk in towns my fill,
With strong resisting blood.

There is no virtue in stark fear,
Whether it be of Sin or Death,
But there is pride in walking clear,
Through Plague's contaminating breath.

Nervous Prostration

I married a man of the Croydon class
When I was twenty-two.
And I vex him, and he bores me
Till we don't know what to do!
It isn't good form in the Croydon class
To say you love your wife,
So I spend my days with the tradesmen's books
And pray for the end of life.

In green fields are blossoming trees
And a golden wealth of gorse,
And young birds sing for joy of worms:
It's perfectly clear, of course,
That it wouldn't be taste in the Croydon class
To sing over dinner or tea:
But I sometimes wish the gentleman
Would turn and talk to me!

But every man of the Croydon class
Lives in terror of joy and speech.
'Words are betrayers,' 'Joys are brief' –
The maxims their wise ones teach –
And for all my labour of love and life
I shall be clothed and fed,
And they'll give me an orderly funeral
When I'm still enough to be dead.

I married a man of the Croydon class
When I was twenty-two.
And I vex him, and he bores me
Till we don't know what to do!
And as I sit in his ordered house,
I feel I must sob or shriek,
To force a man of the Croydon class
To live, or to love, or to speak!

Retrospect

Your talk was most in praise of these poor
    features,
And of my body – not unequalled 'mongst God's
    creatures.
And even did your courteous fancy find
Some small perfection in a woman's mind.
But of my soul, sir, not a word!
Till your quite reasonable anger stirred .
To bring our love to sudden wreck.
'Twas then you stayed my ecstasies
With truth! Which ended in this wise: –
'Woman! Your soul's a stone about your neck.'

Maybe our love had happier consummation
Had this part known more quick consideration!

The Pioneer

God send that never I speak truth again!
It's too strong meat for these most silly men!
God send that never in my life I lie!
God give me blessèd silence till I die!

Traducers

Kinder the enemy who must malign us,
Than the smug friend who will define us.

The Choice

Two lovers wooed a woman.
The first was very kind and courtly, and he
    said –
'I offer you my honourable name,
And all the things there are to do, I do,
And everything you wish for I will give,
And you will be my lady, I your knight.'

But the other smiled and said,
'Our love is late, I have no house to offer you,
But one good gift – yourself.
And you shall walk with me without constraint,
And all your words my wit shall understand,
And when our eyes meet full, we two shall smile,
And you will be my woman, I your man,
And you shall serve me.'
Then the woman came softly to that man's side,
    and sat her down.

The Promise

I will not love you for my duty,
Nor for all your treasure,
But I will love because of beauty,
And because of pleasure.
The boy that I shall bear will be a love-child,
Conceived in holy blindness,
I give him to the world who shall be reconciled
To loving-kindness.
Since I no longer love for duty,
Nor for all man's treasure,
And since I bear the child to Beauty
Because of pleasure.

The Assignation

Gentlemen came wooing me
From north, east, west and south,
And each was afire
With quick desire
With a hot kiss on his mouth;
And there was never joy for me
From this dun, dull democracy.

My King, O my Delight!
Who is so strangely dear,
Kiss me not to-night,
Kiss me not for a year.
Let us live lonely days,
Keeping a holy fast,
Walking rough hilly ways,
So that we meet at last,
Near fir-trees on a height,
In still, kind, perfect night.

Service

I love you so entirely
I cannot think to please you,
My art is wasted.
You are burnt with madness,
My being burns to ease you.
In dreams of utter service
Is all sweetness tasted.

I love you so entirely,
I want you not to praise me!
I would be low in all esteem!
I would be outcast with one thing to raise me,
The hope of service I have gathered in a dream.

Let us go to the mountains, O my Lover!
And make our habitation near the sky;
In clear, cool air we can discover
A plan of perfect living, you and I.

Remembrance

What shall I do with my marriage dress?
In which I walked the lover's way.
Shall I wear it in forgetfulness,
Through a less honoured day?
Shall fastenings he has drawn for his delight,
Be loosed by a less honoured hand, at night?

State Endowment

Flowers all natural sweet,
That women sell on baskets in the street,
Lose half their beauty in my eyes,
They are a huckster's merchandise.

Who offers then to buy from me
That natural service, my maternity?

The Faithful Mother

I could not be withheld from you by iron bands,
All cerements would be riven,
That we should claim our heaven,
But I am here in bondage, to these little, little,
        hands!

If I unclasp the tender fingers and walk free,
Our love shall have no gain
From that poor hopeless pain,
For I shall lose my soul because of infamy.

O! Shall I walk your sunny gardens a cold ghost,
And will you cover me with flowers,
That I may spend sequestered hours,
Weeping the lovelier Blossoms I have lost!

I could not be withheld from you by iron bands,
All cerements would be riven,
That we should claim our heaven,
But I am here in bondage, to these little, little
       hands!

A Boy's Mouth

His lips are open, since his mind
Delights in work his fingers find.
In that red arch I see a gate,
Where gracious Loves might pass in state.
Sure his white body were fit habitation
For a whole fairy population.

The Mother-in-Law

This is what my lover said,
'I kissed your hat because it touched your head,
I kissed your shiny shoes, I'll kiss you all,
I love your house, I'll kiss your wall.
I wish that I could kiss that burning coal
Because it's in your fire, dear Soul!'

My little Son is my fond lover –
It seems no time ago since he was born.
I know he will be quick and happy to discover
The world of other women, and leave me forlorn!
Sometimes I think that I'll be scarcely human
If I can brook his chosen woman!

The Individualist

When I get a child,
I get him with fixed intent,
I don't get him by accident.
I get him because I am content with life,
Satisfied with myself,
And because I love my wife.

When the child is born,
I am full of scorn,
At thought of other children.
By instinct I divine
There never was so fine a boy as mine.
I think this, because I am satisfied with life,
Conceited with myself,
And because I love my wife.

And I want to keep my son,
I want to finish what I have begun.
It is one of the keenest pleasures that I know
To feed a child and watch him grow.
I don't want to give him to the State,
I want to share him with my mate.
I like going into hustling life,
To bring back something for my boy and wife.

I do this because the old Brave
Hunted from the cave.

Because a lion in the wilderness
Kills for the cub and lioness,
And because I am satisfied with life,
Conceited with myself,
And because I love my wife.

A Girl in Summer

She took the summer to her blood
Through her sweet mouth.
Until her sleepy mood
Was warm as sunny walls of the old south.
It seemed the yellow light
Had fruitful powers,
Beneath her bosom's white
Leapt sudden flowers.
Each round as the breast
From whose dear core it sprang,
And in the middle of each flower a nest,
In which a young bird sang;
Sang for joy of a coming
And for joy of a name,
And the petals of the flower
Leapt like flame.
Driving with a sweet compelling
Towards his dwelling,
As her singing birds were telling.

The Song-Maker

I would live for a day and a night,
In the rigorous land where everything is right.
Then I would sit and make a song,
In the leisurely land where everything's wrong.

Imperatrix

Am I pleasant?
Tell me that, old Wise!
Let me look into your eyes,
To see if you can comprehend my beauty,
That is a lover's duty:
I look at you to see
If you can think of anything but me.
Ah, you rememer praise and your philosophy!
My love shall be a sphere of silence and of light,
Where Love is all alone with love's delight.
Here is a woodcutter who is so weak
With love of me, he cannot speak.
Tell me, dumb man, am I pleasant, am I
    pleasant?
Farewell, philosopher! I love a peasant.

Song of Anastasia

Shall I mock you, and tell you that love shall
    endure,
Knowing you know the quality of things that are
    secure?
Let love be fierce as lightning, and as brief
As summer-hail, that is a storm's relief.

Question

If I live all my days by routine,
Keeping days ordered and ways clean,
Will there be room for Love in my life?
Love who is born in storm, and lives in strife.

The Conscience

Deadly destructive to my man and me
Are my rare fits of sore morality.
A mad domestic hell begins
When woman hides her virtues, and displays her
    sins.

Release

I have lived five years of mourning,
I live a bitterer year of scorning.
Now of this service is my spirit free,
Free of my grief, and of antipathy.

The Contrast

I knew a pure man, who was without pity,
I knew the veriest bawd in all this city.
And she was very tender, very kind –
She was most after God's mind.

Tatterdemalion

O I will wear a tattered gown
And ash my breast shall cover,
For my bird has gone to the clanging town,
To the hand of my valiant lover!
But still myself shall sit and sing,
By the bed of the old blind king.

O! If I stept in bright array,
And bound my hair with beauty
I'd follow my bird to a feckless day
And leave this dearer duty.
In ash I'll sit, in rags I'll sing,
By the bed of the old blind king.

The Ghost

I wish you'd a farm on the hills, my Dear,
And need not work for hire.
For though I'm cold in the churchyard here,
And cannot sit by your fire,
I'd walk the paths of your house, some nights,
And haply look into your room:
Then I'd always see my Love's home-lights
When I stood on the rail of my tomb.

The Woman's Mind

Knowledge to me is wearisome from books,
I learn so readily from words and looks.
Give me yourself as free as air and rain.
I'll drink, I'll think, and send you flowers again.

The Avenue

To the tired traveller in summer's heat,
The thought of airy trees is sweet.
Come, in my straight stretched arms discover
A leafy road, thou weary Lover.

The Woman of the Hill

I would be ever your desired,
Never the possessed —
Nor in this will of mine is wantonness expressed.
The desired woman is most dear,
The possessed wanton is too near.

I would be far on unattainable height —
Always for knowledge, always for sight:
While from your touch and kisses I am free,
Our love is the high, perfect thing to be.

The Meeting

When I saw you, you went to my head,
You were like wine to my brain,
I walked in London through the rain,
To see a man who had been ten years dead.
For pleasure I forgot the years,
Old time, old death, old tears.

The Little Language

When I am near you, I'm like a child,
I am still and simple, I am undefiled.
I speak my love in a forgotten tongue,
And use the words I knew when I was young.
My Love! You have restored me in a hundred
        ways,
You gave me back my happy childish days.

Vanity

I saw old Duchesses with their young Loves,
I, in a pair of very shabby gloves,
Even my shapeless garments could not make me
    sad,
For I remembered I was young as you, dear Lad.
That I am lovelier without my dress
Gave me sweet wanton happiness.

Irresolute Lover

I said, 'I will not go to her to-night,'
When I had courage from the prudent light.
My resolution vanished with the day,
When the dark came I could not live away.
O! My dear Love let down your hair,
Make me a tent, and let me shelter there;
That in the darkness of a screenèd night
I live more prudent than in loveless light.

The Silence

When I meet you, I greet you with a stare;
Like a poor shy child at a fair.
I will not let you love me — yet am I weak.
I love you so intensely that I cannot speak.
When you are gone, I stand apart,
And whisper to your image in my heart.

Slave of the Fire

I am weary of my service to the blood of a king,
For my people were farmers out of the West,
I would be wife of this yeoman of whom my heart
  sings,
In his strong love, I would take my rest.
O! That I might raise a man to my kind,
Shelter him in my womb, and feed him with my
  mind.

The Supreme Courtesy

My man is like a good steel blade,
As subtle, strong, and finely made,
His power blue-white
As steely light.
O, he is cruel-quick enough!
But to my touch, as pleasant as fine stuff,
And from a wound of him I'd die,
Happy at such keen mastery.

Wander Song

When I come to the end of the land,
I find the sea,
With edges of cliff and breadths of sand
To pleasure me.

When I raise my town-tired eyes
There is blue and white,
Or kings and castles of stormy skies,
Or joy of night.

When I weary of all I see
And tire even of space,
I hold your love in memory
And your dear face.

The Thief

I said in pride, 'To love's my need;
I will not have him loving me,
I'd walk unhobbled, and indeed
What woman loved was ever free!'

So for a man, I loved a ghost,
And knew chill rapture in the walks of thought,
But when I needed pleasure most,
Imagination gave me naught.

O! Had I given what I fought to take
I had not wept for this cold hunger's sake!

Revelation

'Love has no shame.'
'Twas this you said to me.
Shall Love reveal
Hid beauties that are real
And still disguise the soul's infirmity
In fear of blame?
'Love has no cruelty.' —
See first the wounds that are within
Hidden by this quite sufficient skin.
Loving your spirit, I may not deceive it.
Then of my body, Lover — take or leave it.

Transmutation

There is happiness for me,
In sight of a great sun-warmed tree.
I pray that roots may touch my head,
When I am dead.
Maybe there is some splendid compound rhythm
    in confusion,
And there is hope in dissolution.
I should have little fear of ugly changes, little
    grief,
If the material of my thought were quick
    transmuted to a leaf.

A House in Hampstead

My house is damp as damp can be,
It stands on London clay.
And if I move unthinkingly
It shakes in a most alarming way,
Mayhap it will all come down on me
One day.
But through the window I can see
The most enchanting apple-tree.
In spring-time, there are daffodils
And primroses on little hills,
And high within my apple-tree
A blackbird comes and sings to me;
On the black branch he sits and sings
Of birds and nests and eggs and things.
I can't remember as I hear
That old grey London lies so near.

The Awakening

There is a veteran tree,
With green-stained bark,
Rising like a tower of the sea,
From the smooth park.
He is a giant among trees,
And he has watched this house for centuries.

His bark is hard as rock,
Time and Sun and the Wind's shock
Have twisted his boughs till they are like the
    arms of a great carven figure of Care,
Flung in passionate appeal to the changing
    humour of the Air.
Now on high branches sticky buds appear,
Promise of growth and beauty for the year.
It seems my life is an old tree,
And the young buds are your sweet love for me.

Concerning Certain Criticism

There is no pleasure in hard names for flowers,
Nor in acquaintance with their inner shape.
To ravish Beauty with dividing powers
Is to let exquisite essences escape.
At feasts within a flowery paradise
Parvenu Wit must yield his precedence.
Honours therein are for the nose and eyes,
For that old exquisite, discerning sense.

The Explainers

They have taken the street
From underneath my feet,
Now the great roads appear
Unmeaning scratches on a sphere.

226

They have given every star its place,
They have made a wearying diagram of what was
      boundless space,
Long ago they stole fairies from the trees,
They took naiads from the rivers, and mermen
      from the seas.
I wish that I could tremble now
In fear of a small devil curled upon that bough.
In these imaginings I should find
Relief from the strained stillness, that is my
      mind.

Faith

I keep a bird in my heart,
He lives on sorrow,
His name is Faith.
He is so quick a conjurer that he can borrow
Flesh from a wraith.

He swallows the harsh weeds of pain
And gives me scope,
To tend my little garden-plot again
And wait for Hope.

Insensibility

Why should I weep for Autumn rain?
Give gusty Winter toll of tears?
I know that Spring will come again,
As in the other years.

And there is pleasure in wet ways,
In frozen fields, and mist-strange days;
What were eternal Spring to me,
Whose joy is in diversity!

To Anita the Bountiful Mother

O generous woman! gracious and so kind –
Take a long-needed rest of body and of mind.
You gave so many gifts of service and of
    sympathy
Can you refuse this gift of gifts to me?
Now I desire no food, no garment, and no rose
But the sweet sight of your most calm repose.

The Passer

I love the stone of your threshold,
I love the path without it,
I love the briar in its borders,
With the brave young plants about it.
There is pleasure in sight of your windows,
And passing, in decorous night
I smile my love to your window
And bow my love to your light.

The Sentimental Debtor

Lady, when I recall indebtedness
To you who hid me from my bitter day,
And with kind craft bewitched my griefs away
I would not have my owing to you less!

Untimely night has fall'n between us two.
Mine were the blackness of a dumb regret
But for the dear relation of this debt,
Which still unites my destiny to you.

Thus in my cold a little cheer is found,
The fullest debt will hold me fastest bound.
Here's coin for quittance, yet I will withhold
Return in any service, faith or gold.
And since your due is doubly dear to me,
I will not even give you courtesy!

The Dependence

I am your shadow, since I love,
'Tis you compel my changing mood,
Now to be still, and now to move,
You are my evil and my good.
Smile, Lady, and behold in me,
The grace of mirrored courtesy!

To Anita the Gardener

In summer when my life was cold,
Frozen too weary for desire,
I warmed my heart at your marigold,
As at a fire.

It was the first flower from your new ground,
The first gold largess from the care
And loving, you had planted there,
And in the walks around.

I stole your garden's coin to buy content,
A vision of black earth dug deep for flowers,
Through sunny self-forgetful hours,
With joys, God meant.

In summer when my life was cold,
Frozen too weary for desire,
I warmed my heart at your marigold,
As at a fire.

Verity

What do these outpoured lovings prove
But the long ache to love!
O Fate! You are not kind,
To fill this chasm with cold wind.
When had a woman wealth from dreaming,
Or any solace for love's seeming?
Let it be said, that these are dexterous feignings,
Well stated heats, ingenious complainings.
And yet with loathing is my silence broken,
Had they been true, they never had been spoken.
What fuller happiness were it for me,
To leave a mummer's rages
To fill a footnote in my Love's biography,
And not these loving pages.

Epicurean Lover

Dear! I will love you, though you love me not!
Contempts will never shake my mind!
Misuse and scorn and silence move me not!
But I beseech you, be not kind.
Since loving me, you would approach me,
O, let your distance still reproach me!

For things remembered may be sweet,
As things imagined, and for me
A wearying rhythm of due feet
Were less esteemed than your apostasy.
Then, O my Love! Live still beyond my reach,
Leave me my dream of your dear look and
    speech.

The Poet's Change of Mind

Who prizes fruit and scorns the tree?
Yet this fair Critic says of me,
I love the work, but hate the man!
Show charier charity who can!

My Lady, I was ever loth
To wait inactive to be loved,
I found in insult, whips from sloth,
When I was stung I moved.
But there is justice for whose sake
A sleepy dignity will wake.
If of my book you prize a part,
Honour a hand, deal fairly with a heart.
The thing you love is very me,
Come, eat the fruit, but love the tree!

Diffidence

O time has a kiss
For every Miss
And a bed for every Trull!
But thou, my Dearie,
O! Come not near me,
Our love is a wheeling gull.
Lovely he flies 'twixt sea and skies,
He's a silly bird on land.
No wrath of black weathers
Will ruffle his feathers
Like the touch of a capturing hand.

To 'Nucleus'

'Tis you who hold
My heat, my cold,
My rigour and my ecstasy.
Control my days,
Compel my ways
To action or to lethargy.
You fill my nights
With keen delights
Of a stupendous dreaming.
O! Little Seed,
Who at my need
Flowers to such splendid seeming!

The Neophyte

I carry thoughts of you
As I might wear a charm.
These are my Scapular
Clothing me from harm.

You lock my lips
With a most cunning key,
And all my heart
Is your still oratory.

Absolute

I, your true lover,
Demand neither words nor your silence.
My heart can discover
Delight in transport or in continence.

My faith is zenith, earth, and air,
Ever beneath, about, above,
And when you wander I am there,
So changing-constant — since I love.

The Fallow

Now, Tiller, hold your grain,
Leave her to sun and rain
And the kind air.
Then trench her with a well-judged measure
Of feeding pleasure,
And give her peace
To dream of her increase
And your good care.
Well might you reap miraculous yield
From such a happy, nourished field!

Hommage Eternel
To Anita: 14A Downshire Hill, Hampstead

Hygieia's house gave space for dreaming
And a small place for sleeping,
With laughter for a soul's redeeming
And sweet release of weeping.
Within her walls Disorder's daughter,
Dusty, devoid of hope,
Found unction in kind offered water
And various sorts of soap.

The Return

She gave me tears,
A rain to wash the dust of years,
A silence for disharmony,
For jaggèd wounds a remedy,
Green windy downs for fœtid towns
For slums sweet-scented closes,
And for the thorn of her blest scorn
I gave her thorny roses.

The Winded Horn

Ah! my good Wizard she shall not escape,
Though the soul leave her house in a magical
    shape,
Be it asp, toad or lizard, or tiger or ape,
Sure I will find her, secure I will bind her,
Wherever she fly, in whatever disguise.
I am Love the hunter, all-swift and all-wise,
A torch is my hand and spears are my eyes.

The Little Room

I am my Love's laboratory,
For truly he shall find
The proof of his high quality
Within my heart and mind.
Look down, my Love, my Dear,
At the sure change wrought here!

Modern Anomalies
When a Man and His Wife Are Watching a Kinematograph.

Many a time, seeing their darkened house at close
    of day,
She opened that dear gate, and knelt upon their
    steps to pray.
And through their window crannies crept her
    loving powers,
Till all their dwelling smelt of blessing, as a wood
    of flowers.

The Economist

It must be true I love you well
Since your light words are whips of Hell.
But who has pain has songs to sell.
My profitable Friends, farewell!

Inconstancy

Time was, when I recalled your words, your
    looks, your deeds,
As a rapt nun counts over her blest Beads;
Then was my mind so filled with memory
Love had no room to work his change in me,
And I was faithless from my faith's continuance,
Since being changeless I gave no obedience.

I have forgotten you, for these long days,
All unsustained by you I went my ways:
Now at the end I take you back to thought
To find my action was the thing you taught.
And so in faithlessness is faith's continuance,
Since in a change I do you all obedience.

Song

Not for an hour shall your dear thought escape
    me.
I keep it fast to cheer, to guide, to shape me.
As an old pilot held in sight a star,
As a wrecked man clings frantic to a spar,
So I maintain your love in memory,
My hope of Heaven, my security.

For Pity

Men are brought low by blame,
So that they live with shame.
Kindness and love and praise
Are strong to heal and raise.

De Profundis

How shall I bring this beast into subjection
But by the hope and knowledge of perfection?
Must I avoid all paths my Race has trod?
Shall I not call my vast upholder God?

The Torture

God has raised his whip of Hell
That you be no longer weak.
Because of anguish shall you speak,
Because of anguish, shall you speak well.

Sanctuary

He who thinks a perfect melody,
Lives for that time, in harmony.
Walks for that time in liberty,
Loves for that time in purity.

'Such Stuff as Dreams Are Made Of'

A man can build a bridge of wood and stone;
Exterior forces his trained powers control;
But the material of the Singer is his own,
He cuts his songs out of the raw texture of his
    soul.

Quest

Where is the miracle? In Future and in Past,
Not in the Present, which must ever last.
The Young and the weak Old must live dream-
    fed
On gods to be, and on the holy Dead.

The Song of Pride

We are unwilling to lie low,
Crushed by a cursèd tyrant 'No.'
Give us a fight where we can cry, 'I can!'
To show there is the seed of God in man.
If God shall strike us for our pride
Know that in joy of death we died.

My Lady Surrenders

How did she abdicate?
Was it with soft sighs
And pretty feignings of a lover's state,
Or was it solemn-wise,
With altar offerings and rapt vows?
O no! when Love himself was there,
Most housewifely she bound her hair
And went off across the field to milk the cows.

Counsel of Arrogance

If I were God, I would find equal treasure,
In human work, in courage, and in pleasure.
And I would whisper to the captive soul,
That all these things should be in sweet control.
That man should be from birth-bed to the grave,
Not always busy, not always brave.
That he should gather me the flower of idleness,
And the seed-holding cup of perfect happiness.

Prayer on Sunday

God send a higher courage
For to cut straight and clean!
God send a juster language,
To state the thing I mean!
Here is such random thinking,
Such sloth, such slime, such fog,
I see an old cow sinking
Deep, in a pitchy bog!

Effect of Gifts on a Recipient

When the ape and the wolf bared fangs to eat
A silly dish of praise,
The drowsing master snatched the meat
Which mocked his faithless days.
He grasped the beasts by a hanging chain
And stood in his house, a lord again.
Then out he went through a feeble morn
With the drunken sleep in his eyes,
He begged affront, he craved for scorn,
In mendicant's disguise.
And of these gifts divinely given,
His faith in life, his hope of Heaven.

Sung to the Social Reformer

Leave us our sorrows,
Take not our tears,
For long to-morrows
Of too perfect years.

To the New-born can you deny
The world-old solace of a cry;
Nor to hot Youth the eternal right
To win his having with a fight.

Leave us our sorrows,
Take not our tears,
For long to-morrows
Of too perfect years.

The Viper

I heard a pander say in scorn of a bawd,
'A child should be her reward.'
O, rotten speech!
Whose filthiness should teach
That man shall find
Reward for his lewd living in his mind.

Outlaw

Suppression is the duty of a slave,
Expression is morality for the brave.
If you are born a king,
Fight, love, and sing!
But he who walks alone in liberty
Must face the hordes of massed humility.
Now, as of old, a leader risks his head,
A coward dies an inch a day, a hero is quick dead.

The Fresh Start

O give me back my rigorous English Sunday
And my well-ordered house, with stockings
    washed on Monday.
Let the House-Lord, that kindly decorous fellow,
Leave happy for his Law at ten, with a well-
    furled umbrella.
Let my young ones observe my strict house rules,
Imbibing Tory principles, at Tory schools.

Two years now I have sat beneath a curse
And in a fury poured out frenzied verse,
Such verse as held no beauty and no good
And was at best new curious vermin-food.

My dog is rabid, and my cat is lean,
And not a pot in all this place is clean.
The locks have fallen from my hingeless doors,
And holes are in my credit and my floors.

There is no solace for me, but in sooth
To have said baldly certain ugly truth.
Such scavenger's work was never yet a woman's,
My wardrobe's more a scarecrow's than a
      human's.

I'm off to the House-goddess for her gift.
'O give me Circumspection, Temperance, Thrift;
Take thou this lust of words, this fevered itching,
And give me faith in darning, joy of stitching!'

When this hot blood is cooled by kindly Time
Controlled and schooled, I'll come again to
      Rhyme.
Sure of my methods, morals and my gloves,
I'll write chaste sonnets of imagined Loves.

A Song of Women

When Kings knelt to a Maid and a Child,
In a poor place that kings could scorn,
Was Might exalted in a Maid?
Or stark Strength praised in the New-born?

Then was a babe known as Earth's Lord,
And a maid's arm was God's strong shield,
How long shall this Woman wait her reward,
The honour that her love should yield?

Upraised in Churches shrined in Art,
Ages have seen a Girl and Child.
But fullest honour is for days,
When Life and Faith are reconciled.

When Love is counted strong as Strength,
And all the tongues of service speak,
When you in council hear at length
The guardians of your mighty weak.

What splendid empire can you build?
What destiny in pride and lands,
That is not by our babes fulfilled
That is not in your women's hands.

Now we, the guardians of your Race,
Strong to fulfil your mighty task,
Ask in your Councils for our place,
And you will give us what we ask.

When Kings knelt to a Maid and a Child,
In a poor place that kings might scorn,
Then was our pleading justified,
By that strong Mother and her New-born.

The Foundling

There is a little naked child at the door,
His name is Beauty, and he cries,
'Behold, I am born, put me where I can live.'
The old World comes to the door,
And thrusting out a lip, says only this,
'It is true that you are born, but how were you
    conceived?'

There is an owl upon an elder-tree,
Who opening an eye, says only this.
'That is a lovely child!'
The old World said again,
'Yes! but how was he conceived?'

242

There is a gust of free wind,
And high cloud voices call.
'What can you ask of Love but conception?
Men are born of blest love,
Of evil love is death.
There is but one pure love, the love of Child,
And that is sweet as a pine forest, clean as the sea:
Old World take all your children in.'

Theft

When first I saw the old man dead,
I laid a curious hand upon his head,
To leave that little left in the soul's mould,
The knowledge of the rigour and the cold.
I asked no pardon of the Clay,
For the dead eyes had wandered in their day.
And kneeling ceremonious as his side,
I found a book he'd dropt the day he died,
Verses — which I repeated to dead ears in lieu of
    prayers,
I stole the book, regardless of his heirs,
Asking no pardon of the Clay
For the dead man had loved me in his day.

Solitary

When love is over are we most alone.
When hearths are black, there is the cold of stone.
I rise from my bed and walk the dismal night,
Weeping I seek alone my ultimate right.

The warmth and cheer of Love is but a lure,
By which the blood is cheated to endure.
To each man is a path, by other feet untrod,
Which leads him, lonely, to the hell of God.

On God's cold hill there is a holy height,
Where splendid fires descend to man at night:
On the cold traveller falls the livening breath
To raise him high in life, and proud in death.

From 'THE LITTLE OLD HOUSE'
(Poetry Bookshop, 1921)

The Little Old House

Now the house of your Grandfather Hardy
Was a scented Shropshire farm,
Where a boy might dream in the cinders,
Without a thought of harm,
For he who is burnt finds ointment
As soon as he understands
And the sting of a burn may be welcomed
For the healing of certain hands.

O the hands of your Grandmother Hardy
Were lovely and strong and white,
For she rubbed on their red with goose grease
After her prayers at night.
And they were free in giving
Yet never gave too much,
And not a baby living
Could cry beneath their touch.

Now the faith of your Grandfather Hardy
Was burning and clear and keen,
His heart was like his homestead
Ordered and straight and clean,
And when his work was ended,
Because the light grew dim,
Stole out of the clear cut shadows
A lovely English hymn.

O the love of your Grandmother Hardy
Was good as farm-house bread,
For all that was strong she worshipped,
And all that was weak she led.
And when her man was wounded
By a stray shot on his land,
She chid her eyes for weeping
But could not raise her hand.

Then take the tinker's road my son
Or sit in the courts of kings,
Yet carry from your mother
These two most royal things:
Let the faith of your Grandfather Hardy
Stand for your pride in life;
Let the hands of your Grandmother Hardy
Conduct you to your wife.

The Freeing

True Love came to the Sleepers' town,
Wandering up and wandering down,
I'm looking for the man I know is there
Hidden with cowardice, hidden with care,
Behind false looks and behind false speech,
I will have him out and throne him within reach
Of all men's honour for all men's aid,
And Time shall acclaim the king that I have
    made.
Such a king we have met, you and I, in a dream,
For we two know you are not the slave you seem
But a most royal prisoner to whom I bring release
That you may have God's laughter, and I may
    have God's peace.

A Boy's Voice

So lovely is his voice to me,
That I imagine a young tree
To rain a golden dew
More sweet to taste than wine.
Each perfect yellow sphere
Is as a word I hear
A sunny note, from the young throat
Of this white boy of mine.

Embassy

All the great lovely house,
When he's away,
Is like a bush
From which the rose is torn.
Is like a songless thrush
A flowerless May
Is like a gemless crown
A sunless morn.
Hve you not marked him and his pageantry
Grace and the pleasure which I lack?
But he has left a gallant guard with me:
I will send Love, to drive him back.

The Two Kings

To an eloquent friend I had given the key
Of my heart and my house and my granary;
He flung my heart for his dogs to eat,
And the shift of my soul he spread for his feet,
And freely he squandered my loveliest thing,
He would have me allow him the pride of a king.
Because of his kingliness was I so poor,
That I knocked for an alms at my silent friend's
    door.

Sham'dly and sadly I told him my needs,
And he said 'Long ago friend I gave you two
    seeds
Which I hid in my garden and now they are
    grown,
One tree is my wage, and the other your own.'
Then courteous he led me, 'Come hither and
    see.'
The gardener had nurtured a magical tree,
For the fruit was of gold and the trunk was of
    jade
So I mended the wreck which my false friend had
    made.

Naming the Girl

Soon after I was five, my dear
We lived beside the sea,
And I had such an angry nurse
She took the shells from me,
She hid the crinkly shells away,
For the small faults of yesterday.

And even smiling was a sin!
Nurse took a brush and scrubbed my skin
And when her nasty work was done
They found my brownness was the sun,
And then she coughed and scolded me
For all I did in Italy.

And we'd a great tall house
With shadows on the stairs
And devils in the corners
Who popped out after prayers.
O I can see them now my dear
Though I am nearly old,
But once in that house garden
I found a marigold.

And O it looked so happy!
And O it shone so sweet!
I ran up through the shadows
With dancing in my feet,
And I polka-ed in the schoolroom
When nurse was at her tea;
I didn't hear her scolding
When she remembered me.

And when your Mother told me
Her beautiful surprise,
I thought about my marigold
From pleasure in her eyes,
I said 'If it's a little girl
Who comes to live with you,
Be kind and call her Marigold
After the one I knew.'

Carol

When little Jesus slept
Unguarded in a stable
Out of the grass a Daisy crept
As close as he was able,
And watched the babe with steady eye
While following bees droned lullaby,
'Day's eye, Day's eye, thou blest day's eye.'
Happy was Mary in that hour
At service from so low a flower.

And Cherubim at night
Flew with the tale to God
Who touched the flower from Heaven's height
With a great shining rod
And in the morning it is told
That daisy woke a marigold.
'Mary's gold, O Mary's gold.'
Yet more than gold that mother mild
Loved a flower's kindness to her child.

The Performance

When we played a Greek play to the poor,
A fat old woman quickly sought the door.
She looked like a sad black beetle in her old
    shawl,
A creature that one could not educate at all.
I shall go back to Plaistow before long,
And sing that woman just a silly funny song.

Work of James and the Nation Builders

Jim's a lad that's stout and bold,
Five days more than five years old;
What craft shall this craftsman choose?
He'll wash the hearth and brush the shoes.

Brushing shoes is the queer boy's fun
Yet Master James is a gentleman's son;
There's a trade for the squire to choose
Washing hearths and brushing shoes!

P'raps it's the fault of the poor lad's nurse
That he won't remember that work's a curse,
Maybe his Mother's one whit to blame
That he will believe that work's a game.

All his young life he has never been sick
His eyes are clear and his fingers quick
He's free as a king, and hale as a peasant
His body tells him that work is pleasant.

Who knows but our world has read amiss
The splendid myth of Genesis!
For God can never curse the ground
When man's heart is high and his body sound.

Then let our nobler age confess
God's curse on slattern weariness!
Cursed be such sloth, and let it be desired
That no child ail, so man be never tired.

More blest than Eden is our world of sin
Since curious cleansings can be wrought therein.
Then let our pride contrive a thousand games,
To search and scour with all the zest of James.

Study of a Certain Brilliant Young Actress

She can never do her *Duty*,
She remembers the people who taught her music
When she was a child;
Then from a ravished sense of beauty
She becomes so self-conscious
That she runs wild.
She can't *work*
She functions like a flower or a wheel.
Even in art
She never *knows*, she can only feel.
Leave her alone
She will accomplish what God meant
She'll give you something perfect
As a rose's scent.

Host

When I was host to my enemy
I set him a chair of state
I summoned a solemn company
And served him quails on gold plate,
I pledged him courteous all the night
And this I did for spite.

There was little enough of my pride to see
When I was host to my friend,
I set him a dish of hominy
The feast came quick to an end.
I said 'It is here I have lost my skin
Since I was a hardy fool
Then open your counsel and let me come in
To school myself at your school.'

With the blood of my wounds I pledged my
　　friend
And fitly I had proved
Before that grim carousal's end
How courteous I had loved.

The House of Little Victories

The house is barred unto the lover,
His foot shall not pass over
Stone of this threshold
Though fires be fierce within
The living heart is cold.
This house is open to all covert sin
Free to the poor light mind,
But thou Desirer − Come not in!
'Tis thou wilt loose and bind.
This is the house of an eternal sloth
And they who live therein are loth
To sting and wake.
Leave thou this dwelling
For thy kingship's sake.

Meg and the Witchwight

Muddly Meg was ever toiling
With all her poor thin ugly will,
Muddly Meg was ever spoiling
Muddly Meg was never still.

Meg was working at her children
She took no gracious thought to please,
Meg was working at her baby,
She never stopt to kiss his knees;
Meg was working at her husband
Till that poor man ran mad one day:
He said 'I'll go and fetch a witchwight
There's one sells pipes across the way.'

Thither he came the merry master
Covered the vixen with a motley dress
He said 'Thou fountain of disaster
Thou mother of foul idleness,
Stifler of men, ill architect of children,
Follow pale misery. Come shake a leg.'
And they went dancing down our village
The mystery man, and merry Meg.

Stateswoman and the House

Were there dynamic in a pure democracy
The servants in this house would not reflect my
    mood:
When I'm all inky with my poetry
No thing is found where it but lately stood.

When I'm not willing all this house runs ill
Since for fulfilling I advance the will:
I am their slave, since they will never rule for me:
That I'll not have, and they shall go to school for
    me.

Thus I'll compel them, thus they shall be free,
All power applied conditions liberty,
And the full power of life shall not be known,
Till, through their freedom, I attain my own.

Song for Domestic Anguish

Give me a house where the servants sing,
Fit it with green baize doors
So that the faults of their carolling
Stop at the servants' floors.
Ingenious Love shall bring to pass
This happy Reconstruction,
Stating the difference betwixt class and class
Not in Joy, but in Voice-production.

Due for Hospitality
(To H.M.)

God is a courteous gentleman
And a most genial host.
Such could not rest
If any guest
Should leave his house to roast!
Then fear not Hell
Respect God well
He's great as man at least.
Before you're dead,
See there is spread
Within your life a feast,
Which it is meet
That you should eat,
With courtesy expressed.
Acclaim with mirth
God's pleasant earth,
As fits a gracious guest.

The Fairy Wife

When you have gathered a thousand pound
I'll not let you kiss me,
I'll steal out of the garden bound
And you will never miss me —
You'll buy a farm with your minted gold,
And drowse o'er the fire, as you grow old.

Slippery slippery spending Jack
What wealth would you gather? What gold could
    you keep?
You'd had scarcely a coat for your great broad
    back,
If I had not charmed you full half asleep —
When the good grain's in the great oak box
I'm through the edges as lithe as a fox.

Love! Love! Love, I'm tired of the name
Mine is the wound and yours is the balm
I'm to a duck pond to drown the flame,
When you are master of yon hill-farm.
Sleep sounder sounder slippery Jack,
And quickly gather the gold you lack.

It is my pleasure to walk alone
On the sheer steep above the snow,
I have a cave and a bed of my own
On the blue height where lichens grow,
There I will sing with the deeps to hear
While the stars keep their courses nor swing too
    near.

The Homecoming

I waited ten years in the husk
That once had been our home
Waiting from dawn till dusk
To see if he would come.

And there he was beside me
Always at board and bed,
I looked and woe betide me
He whom I loved was dead.

He fell at night on the hill side,
They brought him home to his place;
I had not the solace of sorrow
Until I had looked in his face.

Then I clutched the broken body
To see if he stirred or moved,
For there in the smile of his dying
Was the gallant man I had loved.

O wives come lend me your weeping
I have not enough of tears,
For he is dead who was sleeping
These ten accursed years.

The Song of the Old Mother

Do you remember the summer
Before the boy was born?
You rowed me up the river,
Between the filling corn,
I see you now as you smiled at me
And handed me ashore
Then we were happier lovers,
Than in the year before.

We wandered in the orchard
Beside the river brink
I saw the young bronze apples
And lingered there to think.
'The child will be here in the autumn,
When fruit is red on the boughs.'
You asked me why I was smiling
As we went into the house.

The last thing I saw from my windows
Were ladders against the trees.
Then I woke on my happiest morning
To see your son on your knees,
And I was weak for laughing
But there were tears in my joy
To see yourself a father
And you a slip of a boy.

And he was brave and wholesome
Like apples. As he began
He always was and shall be,
Your son is a splendid man.
But sure I was never his mother,
For you are my only child,
The lad who stood in the orchard
To help me ashore, and smiled.

Reaction

A certain bitter shrew
Gained sudden courtesy
Until a wonder grew,
That such a change should be.

Said that poor man her mate,
'This thing can not endure.'
And the priest came out in state
Scenting miraculous cure.

He asked 'How is't my child
You who were harsh of old
Are now so douce and mild
And are no more a scold?'

Then did her quick tears start
'I am grown sudden kind,
Since I saw a man of great heart,
And of most gallant mind.'

Counsel to Craftswomen

Deep in the man there is a lonely boy
To life's hard nurture still unreconciled
Starving for beauty and for natural joy:
Go — thou kind woman, and console the child!

There is new truth concealed in this day's night
And man shall find it with a boy's keen eyes
Thine honour is in victory for his sight:
Feed then the child in him if thou art wise.

Make of thy love a pleasant laughing game
And set thy beauty like a birth day feast
Be thou first mother, who art wife in name:
So is his man-hood grown, his power increased.

Yet, for that manhood call him not 'My son'
But at his weakest honour him in word.
So shall a play-boy when the game is done
Prove thy most true and honourable lord!

Song of the Exalted

This child's father is a strong man, is a valiant
    man
He is God's man.
He is lord of anvils, hammers and fierce fires —
With his great hand he fashions a brass pan
And he shall spill in it world's hungers, world's
    desires.

This child's father is a strong man, is a valiant
    man
He is God's man.
He shall stretch his sinewy back and shall exalt
    the pan —
Brimming with tears and grimy sweat and grief
He shall fling it to the stars, for the old world's
    relief
Till the black liquor sinks through crevices of
    night
And the assaulted dome crashes an answering
    light.

This child's father is a strong man, is a valiant
    man
He is God's man.
I am more blest than any other
Since he has called me
For his proud heir's mother.

The Pleader

Love has compelled me subtly to offend
He who is very Prince of Courtesy,
And for his fault I cannot make amend,
I am your suppliant for charity.

How meek is Love who thus will be a mime
To learn if faith be worthy of delight:
How proud! He will not leave the test to Time,
He swoops to knowledge like a spear in flight.

Love has compelled me to forgo my will,
My tongue turns traitor to my heart and mind,
If you believe of me my feignéd ill
I must forswear you, since you are not kind.

House of all dear Desires! There is no cost
But I would pay it to abide in you.
Then yield your little debt lest all be lost:
Pay in blind loyalty Love's chosen due.

The Boy and the Playhouse

Give him two sticks, a flower and a stone,
And the small model of a sheep,
And such a fairy land will be his own,
As you'll not find in waking or in sleep.

Blind educationist, take your proper way!
And never teach a little child to play!
God send our theatre new phantasies,
As fresh and exquisite as his.

Felicity Neat

Felicity Neat the serving maid
Cleared the muddle Queen Order made,
Smoothed her silver dress away
In scented leaves of yesterday,
Then turned a musical handle round
Till people danced to the pleasant sound.
Queen Order laughed to their chiming feet:
O how I love you, Felicity Neat.

Tidiness and Order

Where work is always finished
And nothing ever strays,
There are the sad old children
And the wet empty days.

There are too many servants
So every day is long
And duty fills all silence
And leaves no room for song.

In the house of beautiful Order
Everything has its place,
But a boy may run out of the schoolroom
To kiss his Mother's face.

The Boy and the Scrapheap

Let us find the truth of Stephen
Since God has set the seed of him
So honouring our service
Till man shall have his need of him.
Can we understand his essence
Know the secret of his joy?
Here a woman and her husband
Are joined within a boy.

See his straight lovely body
As he runs across the field!
There is his Mother's courage,
Clear written and revealed,
And his face has flowers and marbles
And stars and firefly light
For he stole his father's spirit
In the silence of the night.

A fairy boy is Stephen
And warden of such gold
That what he steals is given
Again a thousand fold;
I flung him sticks and rubble
For the pleading of his eyes,
And there among the stubble
He built a paradise.

What need have such as Stephen
For a beauty clear defined?
For the Mother of all perfectness
Sits throned within his mind.
There is Old Wit the huntress
With her brave dogs in hand
And Stephen shall unleash them
To riot through his land.

And where he runs they follow,
Hosanna for the chase!
For see within what hollow
They make their sporting place!
Not among flocks and beehives
Not on the beach or down,
But on a builder's scrapheap,
Of this erroneous town.

The Vain Girl

When you left me last night
I dressed myself in shiny white:
I wore my simplest satin dress
Knowing you love my slenderness.
And I was like an ivory snake
And I was this for Beauty's sake.

Note

A fine spirit of hospitality
Has disregard for property
And fine contempt of quality.
It offers all things easy-found and rare
Without words, without apparent care,
As God almighty offers sun and air.

Queen's Song on Saint Valentine's Day

Here are we — You and I
Waiting, waiting!
While the happy birds flash by
Swift to their mating.
In March will fledgelings be in nest,
In March I'll lay my babe to rest
On the knees of the king.
O happy Mother! and O happy Spring!

What shall we do, you and I
Waiting, waiting?
We will bless the birds that fly
Swift to their mating,
And through the house we'll gather wool and
    thread,
That Mistress Thrush may build a royal bed
For her brave children, who will dream of flight
When you my babe have joy of light.

Thanks for your song good thrush
You cheer our waiting.
See I have laid your wool beneath this bush
God bless your mating.

The Eternal Faith

Thou art established in my endless love
Firm as a hill is set upon a plain,
The little torrents leap, the great winds move:
Thou shalt fear changes as the heights fear rain.

My faith shall hold thee in thy chosen way
Sure as that will which binds the stars in place.
Would'st thou mistrust me? Wait that final day
When hills lack bases, and when suns doubt
    space.

To Jane-Across-the-Bay

When my blossomy tree came out in May
To the edge of the sea I took my way
And set a flowery twig afloat:
I thought white petals the sails of a boat
And dreamed kind winds would bring it to land
Where rosy feet touch happy sand.
A flower went down in the foam of the sea,
But a gallant ship was lost to me.

Song

I will sing no more of Love
Love shall sing in me,
I will sing the bird in the grove,
The flower the fish and the bee,
For I love well small things that dwell
On land and in the sea.

Invocation to the Intelligence of a Gentleman

Nymph in a Cloud!
Shy loiterer on a height!
By faith art thou avowed
Thou art not known to sight.
Pity the clod in me,
Frail denizen of air;
I, lacking sight of thee,
Must doubt if thou art there!

Light, the Daughter of Charity

Light, the daughter of Charity,
Kissed her servants and made them free,
Staunched the wounds of their mad carouse
With holy oil of her Father's house,
Then harried them back to Charity,
To sweep in her cupboards and find a key.

Thus she came to her power at length,
Loosed from their bonds young Beauty and
    Strength;
'Hear, my sons for your Mother is wise,
Sorrow has fed her ears and her eyes,
But you for your joy shall be wiser than she,'
Said Light the daughter of Charity.

'Beauty, thy scent shall be truer than Truth,
In strength shall abide eternal youth,
And he shall steal from that poisoner Night
A lovelier gem than the jewel of Light:'
Thus said the daughter of Charity
Who swept in her cupboards and found a key.

On the Day They Took Down the Grille
(House of Commons, 1917)

Now give me a high room and a long taper
Much ink and pens and endless reams of paper,
Then I might well my lyric mettle prove,
For I have made a peace with my true-love.
How were my singing more than raucous din,
With fires and tempests raging fierce within?
I cannot raise a paradise from me
Without some seedlings from reality.
If ever I speak truth or I sing clear
Impute it to my love, that he is dear,
If I show gallantry in any fight
Know a man's courage was his wife's delight,
If I walk comely know a woman's grace
Is but the image of her lover's face.
Go black-cat Misery avoid my pages
Hence clammy Passion with your bombast rages
Tell me some henbird sings upon her tree
And I will raise a natural melody
But if male singing is by God preferred
I will learn silence from the nobler bird.

Dedication of the Cook

If any ask why there's no great She-Poet,
Let him come live with me, and he will know it:
If I'd indite an ode or mend a sonnet,
I must go choose a dish or tie a bonnet;
For she who serves in forced virginity,
Since I am wedded, will not have me free;
And those new flowers my garden is so rich in
Must die for clammy odours of my kitchen.

Yet had I chosen Dian's barrenness
I'm not full woman — and I can't be less,
So, could I state no certain truth for life.
Can I survive and be my good man's wife?

Yes! I will make the servant's cause my own
That she in pity leave me hours alone,
So I will tend her mind and feed her wit
That she in time have her own joy of it;
And count in pride that not a sonnet's spoiled
Lacking her choice betwixt the baked and boiled.
So those young flowers my garden is so rich in
Will blossom from the ashes of my kitchen!

The Woman and the Aeroplane

Here I stand in this muddy Street
While a great plane goes by!
There is a rage of dancing in my feet
And in my heart a mad-ecstatic cry
'He is up! He is out!'
Brave on supremest enterprise
With a swift menace all about
He cleaves new skies –
Insistent as that engine is his mood;
I know it by the leaping of my blood!

The Thrifty Lover

She is so exquisite! I will go hence
To make a singing of her eminence
For if her living lips should touch my skin
Such sweet commotion would abide therein
That I were no more diligent and no more wise
Than to breathe out my happy life in sighs.

For very fear of her I'll go my way
Yet bare her beauty in my heart each day;
A richer treasure shall I win from this
Than will a hardier man who waits to kiss:
From such chaste intercourse might well be got
Songs that will live when she and I are not.

267

Eyes and the Child

Looking from out the gates of paradise
The Holy Child perceived the devil;
Long he regarded him with pitying eyes,
Then said 'Thou art no ugly thing of evil
But a great angel sorely tired
Then come thou, eat and sleep within.'
The devil followed as the babe desired:
That was the end of sin.

The Mirror

'Twas on the eve of Christmas day
I had not hope nor charity,
I met a beggar on my way
Who stretched his hand and grinned at me.
I went into my house and barred the door
'He is not poor as I am poor.'

'Twas on the morn of Christmas day,
Bankrupt in heart and sick in mind
O'er heath and wild I took my way
In haste to leave Myself behind.
When on the hill I paused for breath
I found that beggar still as death.

He said 'Oh thou that art a cold
With fiercer rigours than this blast
I sue for neither warmth nor gold
But this redeeming gift at last:
A soul of your good charity
And grant a spirit room in thee.'

'Twas at the noon of Christmas day
The sun was at his little height
And I went singing on my way

Singing for freedom and delight.
The mendicant who walked with me
Sustained a happy harmony.

And on the night of Christmas day
We two walked homeward through the gloom,
Into the house I led the way
To show him to my inner room.
'Twas then a wonder came to pass
He waited in the looking-glass.

Then I had almost shrieked for fear
That madness should abide with me,
I turned about and *I am here*.
My living comrade laughed to me
I am Thyself. Myself to Time's end
I am thy friend.

The Doorkeeper

Tread soft ye stars and little winds lie still,
My lord Berolf has cut himself a quill.
Here on the board is a new parchment spread
And the long taper mocks the silken bed.
I will have no owls to hoot among these bushes,
No sleeping starlings, doves, nor thrushes
To change-a-leg-in-the-night and make a creaking.
Out bats and mice with scratching and with
    squeaking,
Back to your closes fairies, sylphs to your ways,
Elves to your hills and goblins to your caves.
If near these precincts any woman scold
May a black palsy strike her dumb and old.
Our lord Berolf has cut himself a quill
And by his might I bid this night lie still.

Miracle

I bring you this word –
Truly I was redeemed –
Not by God-Withdrawn – but by living man
A man bred natural in this town.

He gave me great scope
For my faith and my hope
Since he was not of the scatheless,
But a poor sinner.

He gave me my need,
A pod of dream-seed,
And he was not of the scatheless
But a poor sinner.

Such miraculous high things I dreamed of him
That I was quick redeemed of him.
I bring you this word
Truly I was redeemed
Not by God-Withdrawn – but by living man
A man bred natural in this town.

'RICHARDS' SHILLING SELECTIONS'
(1936)

In the House of the Soul
(Harlequin and a Woman under One Skin)

Well, they are gone!
And we are here alone:
I, the mime, and master of surprises,
Who have fooled that mob with fifty new
    disguises –

You, who sit still in the soul
Like a quiet wife;
You, who are Control,
Weaving the long continuous web of life.
I should have little courage to continue with this
     jest
Could I not meet you here, and be at rest.
Sometimes I think that there is nothing of my
     winning,
That all we have of service from our union is
     your spinning.
But when of shame my heart is full —
Then you remind me, dame:
I bring you wool.
It is our business here to make a song —
Whoever is sore, whatever is wrong.

King Alfred and the Peasant Woman

Threw me from the house, did he?
Well, to new chivalry that is no great thing!
I am my father's daughter, Lady,
And he's a pretty figure in the ring.

But my man, my master, there he sat a-dreaming,
While all the house might burn, and he'd not
     sorrow;
Nor had I any warrant that his scheming
Would bring us any victory on the morrow.

And I spoke to him — O I informed him!
He'd be a dead man, if he were not stung.
Could any man keep hands down, and me
     lashing?
Ach, you insult my tongue!

I'd rather he fought me than missed his combats,
Though I'm not built for blows upon the heart.
Give me a breastplate and I'll at 'em –
Though that's fool-woman's part!

I love him, and if he comes back with honour,
After the fight I drove him to is won,
He'll find his woman, with her glory on her:
Please God, the child's a son!

The Venturous Shepherdess

Listen, good Ewes, to this wonderful thing!
There's a troll in your woods, with the eyes of a
    King.
I have marked out the path to his cave with a
    stone,
And I'll drive him with boughs to the height of a
    throne:
For he shall inherit your grazing land,
His head is an orb, and a sceptre his hand.

I'll run to the hills, and run to the glen,
And call to the maidens, and call to the men:
'Wake, sleepy folk, to this wonderful thing –
In a cave of your woods, I have found you a
    King;
In a cave of your woods, I have found you a
    Lord;
His word is a crown, his glance is a sword!

'Bring spears, ye striplings; hunt for his pleasure!
Bring flowers, ye girls, and dance for his leisure!
With rare sweet food shall the King be fed,
And ten white maids shall smooth him his bed;
And I will sit and laugh all my life,
For a keeper of sheep is the King-troll's wife.'

Song of the Lonely Shepherd
(*Written for Mme Nicklass Kempner*)

I found her asleep in the snows:
Her head and her feet were bare,
And she was like a wild sweet rose
By miracle flung there.
I carried her in to my love and my rest,
And I thawed her feet at my breast.

And all the winter long
She neither spoke nor stirred:
My heart made a happy song
(O I was blithe as a bird!):
'There'll be an end to these bitter days;
I'll see her dance down flowery ways.'

And on an April morning,
Alas! I was early abroad
To pluck a crown for adorning
The head that my soul adored –
Alas and alas! I was home too late:
The cruel feet had danced out through my gate.

O little feet, matched like two happy lovers,
Have you no pity on me?
Know ye not that this sheepskin covers
Sore wounds, and my piteous misery?
Your ice has burned a brand on my breast;
Then lead her back, to my love and my rest!

The Heavenly Bitch

Master, O master, turn to me, speak!
Why do you wander, and what do you seek
Long on the edge of this fœtid lake?
Come with me, come for your leman's sake.
We drowned a priest in that horrible hole,
And weighted his corpse with a live man's soul.
The air is thick with his odious stink:
O walk no more by the deathly brink.

Master, O master, why do you stare?
What do you see on the lake out there?
It's only a clot of floating weed.
Why do you wait? O will you not heed!
In the mud of the lake, a saint lies dead
With a live man's soul for a stone at his head.

It is no weed looks up at the sky
As if the mere were a beast with one eye.
This is my winnings, this my reward,
That my soul is tied to a stretching cord,
To the rotting flesh of a silly priest:
It has mounted to air like a bubble in yeast;
It is mocked at noon by the high hot light,
And stars invade its void by night.
Girl, my girl, I would have it again.
My flesh dissolves to ash with pain.

Master, O master, am I not your witch?
See! I am transformed to an old black bitch;
So I run swift through the menacing night
To your cave, to your shelter, to your delight.
And I am a valiant swimmer, my lord:
I will fetch the stone for love's reward.
I'll pay for the gift you were loath to take,
For a feeble, pitiful changeling's sake.

I'll swim to the saint, and swim to the land,
And lay the stone in my master's hand.
The stinking beast with the single eye
Shall not stare in vain at the stubborn sky:
For, if my lord would climb to their Heaven,
Importunate doors of the sky shall be riven;
A bitch shall lurk at God's high gate
And yap and yap at his solemn state
Till she wreck God's peace with her tireless din
And Saints shall open and let her man in.

The Girl and the Jester

As I ran weeping out of the house
Of my foster-mother, Misrule,
Carolling high of the loves of a mouse,
I met the Cardinal's fool.

Now, he was meagre and he was thin,
But a wonderful man to see;
For a curious light shone out of his skin,
And he came and accosted me.

He said with never a smile or bow:
'How little you honour your face;
You're wearing it very uncivilly now,
And so you offend God's grace.'

He plucked my sleeve with his finger and thumb:
'How little you honour your hands!
For over your weaving they wander glum
To sully its intimate strands.

'Come, give me your jewel, my girl,' said he.
I raised my hand to my breast;
And there by unholy wizardry
I found an adder's nest.

Then I ran shrieking back to the house
Of my foster-mother, Misrule:
To my brother the Tiger, my sister the Mouse,
I set myself to school.
Now Beauty and Peace are pensioners here
And all for the love of a fool.

War of the Cave

Old Witch, old Witch, come lend me your
    broom!
Himself is walking the pine-wood's gloom
With Dulcibella, the wench of the farm.
She has a mouse's wit beneath her hair;
We of the craft must have a care
Or he'll take harm.

Old Sloven, Sloven, are you not shamed
Of your sucking Wizard? She's inflamed
To think herself a goddess from his cozening!
She'll teach him flight;
Climb slow before him to a dung-hill's height
And queen it with him for a vassal king.

Ach, you have lost your claws, old Cat!
Time and your sloth have seen to that!
Yet there is virtue in you, *that* I now concede!
By this unwonted courtesy, by this most silly
    honesty,
I beg a broom of you, though I've no need.

Would you withhold him from me − you a fairy-
    woman?
Can you be jealous, like a puling human?
If he be that fine essence you believe him −
If you, Witch-mother, are not blind and daft −
Now, for the honour of our kind and craft,
I must fly farmwards, to retrieve him.

Your broom, your broom, I say! Give it me
    quick!
Else I am out, away, on my own stick:
I'll to the zenith with him in straight flight;
Upwards I'll sweep on a fiend-driven wind,
With your sweet changeling pillioned behind,
To dash his carrion from the utmost height!

Song of Ophelia the Survivor

There is no smirch of sin in you, only its fires.
You are a man burned white with merciless
    desires;
A restless heat consumes you, and your brain,
Tortured to torturing, craves for ugly pain.

Beauty still lives in you, and from her seat
Controls your glances, and directs your feet;
One look from you taught me so much of love,
I have all pleasure, just to watch you move.

That look was like a wet blue mist of flowers,
Which held compelling loveliness and sleepy
    powers.
I dreamed of calling pipes down a warm glade;
By the transposéd music of your soul I was
    betrayed.

Pipe for me, my dear lover! I will come,
And your sick soul shall find in me a home;
I will be your house, clean, high, and strong.
And You shall live in me, all winter long.

As you are fevered, I will be a pool,
Full of green shadows, level, silent, cool.
You shall bathe in me, in my being move;
I will put out your fires with my strong love.

Lament of the Red Knight

Tree-blossom and May
Are vanished away;
The mad merry month is over.
Alas! and alas!
How came it to pass
Not all that month was I any woman's lover?

The Queen sits up in her sullen bower;
Her eyes shoot wrath like darts from a tower.
Such a melancholy harridan never was seen!
But alas! and alas! I love the Queen.
Now I must bear Winter to every warm glade;
For never again will I kiss a young maid.

The Captive

I loved so that my blood became new substance,
Like the wine of priests.
There was no Time for me, but one eternal
    moment of desiring:
The woman had one scented garment;
I had one sense, to find her.

I came to her chamber;
She was upon her bed:
The room was heavy with incense;
It was lighted by high tapers;
The woman's skin shone like as a stormy moon.

She was more gracious than reality,
More lovely than phantasy;
She slept, her upturned palms invited me.

What spell could keep me by the curtains of the
    door?
In the shadows of the walls were pillars the
    height of men;
They were boxes faced with glass:
I stept stealthily, and gazed at them;
They were dead men, coffined dead men.

High in the dome of the chamber was a raven
    chained.
A voice fell like a stone:
'This woman's name is Beauty; her lovers are
    dead men:
Go, bridegroom, to her bed!'
Then I would have gone out into the sun,
Where rosy mothers played with children in the
    air.

The woman's skin shone like a stormy moon:
My soul died like a candle that is blown out,
And like the smoke of an extinguished candle
    trailed my song:
'Let me die, O Beauty, let me die!'

Love Song

I am like sand sucked down by the tide:
Love has compelled my soul:
Not for my fears, not for my pride,
Can I regain control.

I must be still with the thought of fire:
I cannot move for pain:
Woman I am, transposed by desire
To a broad upland plain.

I am a down, spread green by the sea,
And white cliffs are my feet:
My hair is a wood, and the breasts of me,
Hills where storms meet.

Between the hills is a broad white road
Down which a king shall ride:
I am firm earth, with the earth's load —
I, who was drawn by the tide.

When I remember your horse's feet,
I am like mountain grass,
And your young colts so free and fleet
Shall trample me — and pass.

Song to Amidon

Dear Fragrance,
Be no more a man,
But a small hill of herbs!
And I will take you in my hands
And press you to more intimate fine scent;
And I will hold you to my heart
Till I know grace.
The hungry winds shall woo me for your sake.
Incontinent, I'll fling you to high air;
And you, ascending to poor God's assault,
Shall burden Heaven with your subtle sweet,
Till he repent him of old odorous smoke
And fling out bolts to throw the altars down.

Inconsequent Lover

I will drive you down odorous hours
With a whip of white exquisite flowers,
Till, worn by my wooing, you lie
On a bed of delight, and so die.

I will steal from the magicky night
Blue Moth for a young acolyte;
And a sad, solemn mass shall be said
For the beautiful thing that is dead.

The Winds

The quality of your rage is my delight:
I saw a wind in a volcanic night
Incline a fir-wood almost to the ground,
And with such strength that I could hear no
    sound:
So is your anger written for my mind,
In driven trees, and in that mastering wind.

A quality of courage is my gift.
First would you wreck, O Builder? Lift
Your hammer against me, and strike your fill;
Cleave me to dust — and from that dust my will
Will rise in spirals, masterful as flame,
Till whirlwinds march in triumphs of your name!

Song

Your spirit is my treasury,
My storehouse and my armoury.
There rich, bright stuffs are found
And rare sweet foods abound
With curious knives designed to slay
Those prowlers of the night and day
Who ate my noon and took my sleep,
And held me captive in my keep.
Now in your being I can move,
My air, my path, my light, my love!

Garnett's Garden

I look down from my window,
And I see
A ramble of forget-me-not
Beneath a flowery tree;
As if the sky had fallen
To let pass
A lovely girl
To dance upon the grass.
I could lie happy dead beneath your garden
If my soul could walk the skies
With such white lovely women,
In a cool paradise.

Mare Bred from Pegasus

For God's sake, stand off from me:
There's a brood mare here going to kick like hell
With a mad up-rising energy;
And where the wreck will end who'll tell?
She'll splinter the stable and eat a groom.
For God's sake, give me room;
Give my will room.

'Make Beauty for me!' – that was what you said,
While I was cowering at your dying fire,
Laconic, blowing at your chill desire.
Then flame broke out in me to char you dead;
A fierce hope and a more fierce distrust
To char your bones to dust.

My pretty jockey, you've the weight
To be a rider, but not my mate;
And yet your spirit's bold to impregnate,
And I'm a lashing, butting hate.

Since my poor life began
I had desire to serve my man
With all my wit, all imagination,
And every subtle beauty of creation;
And you come late,
And mock me in my masterless hard state.

'Make Beauty for me!' – that was what you said.
Desire rose up in me to strike you dead,
With that mad mare my will
To lash and smash her fill.

Run, run, and hide you in some woman's heart,
In a retreat I cannot kick apart!

Pilgrimage

I think of the room at *Bon Secours*:
The clock on the shelf, and the bare-board floor,
The tallow smell from the out-blown light,
And the laughter and love of the prodigal night:
I wish we were young, dear,
As young and as poor
As when we stole Heaven
At *Bon Secours*.

Call of the Dead

The stone is riven, I'm free, I'm free.
Come out, my Ransomer, out to me.
Leave the wrecked tenement behind;
The night is ours, and the night wind.
Up we ride from the dim places,
Out we swim through the great spaces,
Driven in tracks of liberty
On ether-piercing ecstasy.
Follow me quick, my Love, my Friend,
To the blue steep at Time's end.

The Boor's Wooing

I love her for her fine blue coat,
And for that ivory at her throat
All cut about in charming shapes,
Small flowers, and nests, and birds and grapes.

I love her for her white, deft hands.
With what an art, she smooths the strands
Of Chloe's hair to make a seemliness
Among the gins of that sweet-scented wilderness!

But most, I love the farmwoman who drowses
While my fine lady walks the dim-lit houses:
And by my head! that canny wench shall wake
And laugh and labour for her peasant's sake.

When first I saw her in her painted room
My unskilled silence spoke her doom.
What call had I to waste my power in speech
When what I willed was still beyond my reach?

But I have cut a rope from the tough vine,
And I've distilled a draught more strong than
    wine.
First she shall drink, and then I'll draw her
    hence,
To pin an apron on her elegance.

And she shall kilt her skirt, and bare her arms,
And live about my fields, and on my farms.
Is she thin Venus on a painted fan?
No! she's right woman, and Myself's her man!

The Silent Singer

I have no words that could prevail
Against the furies of my male.
When we go out I come behind,
While he expounds his angry mind:
O I walk humbly in the path
Of his just wrath!
Then he goes singing —

Sings like a mavis, or a boy,
From a still secret source of joy;
And I am all humility,
His pleasure's me.
Silent I follow many a mile —
Trying my hardest not to smile —
To my heart's singing.

The Sick Assailant

I hit her in the face because she loved me.
It was the challenge of her faithfulness that
    moved me;
For she knew me, every impulse, every mood,
As if my veins had run with her heart's blood.
She knew my damned incontinence, my
    weakness –
Yet she forbore with her accurséd meekness.
I could have loved her had she ever blamed me;
It was her sticky, irritating patience shamed me.
I was tired-sick. It was her business to amuse me:
Her faith could only daunt me and confuse me.
She was a fine great wench, and well I knew
She was one good half panther, one half shrew –
Then why should my love, more than any other,
Induce in her the silly human Mother?
She would have nursed me, bathed me, fed me,
    carried me;
She'd have burned her soul to thaw me – she'd
    have married me!
I hit her in the face because she loved me.
It was her sticky, irritating patience moved me.

The Shameless Lady

Said the lass that I love, one flowery May:
'Ho, thou great loon, go away! go away!
For thou'lt not lay thy head to my breast.
Go find some other to share that jest.
It's little grace thou'lt get from me,
For I have all that I need of thee.

'Before this happy year is done,
I'll yield my heart to my own sweet son.
A girl has small need for a man, I say,
With work to be done, and a babe on the way.
I'll bear a boy when my time is done;
For I loved thee well, three months agone.'

And she'd not go to the church that year
Though I wooed her long, for I loved her dear.
And when at last she deigned to come,
The little master slept at home:
Said she, 'I loved for this happy thing,
And not for a farm, and not for a ring.'

A Girl to Her Baby

Thou dear Postilion, who has caught the rein
To set this colt upon her road again:
She will not fear the smart of any spur
For the strong sires who set the seed of her,
For stout hill-mares who fasted in the snows
When frost had blackened such poor grass as
     grows:
Let thy red livery be a note of joy
To all who starve and stray, thou lovely boy!

The Happy Mathematician
(*An Arithmetic Lesson for a Small Boy:*
Written for John Untermeyer)

When he was nine, he thought he knew
All about two times two.
He sang his tables out aloud
And he was very glad and proud.
He thought: 'I'll not be weak or poor,
Because twice two are always four:
I know this now, and I'll get knowledge
Even more fine, when I'm at college.'

When he was ninety-nine or more,
Wise Death came knocking at his door.
Death said: 'As you get nearer Heaven,
Twice two are five or six or seven;
And at the centre of God's heart,
The whole is as the smallest part.'
The old man laughed: 'That interests me.
Teach me your tables, Death,' said he.

The Boy and the Trees

Some day she will come to me
All lit-up like a Christmas tree,
Her arms out-stretched like lovely boughs,
And meet me in my Mother's house;
And so my lips will touch her breast,
And I will be at rest.

Then I will wake in golden morn,
With me and all the world reborn,
And from my window I shall see
My Mother by an apple tree.
And I will call her frank and clear;
And she will pluck a rosy sphere
And fling it from her lovely hands
And laugh like one who understands.
That fragrant fruit so red and sweet,
My Love shall eat.

The Show

I am no man's love,
But a lonely devil
Tossing the balls of good and evil;
Slogging the air:
A mime at a fair!

I am no man's love,
But a bearded wench
Lolling in a booth on a scarlet bench,
Where yokels come to grin, and see
What I be!

I am no man's love,
But a five-legged calf;
And I am penned to raise a laugh;
And now and then I try to run —
And that's the fun.

The Sportsman

I'm watching my power and my rapture
Go by me like leaves on a wind:
If I held up my hand, I could capture
And hold them – if I had the mind.
Is it Hell that I fear for my soul,
Or Heaven I'd come to at length?
No! I'm staking to-day on Control!
I'm backing an ultimate Strength!

Stable Talk

When the hart pursues the hunter,
God send that I'm a punter!
When that strange race begins,
We know which wins.

The hunter will need little start
To get away from the poor hart:
Though he pursued her reckless while she ran,
He'll run, to see a deer turn on a man.

Harts, if you would thrive and live
And keep a thing you have no wish to give,
When first you see the hunter come pursuing,
Go out to meet him with a hotter wooing.

Pugilist

Though I am well-clothed, well-booted, and well-
    fed,
I yet have the hunger of Hell in me
For a dream that is dead;
And that, though I have gained two grades in
    rank,
Have a horse, and a house, and gold in the bank.

My mind is dull with fullness, yet I know
I have one utter need —
To find a foe!
I will strip off this fine constricting coat
And grip Necessity by his thin throat.

The Striker at the Gate of All-Sloth

How long have you lingered on the ways
To be inhabited by the first wanton;
Your guest-chamber befouled
By any insensitive penetrating Will?
Most hypnotisable poor soul,
What is left for honour but your sterility —
That Will, in you, has not consented to a base
    conception,
That you have chosen the ugliness of still-birth,
And have not raised posterity to Death!

The Begetter is come, O Daughter of Joy.
He is enamoured of your shape:
Yet for his love he'll work his way with scorn!
He woos you with a whip. Now you are free to
    fear;
And the fruitfulness in you, so long controlled,
Will break its barriers like a dam its wall
And Chaos shall be all about.
From him, so long awaited, you shall fly!

Long have you masqueraded through a hundred
  false alliances.
Let chastity be your garment,
Go nymph to your cloud!

Now, are you withheld! That last is fit!
Sterility is well placed on the cold height.
I, who will have pleasure of you and the brave
  increase of joy,
Would dream a little of our consummation.
How delicately made are you! How proud am I,
Who hold the living nucleus to induce new
  symmetry.

Times there are when simulated scorn
Grows real in me —
When I recall your dalliance,
How you are lessened and besmeared:
Then my hate is hard and bright as crystal.
Are you fit to be desired?
Shall I leave you where I have driven you,
Till you issue out an ugly harridan
Decked with the rags and scraps of dead men's
  dreams?
No! I have lusted with a sanctifying flame.
You are my tower! I set my flag on you!
Make ready for the Guest:
Send down your serving-men to sweep the floor!

The Dilemma

If he roam far away
From the herd's track,
He may run mad one day
And not come back.

If he feed where he stands,
He will find nothing strange nor sweet:
He must die in home lands
Because he cannot eat.

Conscience
(*Written for Fytton Armstrong*)

I dreamed my heart was a grave
In which were dead embalmed princesses,
In jewelled stomachers and dresses,
Flaunting their never-rotting tresses
For the skull smile of the brave.

I dreamed Dionysius spoke:
A free beast howled from the Christians' heaven;
All ugly cerements were riven;
And breath, and blood, and breasts were given;
And the kings and the girls awoke.

Da Capo

Woo me with ordures;
Calm me with castigations;
Have my lips wet
With the plague's sweat:
Raise me to all prostrations!

To Compassion

Fashion me a garment of repentance,
Lovely as the colour of my sin;
For the livery of God is beauty,
Though Hell carouse therein.

Hide me from my fault within your blindness,
Let your silence comfort me to tears,
For the tongue of God was ever lovely kindness,
And grace, his eyes and ears.

Prayer to Love

Give me the moment of self-forgetfulness,
In which the perfect thing is bred.
Fill this small cup of time with an infinity,
Give us quick union with the dead.

Not till that moment shall I be transfigured to
    beauty,
Now I come out to you by paths well-trod,
You are the wall at my road's end,
Open your gates, and let me through to God.

From 'SELECTED POEMS'
(Chatto & Windus, 1971: introduction
by David Garnett)

Soul Colour

The only real thing in my garden is the scent of
    flowers.
Greenness and growth, thorns and the pink,
All colours and shapes are symbols;
They are controlled by the thing they build.

There is no reality in my flesh,
Nor in work, nor in words, nor in possessions;
All these things are symbols of myself,
The sum of emotion, thought and desire,
Which I call soul-colour
And liken to the scent of flowers.

What is this immaculate hat but a symbol of
        order?
What is money but a symbol of the unattainable
Or of things within reach?

In life I am like a juggler,
I throw about my symbols, I rearrange them.
I fling my spheres and rings into the air.

There is one reality which is personality,
Which I call soul-colour and liken to a scent.

The Woman and Her Initiative

Give me a deed, and I will give a quality.
Compel this colloid with your crystalline.
Show clear the difference between you and me
By some plain symmetry, some clear stated line.
These bubblings, these half-actions, my revolt
        from unity.
Give me a deed, and I will show my quality.

Vocation

I will walk always at your left hand
To have my right hand nearest to your heart,
That from your love I ask and understand,
How best the power in me can play its part.

Discover in the stillness of your soul,
What, for your purpose, you most need of me.
You are my hands' work, and my just control,
That is my happy destiny.

Explanation

It's so, good Sirs, a Woman-poet sings
Sick self, and not exterior things,
She'd joy enough in flowers, and lakes and light,
Before she won soul's freedom in a fight.
Thus half creation is but half expressed,
And the unspoken half is best.

Note:

It will be seen this fact is stated,
Of such intrepid artists as are mated;
A maid, good Sirs, in many senses human,
As artist is a negligible woman.

Personality

A perfect small creature sat singing in a bubble
This was his magical house.
Beetles and flying-things led the assault against it:
They strove to enter the frail walls,
Pressing their black forefeet against an
    iridescence.

The song of the small creature
Controlled the invaders.
A weight of singing thrown against the walls
Kept the enemy from entering.

When the singer sings no longer,
The house shall fall.

A Love Letter

You have given me some quality of the male,
While I have given you some qualities of myself.
You are the father of my action,
While I have begotten in you new courage.
Maybe we are completed by love,
So that we are beyond sex.
We have found the miraculous unity,
To which existence itself implies increase.

I do not grieve away my days
Because you are gone from me,
My mind is stimulated forever by the idea of you.
I do not ask that your love should be faithful to
    my body,
It is impossible that your soul should be faithless
    to my soul.

It is well I cannot eat with you all my days,
I would not take my soup from a consecrated cup.
I have before me a wealth of happy moments
        when I shall see you.
They are like holy wafers, which I will eat,
For stimulation, for absolution, and for my
        eternal hope.
I ask nothing of you, not even that you live,
If you die, I remember you
Till the blood in my wrists is cold.

The Free Intelligence

When I put off the sense in death,
And lose all seeming with my breath,
I will not heed the prejudice of nose,
Comparisons of carrion and rose.

When this now fettered judgment shall be free,
All changes are of equal worth to me.
And I will pleasure in the faultless way
My flesh dissolves to worms and fertile clay.

Invitation to Tea

How cruelly you come my way –
Enough to fill my aching day
With ghosts of singing.
Rhythms unfulfilled
By any tone or meaning
I have willed.

Be more a niggard – or much less,
Cure me with famine or excess.
Let full eclipse repose my sight,
Or honest shining give me light
To set your beauty
Where it most belongs
Within the outline
Of my shadow songs.

Dear Bird of Winter

Dear bird of winter,
On a blue bush,
Translated mavis – marvellous late thrush,
Young wagtail for your swaying lovely walk,
Wren for your heart, and ring-dove for your talk.
Live always in a quality of words
More apt, more swift
More excellent than birds.

The Hare

Love, love, the dogs are after me,
I am transmuted to a white hare.
You sit in the lighted house and cannot see,
I know that you are there.
See where I pass, a shadow on the grass,
Come swiftly
Lift me to your care.

The Child at the Breast

See the little Trumpeter
Blowing to the world's heart.
O mothers and O fathers!
Carry me to the gates of your dreams
For I am the inheritor,
I am that man Love has set in life.

Two Egotists

Two men lived together in a house.
One walked in a sphere of silence,
The other filled all spaces with his talk.
This was well,
For the first feared even to listen to his own
        silence,
And the second had use for all the words in the
        world,
And for still more words.

The talker was busy with interpretation.
He watched life, and was interested in himself
As the live thing of which he had most
  knowledge.
He looked at himself, as a man might look at a
  hill,
Expounding himself, as one might expound
The phenomena of rain and cloud.

He said 'I am a fine fellow because life is a fine
  thing,
And I tell you this splendid story of myself,
Because you too are a fine fellow, and know how
  to laugh.'
There was a day when the silent man
Opening his mouth like a lizard who prepares to
  take food, said
'You talk too much.'

Then the talker said
'I am interested in myself, because I am the live
  thing of which I know most,
And I am interested in you, because you are a
  man
Of whom I know much,
And I think what you say is probably true;
And as far as is conformable with growth,
I will talk less.'
But he still talked a great deal.
He ranged earth and sky,
And one day in talk he turned to consider the
  silent man.

He said 'It seems to me, my friend, that you do
  too little,
You are not busy because you are silent.
In order for you to be silent,
It is necessary for you to keep quite still.'

The silent man said
'In this sphere of mine is perfect order.'

The talker said
'There is no growth in perfection,
The perfect thing is still,
And, in a moving world, the still thing dies.

Outside your order there are burdened women,
Sick children, and workless men.
It seems to me, that there are burdened women
Sick children and workless men
Because of your order.

Your race made you, and the world feeds you.
Sing a little song, O my brother,
A small disorderly song.'

But the silent man's mouth snapt to
Like a lizard's after he has taken food
And a look came into his eyes of ravished instinct.
He got up quite quietly and killed the talker.
After which he lived vehemently,
Still silent.

The Resource

When I gave you honest speech
You were annoyed.
When I gave you honest love
Your taste was cloyed.
And now I give you silence,
And a smile you take for chaste.
In these things I am less worthy than a harlot,
And your pride has worked this waste.

Paradox

My brain burns with hate of you.
I am like a green field swept by scorching wind,
Everything withers.
There is nothing left of promise
But black death. Yet in my heart is our eternal
    love,
Hard and pure as a moonstone,
And like an opal,
Subtle with change.

UNPUBLISHED POEMS

None of the poems in this section has been published, except for a few which have appeared in anthologies, literary magazines or periodicals: 'Weapons', 'The Exile', 'Egotism', 'Give me room . . .' and 'Honeymoon' appeared in *Neo-Georgian Poetry* 1936-1937 (Richards). The ninety or so poems presented here have been taken from about eleven hundred in typescript, or handwritten notebooks.

MARRIAGE

Optical Glass

Your virtue is a lens
Through which I look at the stars,
Your imperfections a smoked glass
Through which I consider the sun.

Woman and a Dilemma

The gentleman I married
Says I ruined his intelligence
By marrying him.
The gentleman I did not marry
Says I ruined his intelligence
By not marrying him.
I wonder if either of these gentlemen
Had an intelligence!
I wonder if marriage
Is an affair of the intelligence.
But now I will borrow a book from a eunuch.
I begin to be interested
In my own intelligence.

The Noiseless Propeller

My love is a great plane that mounts the sky
And from the clouds spills out a deadly wrath.
His busy whirling wheel am I,
To hold him steady on his gallant course.
Then let me still my voice
And make no noise,
Lest the great guns below
Should hear us as we go.

Whilemena Shakespeare

How like a rainless summer is the grace
Which lingers, ever-constant, to be kissed,
But from the sullen beauty of your face
I have the sweets of showers and lovely mist.

Bent roses in the rain affirm the sun,
Since earth has raised their beauty to his wooing;
Love's gracious work in you is surely done,
No humour's ill enough for its undoing.

I think your mother had adored the man
Who sowed such perfectness within her boy,
There never was, since little Abel ran,
Such stuff for Eve's amazement and her joy.

Then frown no more. Your father had betrayed
    you
To my delight, the moment that he made you.

Loving and Wooing

When Anthony and I are wed
I will not share a double-bed,
With joys conveniently to hand
Like bottles on a cruet stand.

But he shall knock upon my door
And, in my honour, cross a floor;
For I will never love for duty
And he need only woo for beauty.

Leverage

When I was in travail,
I planted my feet against the rail of my bed,
And pushed, and pushed with great patience,
Till presently, I gave birth to a boy.

Because of my love of you,
I am like a steel wall;
And I invite you,
Set your feet against me,
Oppose yourself to me,
Do me violence;
And presently, you shall give birth to an idea.
As for me, I shall remain whole and undinted,
Like this bed-rail, after these years.

To Men
(*Variation on Ella Wheeler Wilcox, after a poem of
the same name*)

Sirs – though we fail you – let us live;
Be just, have pity, and forgive.
Think how poor Mother Eve was brought
To being as God's afterthought.

God had a vast expanse of clay
To fashion Adam's primal day;
Yet was the craftsman's limit shown,
His image could not live alone.

Yet God supports eternal life
Without the comfort of a wife;
So it was proved e'er we began
God had miscalculated man.

And of his fault he took a part,
Formed woman's brain and woman's heart
Of imperfections – vainly planned –
To love, to serve, to understand.

How can you wonder if we stray
Through coward night and sloven day?
When power in us can but reflect
God's wifelessness and man's defect.

Had lonely God when earth was new
Some blest remembrances of two,
He had not made one half of life
A shambles and a hell-stung strife.

Do you remember, O my dear,
The seventh night of our first year?
The night when my first son was given
With ecstasy to tutor heaven.

Had God loved thus, all hell were blind
And famine, lust, and murder kind.
Come, my co-adjutor, beloved smith,
Raise thou thy hammer − break the myth.

There is no marvel of creation
Exists beyond our full relation.
Yet God shall strengthen from his sins
To breed us new and breed us twins.

Thou bungling artificer, yet
Thou shall be artist and beget,
And on the form of Chaos lie,
To wash the earth and raise the sky.

Not equal I but counterpart,
And in relation is my heart
Perfect with man's, as with his mind
Mine is all strong to loose and bind.

Come then my husband here, and rest
On my so well-remoulded breast.
At morning we'll go out and see
How well God works for you and me.

Sympathy and a Little Lady

'I might cry all night
And he'd not know in the morning'.
And her eyes were bright
With her angry scorning.

'Yet if I wept two tears
His wit would quick discover
More than my Husband knows from years,
Such insight has my lover'.

Sung in a Graveyard

O I'm a professional wife,
Tra la la
And I'm bound to the trade for my life,
Tra la la.
I hate to be slack
And I hope I'm not wrong,
But I find business hours most unbearably long,
As a thorough professional wife,
Tra la la.

I think in these organised days
They might run my poor job in relays;
I can work very well in the light,
But I'm tired of the business at night,
Although a professional wife,
Tra la la.

I'd carry a card-case and own a man's name,
I'd manage a house and take wage for the same;
But to bear a man's children, and share a man's
    bed,
Should never be paid for in boots and in bread,
If a wench has the heart of a wife.
Tra la la.

Assayer

If you will deceive me,
If you wish to leave me,
If you have not faith,
Then let me know.
After I have given
All I have of heaven,
I have earned my hell of you —
Then go.

There'll be no complaining
Of your harsh refraining,
There'll be no sustaining
Of inadept grief.
I may live in sorrow
This day, but tomorrow
My good sense will borrow
Substance for relief.

I have loved you madly.
If I lose you sadly
Then I judged you badly.
And since love began
Woman must defend her
Heart with wit, or end her
Life in sad surrender
To a heartless man.

Lately I was playing
Acid for assaying,
Your dear rapture staying
With my shrewish speech.
If your gold can bear me,
If your anger spare me
Take me love, and wear me —
I'm within your reach.

If my heart deceive me,
If you wish to leave me,
If your wit believe me
That which I pretend,
I've another heaven,
(I indeed have seven)
Which may all be given
To a shrewder friend.

Evolution and a Red Rose

This is evolution,
Here is a biological development.
I will go into the town
To do business with Simon the Stylite.
What a happy chance it is
That my coadjutor is an anchorite,
It suits my vigorous mood.

I board a bus
Which takes me near to Simon's hermitage,
I meditate on the relativity of Truth,
Prompted by the advertisements.
The man of tickets helps me kindly down.

Across the little river of pavement
There is an isle of flowers (O Tennyson).
Neighbouring the island are twin deities,
A costerwoman and a cabman.

Petulant Isis is discontent at the richness of her
    island,
The costerwoman is low
To have so many flowers left over at the end of a
    day,
Osiris offers her his smiling solaces,
The cabman simply says, 'Cheero.'

Very kind he is,
Rallying the woman from her despondent mood,
To trust the changing luck of the streets,
And see in me a customer.

Since I am suddenly so chaste,
I espouse all the virtues at once,
I become morally polygamous,
In honour of abstinence.

And I have set my mind against expenditures,
Against those frequent silly spendings
Which leave me nothing real in my estate,
But a spent toll of happy moments.

I hesitate,
I see a red rose
Which reminds me of Paris
And a restaurant near the Madeleine,
An exquisite salad,
And a certain gentleman.

O little changing Gods,
I had forgot that gentleman.
I buy the rose
For the sake of the costerwoman's urging,
And in honour of the kind cabman.
The woman spits on my tuppence.

This is a pretty act, and not at all disgusting;
So she unites herself with the hope of better
    fortune,
And sanctifies my tokens with her juices.
It is like the anointing with holy oil.

So I meditate
As I make my way towards the austerities of
    Simon.
The rose is pinched against my purse.
I wonder if its fragrance will be distasteful to the
    anchorite.

I mount his strict stairs,
I am unemotional,
I come quickly to the point,
But I am tempted, by the devil of mischief,
To hold a flower to the nose of the abstemious.

Instead I sign a contract
Agreeing to take a ha'penny on the sale of every
    book.
Then I am downstairs again
In the blue beautiful old street.

Bloomsbury in twilight,
It is as lovely to me, born and bred in towns,
As any virgin glade or naked hillside
Was to a caveman.

Why should I not own it like an honest egotist,
Sing of it frankly
As a lark sings of congenial twigs and worms and
    fields?
For I am not a lark

My wise ancestors came down out of trees
To cultivate their wits upon the ground.
Should I honour my liberal begetters
By walking Fleet Street in a skirt of pampas-
    grass?

Is this a compliment
To our old impatient Fathers,
Who changed all custom
For imagined betterment?

All strong new things alive
Are born because of impudent desire.
It is my quarrel with marriage
That so much is begotten in it from habit.

But of this street?
I love it,
I will embrace it,
I will make a song of it.

O technician, you gibe at us who in revolt
Would use all words to indicate a meaning,
You would have been an artificer.
Then I will sing this street in all your metres.

In sonnets and in odes and triolets,
I'll be Elizabethan, I'll be Provençal.
And if there is a Patagonian poetry,
I'll steal its verse forms to express my
        Bloomsbury.

Doing this – I am Lloyd George in woad.
Reverse me, you have Plato in a Burberry.

So I think as my feet
Lead me down Holborn.
I catch sight of a rallying girl behind a bar,
And like her better than a fancied milkmaid.

And, O my feet, where are you leading me?
I hold the rose to my face,
It is dark,
I cannot see the colour,
That is good
The red reminds me of Paris,
Of dinner, of a salad,
And a most unnecessary gentleman.

Down Chancery Lane, across the Strand,
Past the Adelphi, I walk
Allured like any she-wolf
By a compelling scent.

Now in a little street
I stop beneath a window,
This is the seat of an ambitious enterprise.
The man is still at work.
Shall I enter and own his mastery?
What then of all my contracts,
And my song of streets,
Of that proud poise on a new hill?
What becomes of a biological development?
The man behind the window is an atavism,
The old male,
He would keep me sitting by a fire
Sewing a little, but unoccupied.
No, I will make all contracts with Stylites.

But this tormenting rose?
I pass and repass,
I cannot enter,
So I think a melody.
I sing it, sing it softly to a window.
I become a troubadour,
Is this a Florentine revival?
No, I am a woman born in Wimbledon
In that year Shaw was first a Fabian,
A Georgian drowning passion near the Thames,
And humanising opera with an essential song.

A policeman passes, he suspects me.
You are right fat man about sobriety.
I will go home,
And sleep out drunkenness in my own house.

LOVE AND SEX

Page Ending

My wrecking lust has no just bounds
When I know beauty and love wounds.

The Dove

O thou great ship on the terrible waters,
Open thy door,
Let me fly in through the gate of forgiveness
And leave you no more.

Wild Horses

My horses drew me gently in the town,
They raced like furies when they reached the
     down.
My seat was struck from me before I knew,
Still clinging to a rein, I flew, I flew.

Their stamping feet climbed the steep slopes of
     air,
I flew behind them like wild wind-blown hair.
Looking down, I saw the smoke of a dear house
     fire;
I was drawn to the tempest by the horses of
     desire.

Ireland

Poets fight for Ireland
The whole world over:
For Ireland's a woman
And God is her lover.

A Woman of Intelligence

When I discourse I show sagacity,
Acuteness which is superhuman.
My silly lover kisses me
Solely because I am a woman.

For this I hit him with my scorn
Then, for his folly, I sit dumb.
It's ill that he should love what I was born
Rather than grace, to which my mind has come.

But at my anger he makes this demur,
Which I will answer when I can,
'Honour a saint and a philosopher
But come, I pray you, kiss a man'.

Dissolution of a Saint

Poor Lad, Poor Lad.
There's been no fool like me since Time began,
For I have used you like an archangel,
And you are but a man.
And I have flouted your humanity
With my mad melancholic purity.

A woman well deserves the rod,
Mistaking man for God.
Come kiss me!
We'll thank Heaven that we're alive,
And I'll choose piety
When I am fifty-five.

Importunate

You do not honour me: but this mad day,
When from perfection of my love you make
Excuse to love all women for my sake,
I beg you love me in some older way.

The Kill

Good, that is over!
I have loved once for all
And have discharged my lover.
He would have had the hen-bird all in brown;
I was the thrush to screech a peacock down!
Who knows he had prevailed
Had he been scrupulously tailed.

Cock, there was too much boasted, and too little
     done,
And the poor hen
Has won!

Multiplication
(*For D.H.L.*)

Had I married you, dear,
When I was nineteen,
I had been little since
But a printing machine;
For, before my fortieth year had run,
I well had produced you
A twenty-first son.

Your ingenious love
Had expressed through me
Automatic, unreasoned, fecundity.
I had scattered the earth
With the seed of your loins,
And stamped you on boys
Like a king's head on coins.

Function

I do not grudge you to your wife,
But take a mistress
And I'll have her life!

Deadlock

If one of the four of us should die,
You or my husband, your wife or I,
Even such change would be happy release;
There could be pleasure, or there would be peace.

The Arrogant Lady

How like a bladder is this lover
All wind and skin!
Nor could God's magnifying eye discover
A living core within.

High is his mood,
And he is well content
To bounce on every field
Of sentiment.

How well designed is he
To be spurned with the foot:
And it is fit in me
To up and do't.

Song of the Old Sinner from Oxford

In the bed of my Love
Was a text-book on Conics,
In the bed of my Love
Was a compass and rule.
So I cried out my youth
On her horny old bosom,
Then laughed for a morning
And went back to school.

Difficult Dame

Sometimes I wish I was a lady
All smooth and scented
With breasts that never fed a baby:
I'm not contented
With male maternity
Matured in me.

319

Sometimes I wish I had a bathroom
Crystal all over,
An eider-down shift
And a property lover.

Sometimes I feel
Stark life too real.
But had I been a lady
All smooth and scented
With bottles in a bathroom
Some bastard rented,
I'd have bought a child,
That's me all over,
I'd have torn me shift
And shot me lover.

A l'Amazone
(*On translation*)

Bugger de Gourmont, let me speak:
God Almighty, you're not Greek:
Damn him, Damn France,
Damn all your metaphors of casque and lance.
'Twas Britain bred you,
Jews refined you,
Now let time know
That *I* defined you.

Maud in a Monocle

There is a gull in you
Swirls to my breath,
When I cry carrion,
Where I call death.

There is a flower in you
A sick blue rose
Thin like the power in you
Useless to nose.

There is a boy in you,
A thieving page,
Who steals my joy in you
And serves my rage;

Carrion! yet in you
Peerless and bright,
Her I'll beget in you
One angry night.

There is a girl in you
Lovely and free
Set like a pearl in you,
Slug of the sea!

At Lunch

The elderly woman with the masterful face
Told how she loved her sisters-in-law.
This, of course, an extreme case:
She loved all women. She'd a saw
To prove Man's baseness, his incontinence,
His vanity, his weakness, his pretence.
But her daughter, till yesterday an intellectual,
Now in a cherry gown to her mind's detriment,
Set out to prove her Mother ineffectual
By an unfilial heat of argument.

'Woman is not for Woman', the girl said,
'Neither for friendship nor consideration,
Woman's for Love'. One vast transcendent bed
Filled all the cherry girl's imagination.
'Only last week I put my books away,
For now my mind is governed by my heart.
I've thought about the subject and I say
Love is a woman's all controlling art'.

O Greece, O shade of Ovid too,
Have I an Adept or an Amazon for my new song?
Or is the woman the eternal shrew,
And has the girl remained a maid too long?

Discipline

If I write verse for you and you reject me,
And if I dream for you and you neglect me,
Great golden Snake
I'll strangle you for Beauty's sake.

'Give Me Room'

Give me room, a little room
And I'll build you a king's tomb;
The perfect peasant shall be there begotten,
And harsh empires all forgotten.

He who rules need never wreck,
For my jewel is his neck,
And great towers are his thighs,
All regalia's in his eyes.

Give me room and give me air,
And new Beauty shall walk bare;
No restraint and no excess
Lives with holy loveliness.

Technician

So I made love to you: removing you
From my nerve tissue,
Thus to save me loving you,
Till — by intention — I was all bereft
And had no scent nor tincture of you left.

But now I am a clear passivity,
Fine sublimation of my destiny,
And you may fill me as the light fills air,
And where I am, you'll know yourself is there.

Although my words come not to you again
Nor my hands move — to work your peace or
    pain.

Honeymoon

Do you remember Mechlin chimes,
Falling like elfin music from the tower,
As if a carven goblin laughed four times
In every happy hour;

And how we listened to the merry thing,
I, even with feigned joy, to win your laughter;
And when I thought I'd lost my wedding ring,
I heard no bells for grief, in the hour after?

Lately I thought your love was lost to me;
Above the tempests of that bitter time
I heard one mocking maddening melody:
It was the Mechlin chime.

CHILDREN

Pride of Women

God shall accomplish his noblest plan,
All that is dreamed shall be done,
When the lover loves most the child in
    her man,
The Mother the man in her son.

Mothering

Aunt Justice
Weighed the nurseling
For she knew.
But mercy
Watched her baby
And he grew.

New Eve

Why was I born beneath two curses,
To bear children and to write verses?
Either one fecundity
Were heavy enough destiny.
But all my life is penalty
From the two sides of me.

I was a child, I dreamed a son,
A man desired me and the thing was done,
I lured a husband to begetting,
I couldn't lure him to forgetting
Or to forgiving my apostasy,
After fecundity.

When I had borne the increase of his bed
My mind and spirit were not dead,
Men don't keep babes for beauty,
Posterity or duty,
But for the delight they find
In wrecks of woman's mind.
And spiritual castration
Must follow procreation.

But I had great vitality,
And agilest morality,
And somehow I escaped
Alive, though misshaped.

So now they'll sacrifice my son
For all these freedoms I have done.
I wish I'd died in my Mother
Rather than be another.

Nursery Song

Too-well-done
Has blown out the sun;
She made curdy puddings
Till milk there was none:

And the baby starved
For all he was clean
And the cat ate my thrush
And still looked lean.

Such ugly confusion
There never was seen
Since Too-well-done
Has blown out the sun.

La Voilà

The universe consists
Of what is me
And what is not me:
That is the great antithesis.

The Widow of Aberdeen

We have a hold in Cumberland,
My pretty child be brave,
Our house is lost and our land is lost
But we still have your father's grave.

Why should he fear the Southland?
Yet wind, like a traitor foe,
Threw him down in a stream of their hills,
On a night of blinding snow.

At morn a shepherd sought his sheep,
Brave sheep who wandered far,
And above the waters he saw a hand,
White like Christ's early star.

They brought him down to the Hamlet
Where he had thought to sleep.
Six feet by three is land to me,
His pride and faith's my keep.

We have a hold in Cumberland,
My pretty child be brave.
Your uncles have a mortgage,
But we have your father's grave.

The Woman's Harvest

Summer is three days past her prime,
Now sun-dried leaves presage a leafless time.
My thought turns, a sick bird on heavy wing,
To the sure suns of early spring.

What have I here of solace now those suns are
     gone?
And what shall comfort me when sad, dumb days
     come on?
Today, I have this apronful of roses sweet and
     wild,
For this day, and tomorrow the dear body of a
     child.

POETRY AND CREATIVITY

Suppression

If you deny her right to think,
If you deny her pride of ink,
She will smile like a slave,
Trick like a knave,
She will be lonely as a wild boar,
And quick companionable as any whore.

Note on Method

Here is no sacrificial I,
Here are more I's than yet were in one human,
Here I reveal our common mystery:
I give you *woman*.
Let it be so for our old world's relief
I give you woman, and my method's brief.

Some Criticism

I see how Phrase is shaped
But how is she 'raped'?

Come clean, poor lad, come clean,
Know what you mean!

I want fine detail and docility,
Not jerry building and pomposity.

Take time, and think,
And *then* spend ink.

(Moreover proper kings
Wear better rings.)

The Cave

Our father Ape, hairy and bold,
Took himself northward to the land of cold:
The tooth of winter bit the brave,
And he took shelter in a cave.

He and his sons all winter long
Dreamed them of food and of Art and Song:
In order to cheat their enemy, the wind,
They boasted pleasure in being so confined,
That the just services of Wit should be
To add a glory to captivity.

There was the start of Painting born
In this bric-a-brac of stone and horn:
Against captivity is Music proof −
Their songs, like smoke, rose through the
　　　creviced roof.

How to Be a Good Diseur

Switch yourself on to the spirit.
Hope to be a medium.
Always direct your attention to −
　　　Either
　　　　　　Your audience
　　　Or
　　　　　　Your own consciousness (soliloquy)
　　　Or
　　　　　　Your vis-à-vis.
Make your melodic, aesthetic and dramatic
　　　meaning
By infinite changes of vocal colour and facial
　　　expression:
　　　Be always in control.

If your attempt is faithful enough
You may hope the spirit will fill you,
And you will be a supreme artist, the vice-regent
　　　of God.

When lazy and ignorant artists *leave everything* to
　　　the spirit
They are possessed by Hell.

Killing W.B. Yeats

Anna: 'Beat thou thy drum outside my gates
      And I'll kill Yeats'.
J.G.:   'Query! What with?'
Anna: 'With a sheer blast of melody, boy'.

Night Wood (Duo)

Miss Djuna
Barnes: 'So I say — what of the night —
      the terrible night?'
Poor
Anna: 'What of the night? The night's all right!
      Pain and Pox
      Come at all o'clocks,
      But chiefly delight, through the happy night.
      Darling, take heart,
      Make hay, make a start,
      Learn Peace, learn Power
      From the zero hour.'

Attitude Eight

No emotions,
No damned poetic notions;
No smoking,
No ingenious joking,
No religious feelings,
Fewer amorous dealings.
No chemist's stuff
A minimum of bluff;
No conscience,
No bloody nonsense.

Be civil to your relations,
Remember Jane's theory of combinations,
Feed,
Read.

Woman and Artist

If a woman is to be an expressor
And avoid most desperate confusion,
She, more than any, must compass Soul's
    exclusion.
There's no excuse for expression from a woman
Unless she be a representative human.

If an artist must suppress sex too much is lost;
The product, thought, is purchased at too high a
    cost.
The singer must stand proud alone
And claim a little eminence that is her own.

Yet woman will confuse and vex
If she is dominant in things of sex.
The intellectual hermaphrodite
Must stand unified and subject for delight.

In this there is great strain
And sore irreconcilables for one poor brain.

Nonsense

Of water in the world there was no lack:
It trickled down the high magician's back.
So he transmuted it to steam.
Making material for his Dream.
He watched it writhe and twist about the roof,
And so, to wet annoyance, he was proof.

Genius

Genius swallows the past to nourish the present;
Genius destroys the present to give air to the
    future.

Herman Ould and Anna at the P.E.N. Club

Look at him and look at me –
Very like the bourgeoisie.
Although we're writers,
We're well-bred hacks not biters.
Swift could bend his livid tongue
To vivid ends and mention dung.
But his position
Is scorned by our condition.
We meet the muses where they dine,
Our Phoenix is a judge of wine.

Pope was lame, and Johnson gruff,
Spencer never wore a ruff.

To Harold Monro

You bloody Deaconess in rhyme,
You told me not to waste your time –
    And that from you to me!

Now let Eternity be told
Your slut has left my books unsold –
    And you have filched my fee.

Loose Writing

If I knew Noësis I'd define him:
If I comprehended, I'd incline him
To abstract passion, free of time,
Of landscapes, seasons, right or rhyme.

I've no conception of his essence
From mere illusion of his presence.
With what decorum can I speak
Not knowing if he's Dutch or Greek?
But from his verses I can see
He has had trouble with his botany.

The Exile

I wish I were at home in the world,
As when I was a child.
I am like a traveller walking a lone wild;
I hurry on, through the black land with fear,
My only solace that the wood is near.

O wood of fir-trees, where the soul is free,
Within your depths is harbourage for me!
In a green close, behind your high tree-gates,
The woman of all desiring waits.
Her voice comes out to me upon your breath.
Hide me, O hide me, Glade of Death!

Three Questions

Why should I spend my days
Hunting a perfect phrase?
Why should I fret and long
To sing a perfect song?
Why, if all were said,
Am I not dead?

Weapons

Up the crag,
In the screaming wind,
Naked and bleeding,
I fought blind.

Then at dawn
On the snowy height,
I seized a spear,
By the eastern light.

On I trudged,
In the eye of the sun;
Past the cromlech
I found a gun.

Then I strayed
In the cities of men;
In the house of my love
I found a pen.

CLASS WAR AND SOCIETY

Laura Grey
(Died June 1914, in Jermyn Street)
This poem was published in the *Daily Herald*, 16
June, 1914.

A woman with child lies dead,
Stricken by her own hand,
And every pitiless thing has been said
Throughout this faultless land.

For the just makers of the laws,
Through the dead woman, hit her cause,
They have made all the vile capital they
    can
– But who has asked, 'where is the
    man?'

The child, dead in the womb,
Who will not see the light,
Shall find a voice from the tomb
To ask the mother's right.

When will this old world begin
To see man and the woman equal in sin?
Condemn her lonely if you can
When the child has asked, 'where is the
    man?'

The Toilet

All my poor life I longed to have clean hands
And the high powers of willing clean hands
    mean,
But small detachable things denied my will's
    demands.
Not for the sake of all desiring would my hands
    be clean.

The little shrines where our high race prevails,
The temples twixt the finger-tips and nails,
In me, polluted by small foreign shapes,
Were like uncleanly crevices of low-born apes.

I knew that the high powers of life begin
Where life can hold environment in check.
I could not hold environment from off my skin,
I could not keep clean hands to save my neck.

Then I began to work with smaller things,
Cubes and small spheres and pyramids and rings,
With different textures, with my money, clothes,
    my chest, my bed,
And all the multitude of shapes of which I stood
    in dread.

When I reflected, it was not quite clear
Why I should hold my moveables in fear.
And I determined to give each its place,
To give it fixed relation to all space.

A Party

I didn't tell the butler,
I went and told the Lord.
I said, 'O Christ,
Keep tryst, keep tryst,
I'm bored'.

Too Much Washing

I plant my hope
On my Irish view of water
And my Italian attitude to soap.
I am my father's daughter.

I bath by spells
At holy wells;
I take my works
And wash them with the Turks;
Then without sin,
I disregard my skin,
And thus I know
Old Stratford-atte-Bow,
The sweats and smuts and anguish of my Lord,
All saints and sluts, before the Water Board.

Young Fancy came to wreck,
From too much washing of the Heron's neck.

Suez (1946)

She is failure, she is folly,
She's the stink of melancholy,
She's the worm that takes the pleasure from the
    peach.

She's down among the Arabs,
Stamping on the scarabs,
And she's quite the chic-est woman on the beach.

Proud

God bless the middle classes,
Though lawyers must be asses
We have to state our love of them aloud;
And we'll only call a truce
With the lineage of Bruce,
For we were born in Streatham
And we're proud.

Though there's something quite pathetic
In Cheltenham's aesthetic,
The major is distinguished in a crowd;
And we never want to smother
All the loveliness of mother,
For we were born in Streatham
And we're proud.

Grave men, brave men,
Keen men, clean men,
Men that stand for rugger,
Never hugger-mugger,
They're still the heart of England
And they're proud.

Little Soliloquy

That lovely hostess has explained her guests to
    me,
As she has beauty – why not charity?
When I go out, where will she bear the news
Of my gruff manners and my shapeless shoes?
Exquisite lips, instruct a silly heart
In grace, in silence and in art.

Comments of Kate the Cook

There is most pitiable waste,
For there is so much effort and so little taste.
How well, if all the hands of a democracy
Were in control
Of one great motive soul,
This might be compassed by religion
Were she free
To deal with life on earth,
Rather than life-to-be.

The Butler and the Gentleman

The gentleman who had been at Winchester said
'When I made my first call,
After I took over that motor agency.
They showed me to the servants' hall'.

He said how hugely he had been amused,
How a man's butler had been confused
To judge a gentleman, not by his speech, but by
    his face,
And show him to that ridiculous and most
    unworthy place.

While he told us this delicious tale,
I watched a woman, delicate and pale,
With charming eyes and smooth gold hair,
Holding potatoes by the speaker's chair.
I liked the girl, and thought that he
Might choose to stay where she was doomed to be.

Daughter of the Horse-Leech

I make demand,
I stretch a most importunate hand.
How take you that
My good aristocrat?
Doubtless with certain unction, with your chrism
I am anointed priestess of arch-egotism.
Come, be consistent Sir, my reason spurns
Him who is Buddhist, Christian, Rationalist,
All by turns.

You will concede our civilisation
To be the flower of God's creation?
You would not fill your inner rooms
With woaded weavers at hand-looms?
You, who are complex and so clean,
Will not neglect the new machine?
Then how did cavemen leave the mire,
But to the driving of applied desire?

Behold, your woman stands
To make most clear conceived demands.

Morals

Thomas, the cross-eyed policeman, saw
Right was both in and out of law.
He would these curious lines repeat
As he walked lonely on his beat:

It is not kind
To rob the blind,
But he who cheats the C.O.S.
Should be rewarded for success.

It is not necessary to
Boil every man who is a Jew,
But he who gives it Gluckstein warm,
The State should guard from hurt and harm.

He does not choose the better part
Who wilful breaks a maiden's heart,
But he who kisses Caesar's wife
May risk his skin, to save her life.

Women to a Philosopher

Let us consider the Superman,
Him who is to be more than human.
He must lie nine months alone
Hid in the dark with a woman.
Is she to be a thing of scorn
Before the prodigy is born?

Poor man who in the end ran mad
And died so less than human,
Saw you not the brain-wrecking absurdity
Of preaching superman and scorning women?

341

The Indictment
(*To H.M.*)

Your woman breeds dogs
Like an old ham
Breeds maggots.
To all such dreary,
Spavined, skinflint faggots
Commend me.
And you enjoying me,
Cloying me even
With your appreciation,
Fling to her the fees and usufruct
Of my creation
With hope to end me.

FREEDOM, WILL AND COURAGE

Men of the West

I have been too long stranger
To my old lord, Danger;
What rapture shall I know
Who dare not risk a blow?

I have grown fat
From my prosperity,
My flesh is rank
From inactivity.

I have gained a paunch
From this orderly town,
And with it such disorder
That to keep my dinner down

I swallow superfine products
From the druggist on this clean street,
And, in honour of confusion,
Thank God that pills are neat.

Note on Will

My will is free,
Yet in control
Of infinite tensions.
In the soul
A moving storm
Is under governance of laws,
Yet free to induce form,
Yet free to cause.

That will is free
I clearly prove,
When will in me
Is felt to move.
Freedom on earth has never absolute existence.
It's power to move,
To overcome degrees of earth's resistance.

The flying bat is free in air,
Since he meets small denial there,
Yet if he flies against the wall
He is refused, and has no liberty at all.
I am given the world which lies rhythmic and
    still.
I am given hot, climbing fire, and that is will.

Last Lines of Lily
(*Resolution of an old whore*)

Damn and again damn
My métier de femme;
Many a bloody fool
I've taught to rule,
Most by burlesque,
Some delicate grotesque
That no mind but mine
Had humour to divine –
For never I saw eyes
Faithful enough or wise
Enough for loveliness.
O my poor heart's distress,
For all my world's a strutting place for kings –
My wit begot on mud –
And I exhausted, lacking pith and blood,
Must turn to holy things –
Tired of my breasts, my brains, my womb,
Adore the tomb.
No, Christ, I'll leave thy stained emphatics
To study mathematics.
Jesu – thy saving word,
What is a surd?

The Freeman

'It is more blest to give than to receive'.
That is a truth that I can well believe,
Without imagined mansions in the skies
With God to square a debt in Paradise.

For often have I seen in charity
The measure of a most destructive vanity.
If it be kingly to possess,
It is more kingly still to grant largess.
Withhold your gift for dignity's my want
That I forgo when I'm your mendicant.

The New Lease

I have spent all my days in confusion,
I never came to any clear conclusion;
I have lived by rules my reason has not tried,
So every honest instinct was denied.

But a day comes when I shall leave old haunts
And walk and wander as my spirit wants.
Then for a year I'll live supremely free,
And Hell shall have what there remains of me.

Courage

Let us deny the devil
And formulas of evil,
And trust at length
Courage and Strength.

Let us gain skill
To rule the will,
So that we hold the dead and quick
Beneath the rules of plain arithmetic.

Disgust

The cup that held blest ointment
Shall not be filled with lard,
Nor by a baser function
Shall my good flesh be marred.

I had a settled purpose
To do some one thing well;
If my rank flesh betray me now,
I'll fling that flesh to Hell.

Defeat of Pain

Pain is decay,
Yet seed must rot in earth
That a March day
Should see green birth.

But if I live in pain
When winter's fled,
My days are vain
And I were better dead.

Egotism

Consider the brave young egotism,
Which fights at crowded paps,
Claiming its fill of milk for the new day,
No matter who snaps.

Think of the old egotist of the woods,
How he insists
In getting something in his heat,
No matter who resists.

346

Consider the later egotism,
With brush and pen,
Which will expound itself in paint and ink
In spite of men.

GOD AND EPIPHANIES

A Dancing Christ

I saw in a provincial show
More East than Stratford-atte-Bowe,
That time I kept a dismal tryst,
Full miracle − a dancing Christ
In excellent exemption
From crosses and redemption.

Bonds

He who surrenders liberty
A sick, sad slave shall be.
Nor can the Lover give
His soul to love, and live.

Man's arms are stout and fleshy bands,
He shall grasp the world with his hands,
But a straight ray from God's great eye,
Shall hold him fettered to the sky.

Not Alone

God is woven in the mesh
Of my eternal flesh,
Which, though it change from hour to hour,
Is fruit of all time and all extending power.

Form is an aggregate of Cause,
My shape is symbol of interacting laws;
Like cause invoked my curvéd eyes,
And drew the vast elipses of the skies.

I do not stand alone, but am in bond
Of the thing near, and ultimate things beyond.
There is connective thought in me.
Where is divisibility?

The Rescue

When all my prayers were fear,
My ally was the devil,
And praying drew him near,
With his foul scent of evil.

But when such grace was given,
That I could pray in hope,
High God leaned out of Heaven,
To fling me down a rope.

To a Crucifix

O courteous Christ — kind guest, most gracious
    host,
Which of these ugly things had pained you most,
That silly priests repeat your words for gain,
Or in your house hang symbols of your pain.

How had you withered at the servile breath
Spent in the praises of your common death,
Scorning these claims to honour and to pride
For such a death as multitudes have died.

Not in the cross was such indignity
As these acclaiming Christian ages see,
When you who lived for cure and for relief
Are most remembered for your wounds and grief.

Pain

I

God loved the world
And gave his son:
Now was this well
And fitly done?
What is so wise
In sacrifice?
Why final gain
From ugly pain?
Pain follows fast upon rejection
Of laws conditioning perfection.
Is it not rather evil
And adjunct of the devil?

II

What hope for an escape from war
Where agonies and crosses are
Extolled and raised for veneration
Implied essential to creation?

The hope of peace is vain.
War's increment is pain:
Pain shown expedient in the cross
Is an excuse for war's whole loss.

The Last Round

Clasp you the God within yourself
And hold it fast;
After all combats shall ye come
To this good fight at last.

God is a mighty wrestler,
He battles in the night;
Not till the end shall it be known
What foe you fight.

When God in you is overthrown
He'll show a light
And claim the victory for his own,
And crown the fight.

Curves

I saw squared logs in a lumber yard,
They were the length of trees.
Yet one live branch in my orchard
Seems twice as great as these.

Curves give me thought of growing things,
Of the expanse of time and air.
But the idea of man's decaying use,
Is prisoned in the Square.

The Lens

Will Time and God give us an hour
Of perfect freedom and of power?
Or shall our longing be denied,
Our hunger still unsatisfied?

The hour of self-fulfilment were it real,
Would be a disc of some transcendent steel.
It would be brittle, hard, and bright:
It would reflect to blinding, God's straight
    light.

All Creation

There is a silence not of night,
It is a sphere of perfect light,
The stillness of an infinite vibration.
This is the womb of all creation.

And at the margin of the sphere,
Is that pure light refracted clear;
So the enveloping depths along
Sweep great tangential rays of song.

PROSE

❖

PROSE

THE SPIRIT OF THE LAWRENCE WOMEN

Our communion was profound and exceedingly serious, and Lawrence very kindly did not insist on its being in the form of his monologue. He not only let me talk but appeared to be interested in what I said. He relieved me of the burden of my mind, and at the same time tried to reveal what was in his mind to me. Our words plumbed beyond meaning. We discussed the granular quality which is the nature of cause.

The scent of such phrases remains with me, though I can recall nothing definite that was said either of granularity or of cause. But very clearly I remember Lawrence. My nerves remember him, and, perhaps as he would have liked it, also my blood. After sixteen years it is as if he had just gone out of the room.

Our talk was never of personalities; he never told me of coal-mining, nor of his uncles and aunts, and my story was made clear to us only by one or two of my children, who stalked us on our long and pre-occupied walks over Hampstead Heath. The children resented the pre-occupation, and my son John still remembers that no man was ever hit more clean and palpably with a snow ball than D.H. Lawrence. This variation on the theme 'Destruction of the Interlocutor by the Son' seemed fair enough to me at the time because of Lawrence's very curious attitude to the whole subject of reproduction.

One of Mrs Carswell's letters from Lawrence reveals a state of feeling, which he exuded rather than expressed to me, about the time of the throwing of the snowball:

> There are plenty of children, and no hope. If women can bring forth hope, they are mothers indeed. Meanwhile even the mice increase − they cannot help it. What is this highest, this pro-creation? It is a tracing back, when there is no going forward, a throwing life on the bonfire of death and oblivion. This is winter. Children and child-bearing do not make spring. It is not in children the future lies. The Red Indian mothers bore many children, and yet there are no Red Indians. It is the truth, the new perceived hope that makes spring. And let them bring forth that who can; they are the creators of life. There are many *enceinte* widows with a new crop of death in their wombs. What did the mothers of the dead soldiers bring forth in child bed? death or life?

Lawrence would no more have thought of writing like that to me, than he would have thought of offering his mother a bad half-crown. He would have known that I would have been merciless with his loose thinking about the Red Indians. So long as Red Indian women produced enough papooses to compensate for wastage by war, epidemic, and inevitable death, there were Red Indians. When Red Indian women were discouraged in this, there were not Red Indians. This is not a mystical region, which excludes the truths of simple arithmetic. No twist of the significance of spring, no special interpre-tation of the nature of hope, on the part of Lawrence or any other, can alter it.

Moreover, I should have objected then and always to his depre-ciation of *enceinte* widows. My grandmother was posthumous.

He had no right to use the phrase '*enceinte* widows' symbolically, in some special sense, without giving a code to make his meaning clear. Lawrence does not attempt to put a meaning into words, he allows it to float on the breezes, odours, and free open spaces between his words. As he does this he extols the saving quality of truth. He has a general impression that men with diabetes are not likely to beget anything vigorous within nine months of their death. He forgets that heroes are killed on the hunting field and strong men struck down with pneumonia six months after they have made their wives pregnant.

An *enceinte* widow may go forward into the future till she gives birth to a child who need not be even symbolically death. That child will not be the future. In the way an egg is not perspicacity, or an ostrich soap, or any one kind of quality or thing ever entirely another. But the child living into the widow's future will condition it. If the widow were not at this time *enceinte* her future would not be conditioned by a particular child.

Now Lawrence was quite capable of seeing all this. But here words are used deliberately to confound meaning; meanings only felt are allowed to arise like an odour from a decay of phrase. In her book Mrs Carswell strikes to the ground Middleton Murry, a critic so lenient with Lawrence, that he calls his book 'Son of Woman', stating some imagined relation between Lawrence and Jesus Christ. In the mists of Mr Murry is implied some finer, some more delicately suffering Christ. It is strange that Mrs Carswell will print this passage, and leave it for critics less partial to see that for his simple offences against logic Lawrence is the very devil in dialectics, and that by his depreciation of what must always be the supremely essential function of women he proves himself to be their betrayer and their scourge. This is a hard way to talk about a friend and a dead friend. The Lawrence I remember dealt honestly with me about things of the mind. But the Lawrence who let me speak is not the Lawrence who writes so portentously from the page. This man – this manifestation – writes not like an artist observing but like a nahbi, hot with some madness of preconceived truth.

Lawrence's work is a sort of miasma of menace towards women who detach any considerable portion of their energy from their purely sexual function. They work only to keep themselves, and that in the economic defection of some man. Young Morel, the central figure of *Sons and Lovers* and the representative of young Lawrence, is good enough to teach his mistress Miriam French. But he gives her a suitable number of mistakes. Outside the 'realities' of Lawrence, there are women who speak French very well. It is to be admired that

Miriam uses her French exercises to express her feelings for her lover. It is clear that she is reading Verlaine with the hope of assuming some new tenacity of erotic attack. She talks about the Christian mystery, but this sort of thing is inferred to condition her physical failure.

Lawrence the writer does not allow a reading woman to live, but the Lawrence of life had more than patience for that virulently detached type of reading woman, the woman artist-writer.

Lawrence contrived no annihilation for me, who, at this time was putting what might have been my erotic energy into verse at the rate of a hundred lines a morning, with only half an eye on the kitchen and nursery. Mrs Carswell records that Lawrence was kindness itself to her about her novels. Miss Rebecca West found that Lawrence had Caritas: having noted a quality, she expressed it at once in a foreign tongue, with no fears of attack on her syntax. I was not and Miss West and Mrs Carswell are not types calculated specially to inspire sexual anaesthesia.

There is a discrepancy between the practice of the man and the precept of the prophet. There was a fission in this over insistent self.

The bitter sympathy between me and Lawrence had roots deeper than a common turn for metaphysics for we had both suffered from the Board School, and I had suffered with, from, and for Board-School teachers.

In my early childhood, my mother went back to a Board School as an assistant mistress – the trade of her youth. The asphalt of what was called, for the sake of euphony, the playground, still grates in my soul as shrapnel grates in a wound. I sat in my mother's class-room, too young to share the work of the fifth standard, excused from sitting with children of my own age because of my social superiority as the child of a teacher. I was thus made early aware of the bitterest phase of class war, the antagonism between the ascending section of the working class, from which the majority of the teachers were recruited, and the rank and file of the working class whose children were dragooned into the Board Schools. I can remember a feeling of shame, when one of the teachers dealt critically with two of the poorest of the children, who pretended not to know the colour of gin. All knew that the poverty of the children was due to the drunkenness of their home. Lawrence had suffered in the same way. And on our escapes over the heath as we exchanged our liberated phrases, we

358

were like a pair of cold children shut out of a tenement together. As we shivered we talked of the granular quality which is in the nature of Cause.

Lawrence's parlour in the Vale of Heath was not bigger than a workman's front room, and his small flat was not more highly rented than a prosperous workman's dwelling. Like the sitting rooms of the up-breeding workman or small bourgeois, it contained merit-conferring articles of property. On Lawrence's wall was a blue Persian rug. It was his totem symbol.

In Lawrence's room I was at home again. I was back to the thrift, pride and diligence that had built my grandfather's house. I was a little guiltily, more at home in this house than its mistress. Better than her I understood its criteria, and its values. Frieda Lawrence was at this time less its mistress than its supporting pillar. Her inbred sense of government told her that her battling peasant might well be emperor of Rome, if he found the right Javelin, and was allowed enough time. Lawrence's insistence that Frieda should be house-mother and only house-mother, made him a sort of cartoon of man-hood, and raised an atmosphere of burlesque. The necromancer had not enough magic to compel the tiger to be a shrewmouse. But con-tinuously he made his attempts.

He had no hope from the beginning of making any lasting impres-sion. Frieda was spiritually and physically too big for it.

At the time Lawrence was cutting his prophetic teeth. This induced in him a perverse over-decision in judgement, and an extra-vagance of psychological diagnosis. He decreed that I would become too engrossed with Frieda. She was like some over-adventurous and complaisant captive in the hut of a holy but impertinent swineherd. The serf in me was faithful enough and arrogant enough to feel pity for her. She had backed her Goth too far. It was Frieda who could have gone out and killed Romans.

Meanwhile she appeared to fall in with Lawrence's ideas about the house-mother. She helped with the housework. In spite of Lawrence's insistence on the clear limits of sex he had a talent for housework. It is to be remembered well of him that he had the grace to trim Frieda's hats.

Lawrence led all our social meetings. He thundered at us about his bi-polarised Absolute. He must have got his ideas about polarisa-tion from a textbook but he told us that all activity in science was a

359

waste of human energy, which, it was inferred, was best devoted to erotic calisthenics and intuitions about bi-polarised absolutes. Mrs Lawrence, concerned about the quality of her hospitality, tried to put in a restraining word, but had not the rhetoric equipment. I, the small bourgeois, knew that Lawrence was talking like a Board-School teacher. I felt no class solidarity, but impatience and scorn.

At this time Lawrence's friends were leaving him. Even the Murrys had begun to be disaffected. Lawrence would read out some letter of detachment from a disciple gone the wrong way. At this time even the keen eye of Miss West would have seen no Caritas. The incandescence of Lawrence was an incandescence of hate. As his friends left him, he shook the dust of Sodom and Gomorrha from the footcovering which was part of his fancy dress. Bitterly he demanded more joy. We should dance through the night on Hampstead Heath without woad but in some décor of oak leaves. The merciful inertia of Mrs Lawrence prevented this. He became more severe in his judgements of everybody. The verse of an amiable and philoprogenitive minor poet was aesthetic masturbation, and he said a pregnant friend of mine should be deterred from parturition by the State, though she is now the mother of a nice little girl of fifteen who is learning to be a shorthand typist.

Lawrence's most effective patronage had been from the Board School. His way of escape had been across the asphalt pavement and his associations with it were as gloomy as my own. Whatever may be thought of the main psychological proposition of *Sons and Lovers*, much of the detail in the book gives the impression of observed and experienced truth. The delicate son of the miner sent to draw his father's wages, is shy and is ragged by the cashier. 'Can't you count – what do they teach you at the Board School?' He goes home to his mother and complains bitterly of the insult. This little scene illustrates the war, the irreconcilability between the rank and file of the working classes and their sergeants. Lawrence could never go back to the country in which he spent his childhood without nausea. He developed a new Moses complex, a desire, which held too little of plan and too much of pride, to lead a chosen remnant out – somewhere, anywhere – to Deal, to Florence, to Venezuela. Only towards the end did he realise that anywhere the sun shone, his wounded youth accompanied him.

From pressure and inequality in childhood, he passes to a new pressure and inequality during adolescence. He becomes a teacher and, to an extent is differentiated from his class. He fears his class, the great mass of ordinarinesses and hard duties from which he has emerged, and which, if he steps back, will engulf him.

A teacher is a brainworker – the textbook is his tool, no longer the hammer or the pickaxe with their associations of dirt, sweat and old servility. But it avails the teacher little if he, like young Morel, procure for himself dress clothes; he will not be merged into the brain-using class. He has not the status, and chartered accountants will not receive him. He is in a social no-man's land.

Mrs Carswell tells us that, though Lawrence passed his examinations highest in all England, he would not have been received into Professor Weekly's house while he was merely a teacher. Only when Lawrence became known as a poet was he received by Professor Weekly. But Lawrence the teacher and Lawrence the poet had long lived together under one skin. Is it any wonder that he takes reprisals on the class of teachers who shelter in the universities? He steals a woman from it. What better panacea for a man's hurt dignity, and what more dangerous one?

When Lawrence wrote first to his friends after his marriage he wrote on Frieda's notepaper with her crest upon it, and underneath the crest he wrote 'My wife's father's a Baron'. This was taken by his friends, unacquainted with his class code, to be an endearing and amusing little piece of snobbery. But the fact that he wrote about the baron showed he was untroubled by him. He had no concern with German barons: his corrosive, silent pride was 'I stole this woman from the universities: she came with me'. Frieda had left her children with the university set-up; and Lawrence was baulked of his victory over the superior people, because he could never completely own this woman whose heart was with her children in the university. He began to associate children with his failure, to disparage all children, and the bearing of them, he who had written so tenderly of a woman with a baby in *The White Peacock*.

The fine flower of manhood is in that more than womanly tenderness which is in the spirit of fatherhood. Lawrence understood this spirit in his supremely beautiful portrait of Morel, the miner, in *Sons and Lovers*. Morel is not insisted on. He is presented with delicacy and fine reserve. His drunkenness, his brutality, his exhaustion are shadows which throw into relief his tenderness, his fidelity, his

361

exquisite natural manners. As late as *Sons and Lovers*, Lawrence respected the spirit of fatherhood. That spirit which remains with his children, even if it is moved at times to chastise them, nurtures them, and builds with his sweat a home for their mother. As he is exhausted in the caste struggle, Lawrence departs from his fidelity. In *Lady Chatterly's Lover* one child is begotten, as if in concession to old custom, after a great deal of love. The child is not endowed by the father, but presumably out of the inherited income of the mother. In 'The Escaped Cock', when Christ thinks better of the resurrection, he justifies his flesh by going to bed with a lady in Egypt. He fertilises her and passes on. He does not regard the sight of his child among physical delights.

One knows from the pattern of *Sons and Lovers* that old Morel would have had his son a miner, or at any rate a workman, for in that condition he could have remained a man. It is his mother who set him to the teaching, by which he becomes a spiritual eunuch, or at most, a begetter of wind.

The incest theme of *Sons and Lovers* rings false. The pattern has no symmetry. Neither of young Morel's mistresses were in any true sense his mate. Miriam is shown to be a physical coward: she is intrinsically unsuitable. There is no need to argue an attachment to the mother, when a perfect relationship was outside the range of possibility. Marion does not appear to have been even a good whore. She symbolises her emotions in terms of chocolate creams, and Morel clenches his fist too much, strains, sweats and staggers in a way that proves he could never have been near to erotic tranquillisation in her society. When this book was written Otto Weiniger, and Freud's incest theme were not unknown. It is the male milliner in Lawrence who insists on it. He is twisting his material into a new and fashionable mode.

But the hate theme is clear enough. The murder of the mother has not its cause in any perversion of physical desire. Though near death with cancer, she wants to continue living and to remain a mother. Morel the son broke a woman's will. Lawrence the symbolist, murders a mother half dead, as he attempted to kill all motherhood in his letter to Katherine Carswell.

It may be that I am taking Lawrence's sentences too literally, but while the Red Indian women were fully fertile there were still braves. Lawrence reports in 'Mornings in Mexico' that there are still

362

Indians who, driven off the war path, have kept their racial religion. Just as reasonably it might be said that Jewish fertility was futile because of the Roman domination. But before the fall of Jerusalem, Jewish woman bore Jesus whose aphorisms destroyed Rome when Hebrew hosts were scattered. Jesus did more for Jewish world dominance than David. While there is life there is very definitely hope. If Red Indian women had wholly failed in fertility, there would be no sort of Red Indian hope.

The Jews have survived because of the Messiah dream of their women, and down the ages there have been very few Jews under arms.

I have been told that Lawrence scorned logic, and that he should not be looked to for consecutive thought, that he desired always to give rise to a sense of feeling. What possible sort of feeling could the passage I have quoted arouse but one of distrust of procreation. The spirit of Lawrence here shows itself too universal a contraceptive. Lawrence exalts creation of hope above creation in life. Creation of hope is inferred to be male fertility, creation in life the silly yeasting of women. The purest artist must have population or there is no public.

The exaltation of male fertility above female fertility has been too common in world teachers. Buddha leaves home the night his first child is born. Jesus denies his mother: Marx exalts economics above the womb. Rousseau makes foundlings of the increase of his wife, even while he is inducing hysterical displays of breast-feeding among the *mondaines* of Paris. It is perhaps for this reason that we are faced with a new dark age, in spite of so much light flashed from prophetic foreheads.

Lawrence says if the mothers can bring forth hope they are mothers indeed. Is this a taunt, a challenge, or an invitation? In Russia there is bad feminism: childhood is socialised so that women may be free for the factories: motherhood has a new right, the right to abortion. In Russia they are growing food not to feed men but to break markets. If women could be allowed some small fertility in dreams, might not some mind, informed by a womb, dream that all men should be fed, and greater than the sagacity of governments when such things can be, is the common sense of a cook.

Lawrence's irritable, ill-stated depreciation of procreation is the climax of his attack on women, the reduction *ad absurdum* of his hatred of them, hatred as sterilising as that of the early Christian ascetics, and it has less excuse. Lawrence cannot push his problems into the lumber room of paradise, or count on Jesus coming to liquidate his world.

Lawrence's pirate flag against women went up as soon as he began to write. He called his first book *The White Peacock* – why? Perhaps the white peacock is a symbol for the will of the woman who was behind him when he wrote it. A friend of Lawrence's early youth, like Lawrence, a school teacher, she sent his first poems to Hueffer at the *English Review*. She may have given her creative life for Lawrence's, for she wrote a novel about the same time that he wrote *The White Peacock*. I have been told by a friend who read the manuscript that it was a very good novel. There is no trace of it or of the survival of the young woman's talent. I wish this could be found. I have also been told by a society hostess that when she entertained Lawrence and his young woman to lunch, the girl wore her gloves till the first course was well upon her. Everyone thought this very funny at the time. This hostess walks like a grand dame, but has not quite the code. I suspect that she is not telling the whole truth when she says that the girl was rejected for sexual inadequacy.

The White Peacock may be a symbolisation of Lawrence's sister. It is an imaginative picture of what Adler calls the family constellation. Most of the characters had representatives in life, but they could not have been very like life. The scene is a wish fulfilment. He declares his world to be bankrupt, since there is no hope. Is he speaking from his irritated nerves, his violated heart, his exacerbated solar plexus or from some surer source of truth? To the world of the early Christians there was no hope, and they invented mansions in the sky. Heaven was a sustaining dream, an anaesthetic, when imagination was too much pained by disaster. But life survived even the narcotic poison of a materially symbolised paradise. Enough of Rome stood for a Roman to dream and accomplish St Peter's. There is more hope for our world than there was for the Roman Empire in the first Christian century.

There is hope in the aspiration towards great tracts of peace, there is hope of man's mastery of the machine, there is hope from speed, there is hope in the liberated spirit of women. It may be the heavy responsibility of this spirit to validify these other grounds for hope – to hold for life what man has won by the ardours of his mind. The activity of man's mind, in town planning, in hygiene, in improving the condition of living, has freed women of what was once their pitiless burden of child bearing. The infant birth rate has gone down and because of that there has been a vast saving of woman's energy, pain and time. Orpheus has carried his Eurydice out of this Hell of profitless parturition. When the tiger is wounded in the cave, the tigress comes out to kill for him. That tiger of man's imagination, who has dragged down the furthest stars for his delight, may well be weak in the cave from the wounds of world war. The tired tiger in the cave may lose conceit of his claws. Then the jackal is king of the forest and Lawrence yaps to the austerities of Eddington that the sun must lie with the moon.

Let some girl from Girton say she loves her man's mind, and let the man free her a little from her duties of coition, and she will make a song of her delight in his mind. He may be as benefited by her singing as he is by his activity in lying with her. Mr Bernard Shaw showed that he feared this female redeemer when he sent up his flare about Joan of Arc. Men burned Joan of Arc, and Lawrence's imagination held torture for the woman who rode away. What is the spiritual effectiveness of male will rooted in the ritual submission of women, a submission which must be a lie and a piece of obscene mummery, if the will of women is as effective as men's? The liberated spirit of woman – a little licentious – is impatient at this old bondage of lies. Women who have taken off their corsets have a new indolence – they are so lazy that they would rather work than lie. 'God so loved the world that he gave his only begotten son.' While that word beats across the world, what hope is there for the prevention of war? It is the eternal excuse for sacrifice. Every young man who is tortured in war may be interpreted to be fulfilling God's will. In the cave the women protected the young men from the old men. What hope is there for contriving peace or wide tracts of happiness for life, while there is this almost universal belief in the creative value of pain? Men are brought forth in pain, by false analogy it is inferred that pain is accompanied by birth. There are better exercises for the control of the will than pain; there are all forms of work which may be accompanied even by joy. Ninety-five per cent of pain is a waste of energy – a waste of life. And it should be the privilege of women who are the givers of life, to economise it. In St Peter's at Rome, Michael Angelo, who was no lover of women, has set up his great symbol, *Mater Dolorosa*, in which it might be the point of departure for the most significant of women's revolts. Women might determine that for that old mother of sorrows they might establish a mother of strength and joy. Twilight sleep is flouted by prophets such as Lawrence as a sign of racial degeneracy. Of all pain, birth pains have an immediate justification. At the end of labour there is a child, but at the end of a crucifixion there is as likely to be a devil as a God. There is sense in birth pains, but there is no sense in a shrapnel-torn arm or a gouged-out eye. Women might destroy war by claiming a prerogative of pain. But where is the woman in the trinity — absent, or diminished to a dove? And so we have the absurdity of the sacrifice of the son.

Let us invent God's wife . . . she alone will say the word to end war. She will speak scornfully to the Old Mechanic, whose creation is so imperfect that it has to be cemented with blood. Let the irritated imagination of Lawrence beget this new redeemer on the body of peace. Meanwhile, let us make an inquiry into the roots and scope of his hate. We have our biological justification. It is for the judgement of the hen that the cock displays his spring plumage and for her gratification that he sharpens his spurs.

I have to confess that this particular cock escaped me. I am the female of the species. Lawrence asked two things of me: that I should talk to him, and sing hymns with him, the lovely hymns of our grandfathers, the weavers, the farmers, the shopkeepers, the millers, songs scented with the courage and tenderness that is in English land. I inclined my will; as I have said, I was not likely to inspire sexual anaesthesia. This he entirely disregarded. A little chagrined I wrote to him:

> Had I married you, dear, when I was nineteen
> I had been little since but a printing machine.
> For before my fortieth year had run
> I well had produced you a twenty-first son.

But to revert, *The White Peacock* contains a record of the social ambitions of the Lawrence women. The atmosphere is very genteel. Lawrence has several suits and some very fine flannel pyjamas. In *Sons and Lovers*, he tells us that pyjamas are a caste mark, the work people do not wear them. There are complicated forms of food.

Salad strikes a sense of uneasiness into the nice son of a tenant farmer, and the Lawrence women are rather nasty to him about it. The tables are turned on the tenant farmers because, in the original design, there was likely to have been more and better food on the farm than in the miner's cottage. Mrs Morel's housekeeping allowance could not have run to all that blancmange. The manners are very good and very careful. Cyril – the Lawrence symbol – says, 'My mother told me that the men could smoke'. The phrase creaks a little. Nice men don't smoke without waiting for permission. The conversation is beyond reproach – of pictures, Debussy and Strauss. There are photogravures and Botticelli. There is a meeting of university graduates, and everyone talks of the good old 'coll'. Lawrence's sister is the best conversationalist. She quotes little bits of Latin, and quite goes on about the scenery. She is like a dream figure of certain aspects of Lawrence, dressed in a Leghorn hat and a feather boa. And she is socially seaworthy. She marries the son of a mine owner, and mercilessly high hats the nice son of the tenant farmer who is in love with her, though he has at the same time a fixation on her brother. The young farmer goes to the bad, and treats his youngest son abominably. But there is nothing to show that this is due to any of the women, because the young man is stated to be overbred as soon as he appears, and he is shown to be homosexual.

The motive of *The White Peacock* is sounded by Annable the keeper, very much Lawrence, as Cyril, the chief figure to whom everything happens, is very little Lawrence but a two-dimensional figure which moves across the scene as if on wires. But one recognises the personality of Lawrence in Annable as one recognises the likeness in a portrait. 'Ah, you don't know what it is to have the pride of a body like mine', reminds us of Lawrence's courage and his fine energy. Annable stands for two things in the design. He represents Lawrence's moral brawn, which enables him to survive his periods of poverty and failure. In relation to his second wife, Annable symbolises Lawrence's creative consciousness. Annable a university-educated man, the son of a failed cattle dealer begins life as a parson and marries a woman of title, who keeps him as a sort of professional lover: she will not have children because of her physical fear. He disappears, and marries a peasant by whom he has a great brood of children. He says to Cyril, 'You know them, do you, sir? Aren't they a lovely little litter. Natural as weasels, that's what I said they should

be, bred up like a bunch of young foxes, to run as they would.'
'They'll get nicely trapped one of these days,' says Cyril. And
Annable goes on: 'I watch my brats, I let them grow. They're
beauties, they are sound as a young ash pole, every one . . . They can
be like birds or weasels or vipers or squirrels, as long as they aren't
human rot.'

Here Lawrence is expressing pride in what he knows to be his
great fertility. With his weak chest and slight body, he could never
have estimated this to be a physical fertility. He is expressing his
faith in, and his hope for the works of his imagination. Cyril sounds a
note of prophecy and warning, 'They'll get nicely trapped one of
these days.' One of these brats was certainly trapped in the burning
of *The Rainbow*.

The creative consciousness of a pure artist is bisexual. There is a
marriage in the house of the soul. The female principle produces the
myth from some source within herself, and fertilises it with her
essential energy. The male principle is intellectual, ranging the
world to select material. He is critic and scholar, and master of char-
acterisation. He fertilises his wife from what he knows, and the result
is a work of pure imagination. This is expressed more clearly than I
can state it, in a poem by John Oland:

> Well, they are gone!
> And we are here alone.
> I, the mime, and master of surprises,
> Who have fooled that mob with fifty new disguises –
> You, who sit in the soul
> A quiet wife;
> You, who are Control
> Weaving the long continuous thread of life.
> Sometimes I think that there is nothing of my winning,
> That all we have of service is your spinning.
> When of this fear my heart is full
> Then you remind me dame, I bring you wool.
> It is most bitter for me when flesh drives me to sleep
> With some one-sexed partner, and you sit by and weep.

These verses, as well as expressing the bisexual principle in creative consciousness, reveal the chastity desire of the artist, who wishes to keep the whole of his energy for his supreme purpose. This chastity was in Lawrence. He has been called a sexual failure, and on no grounds. There is no reason to think he wished to succeed at practical sexual exercises, to convince anyone in bed. Lawrence had, to use his own phrase, his sex in his head. When he had any kind of erotic experience he wrote it out, for writing was more important to him than love. It is the primal male principle in Lawrence, speaking through Annable, who states his hatred of women and gives a clue to its cause. In the churchyard towards night, a white peacock flies up and perches on a tombstone. Annable says, 'The proud fool, look at it, perched on an angel too, as if it were a pedestal for vanity. That's the soul of a woman or it's the devil. That's the very soul of a lady, the very, very soul . . . God there must be plenty of hearts twisting under here,' and he stamped on a grave, 'when they hear that row'. The peacock flapped away, down the tombs over the terraces. 'Just look', he said, 'the miserable brute has dirtied that angel, a woman to the end I tell you, all vanity, screech and defilement.'

Who is this lady whose screech has maddened Lawrence to this explosion of hate? Who but the spirit of the Lawrence women. If ever there was a living screech, it is in Lettie, the sister. The statement of the ambition principle of these women, the spiritual truth of this family, is stated in this book, as the truth of its circumstances and the detail of its history is stated in *Sons and Lovers*. In *The White Peacock*, the father dies a broken drunkard away from his family. This was evidently Lawrence's estimate of the truth, but there is evidence, from old Morel in *Sons and Lovers*, that there was no final destruction of the father.

It is significant that Annable is killed by the falling of stones while climbing a wall. This indicates a disintegration of personality in Lawrence, and it follows, as effect follows cause, the expression of his hatred of women. His psyche not strong enough to contain this hatred is broken by it; he is no longer pure artist but half artist. All Lawrence's work proves this.

Lawrence seldom creates a character, he presents a great gallery of faked photographs. He is so little a scholar that he cannot perfect himself in physiology, so invents a gibberish of ganglions. He is so little a critic, that defects of reasoning have to be counted in him as a

369

charm, and in argument he seldom makes a statement without giving his position away in the next one.

The female principle of the creative consciousness of Lawrence was so immensely energetic that it is fertile long after it is bereft. But the conceptions are not legitimate. Impregnation is left to airs, to odours, to phrases of Freud, to a word or two read about Einstein, to chapter three from the physics book – particularly to that paragraph which contains the word polarisation. There are indications that the first of these casual impregnations was from Aubrey Beardsley. A book of Beardsley drawings, interests both Cyril and George. The young tenant farmer, influenced by the shape of Beardsley's women, takes heart of grace and tells his love to Lettie, the sister. What remains of Lawrence's creative consciousness becomes impregnated with a handful of pomegranate seeds, and we have our first seduction. Up to the death of Annable, and the influence of Aubrey Beardsley, the book is as decorous as a churchroom. If the quality of the writing is a little reminiscent, one forgives it because pains have been taken. But suddenly, for no apparent reason, the ground gives under our feet, Lettie invites her fiancé to stay at a her mother's house, and in the morning she is too embarrassed to eat her boiled egg. Around this seduction there is an unnecessary atmosphere of regret and gloom. Nothing follows from it; Lettie marries her young man who becomes a Conservative candidate, and one feels that Lawrence might have spared his mother's house the indignity. There is a better flowering of the pomegranate seed in a chapter called 'A Poem of Friendship' in which a rather more than normal tenderness is shown between Cyril and George: the quality of the writing improves with the loosening of the moral tensions.

I have argued that the explosion in Lawrence's psyche was caused by a hatred for the women in his family, a hatred so deep that it grew to include all women. Let us examine Lawrence's next book of importance, *Sons and Lovers*, which is said to be very reliable auto-biography. Lawrence himself justifies such analysis in his preface to 'Studies in Classical American Literature'. 'The curious thing about art-speech is that it prevaricates so terribly, I mean it tells such lies. I suppose because we always, all the time, tell ourselves lies. Truly art is a sort of subterfuge. But thank God for it, we can see through the subterfuge if we choose . . . The proper function of the critic is to save the tale from the artist who created it.' How is the tale to be saved from the artist who invented it? Plainly by an examination of the tale, of the facts which are known to be true of the particular case, and of what is known to be widely true for life.

In *Sons and Lovers* Lawrence suggests that he has some sort of incestuous attachment to his mother. Mrs Morel unsatisfied in her relationship with her husband exploits the love life of her son so that he can never form an entirely satisfactory love relationship with a woman, at any rate till the mother is dead. There is a distressing implication that it would have been better for the mother to have died a good deal earlier, and that young Morel is somehow crippled and destroyed by his love for his mother. There is an atmosphere of doom round the relationship, which is deepened by critics who say that it would be better for a boy to be dead than to have such a relationship with his mother. The following passage from *Sons and Lovers* has been taken by critics to reveal more than Lawrence implied about incest:

> Paul was very ill. His mother lay in bed at night with him, they could not afford a nurse. He grew worse, and the crisis approached. One night he tossed into consciousness in the ghastly, sickly feeling of dissolution . . . and consciousness makes a last flare to struggle, like madness. 'I s'll die mother,' he cried, heaving for breath on the pillow.
>
> She lifted him up crying in a small voice 'O my son my son.' That brought him to. He realised her, his whole will rose up and arrested him. He put his head on her breast and took ease of her for love.

The scene should not be thought to contain any element of sexual feeling. The boy is gasping with bronchitis, the mother lifts him up so that he can breathe. In his exhaustion his head falls on her breast. He draws a little necessary strength from her health. The contact reminds him of the days of his own health. Children are constantly seeking that kind of physical contact with their parents. A normal boy will hurl himself on his mother's knee till he is twelve. Lawrence, we are told, was young for his age. To pervert such a scene is to poison the roots of life. That Lawrence should expose such a scene shows a morbid lack of reserve. But the morbidity is not in the scene, but in the writing about it, which came later.

To expose as a public example, a mother whose tenderness had saved him from death shows the essential unlovingness of the manhood of Lawrence. Emotionally he was a changeling. Perhaps his circumstances induced in him an irritability which threw his emotional system out of gear. If *Sons and Lovers* is to be taken as evidence, it is clear that by early manhood Lawrence had, on the threshold of consciousness, a very definite antagonism to his mother.

LECTURE: SCHOOL FOR MOTHERS
(Probably written 1909 – 1910)

In the work of the School for Mothers we are constantly meeting with the necessity to provide meals for certain of the pregnant women and nursing mothers. The School for Mothers is an educational centre where women are taught what I will call the technique of mothering. However talented and however educated a mother is, she cannot do her work well if she is denied the necessities of her work, if she has no food to build her child before it is born or to nourish it after its birth. The phrase 'the new born dies at the empty breast' can be extended to an older child. What a waste of the work of the mother, and of the hard-pressed hospitals!

We hear a good deal nowadays that our country is increasing itself from the lowest ranks of the people, that decadents and unfit people are being born. This statement is hurled at us as some sort of argument against our work. The truth is that we are increasing from the strata of society which have the courage, the recklessness if you like better, to give us children.

It is difficult to get statistics about rates of increase of population in different classes, but I have it from Mr Bernard Shaw that marriages in the Fabian Society produce one-and-a-half children per marriage. Now that is a decrease of twenty-five per cent per generation without allowing anything for child death rate. The educated classes, the comfortable classes, are not keeping their ranks filled up: we are getting our population from the cottage and the tenement. It seems to me that God's poor are doing God's work. We have to look through the veil of dirt and ugliness in their houses, the rags and sometimes the unloveliness of neglected children, and see human souls, and do the best with our material. And we really have to decide that the material is not so bad after all. We know that the greater number of the children are born healthy, that a half-starved mother, at the sacrifice of her own body, will produce a finer child than we have any right to expect. And we know the tremendous influence of environment and nurture. If the good children that Providence gives to us were treated well by us, we should not have so much to say of decadents and failures.

We do not for a moment deny sin, incapacity and drunkenness; but the parents of a starved child need not be either particularly sinful or drunken, nor, according to the standards of their class, incapable. A man is thrown out of work through some change in trade, a fashion is altered, there is another strike, and his living is gone; there is no food for the mother and for the child. Now this is very unfair; and in a great, rich town like London, in a town so full of clever people who can contrive, of women who are good house-keepers, it seems a stupid, thriftless thing that pregnant women should be without food. By starving a baby we are multiplying our troubles, the work and food we withhold will cost us a great deal in the end. If every thrifty person would take a little trouble now, the gain would be at a money-lender's rate of interest.

It could be argued that the most thrifty thing you could do with an unwanted baby would be to let it die. And yet there is no more unsatisfactory thing than a dead child. One of the poorest of our women at the Welcome came in to us and said that her sixth child was dead. And the woman cried for the child that had been a burden, and we said to one another that it was a mercy that the child was dead. But afterwards the mother asked me to go into her house and look at the child, and I could not for I knew in my heart that it was not a good thing that the child was dead, and that I had no right to say that it was good for the child to die.

Now, we women who have the means to be good housekeepers and managers should co-operate with the mothers who are at a disadvantage.

NOTES FOR A LECTURE
(Probably written 1909 – 1910)

I am to speak to the title 'The Effects of Gifts on the Recipient'. I think it is a difficult title for it seems to imply that I must take a positive point of view and say that all gifts have a certain kind of effect, and the same effect on all recipients. Now I don't believe that. I can neither say that all gifts have a demoralising effect, nor that no gifts have such an effect. It seems to me that as there are many types of recipients, there are many types of giving. I say that the effect of a gift varies with the character of the recipient and the spirit of the giving.

I am very glad that I have been forced to think on this subject, for the effect of gifts of various kinds is a problem that has often to be faced in the work of the School for Mothers, and in other branches of social work. In such work we are constantly concerned with giving, we are always meeting the need for gifts of money and food, and we are all very interested that our gifts should be constructive and not destructive.

Looking back we see two great roots of giving. One is buried deep in parenthood, the other is found, later, with the sense of property. The first of all gifts was the great gift of life. Away back along the life-stream the living organism split itself into two, and gave half of itself to make a new organism. Later we see mammals give their young the gift of milk. And so it seems to me that out of the relationship of parenthood developed tenderness, care and all good gifts. The parent gives life, milk, care and this giving has always been constructive giving. The parent is driven by a great natural impulse to care for its young. The parent is concerned only with the welfare and development of the young. The beauty and perfection of the new being is the reward of the gift. Now this old spirit of giving has endured and has been growing since the beginning of life. At first it made life possible, in the end it will make life perfect.

I have said that the first spirit of giving is as old as life, and the second is as old as property. The second spirit of giving is the spirit of the sacrifice. Men have always given to the strong, to the conquerors. They did this when they found how pleasant possessions are, to appease and win the good will of the strong. This spirit of sacrificial giving is found in the peace offering of primitive peoples, in the modern dinner party, and in all religions. These are gifts of propitiation. The phrase 'God's poor' shows this spirit, also 'who gives to the poor lends to God'. God was propitiated with gifts, all sorts of gifts. Then when religious ideas became more spiritualised, when the gods became less manlike, when it was understood that God had no need for food offerings and no nose for burnt offerings these gifts came to be given to the poor; they were not given for the sake of the poor, but in the spirit of sacrificial gifts.

Now I think that if you give sacrificial gifts you may be doing something dangerous. But if you give in the great old way, if you have all your attention on the development and the advantage of the recipient, if his well-being is your only reward, if you have none of your own irons in the fire, then I think your giving will be constructive giving. We must give for man's sake, never for God's sake. We must make the poor man our son, concern ourselves only with his well-being, look for his improvement but never for his gratitude. To do this we must give cleverly, we must give the right gifts, we must take a good deal of trouble to understand the need. Now, we often hear that charity undermines independence. That word 'independence' seems to me a stupid one to use towards a working man in a large and highly organised society. We worked and fought very hard for some hundreds of years for something we called freedom, and we are only just beginning to realise that it is impossible for a working man living in a society like ours to be free. A workman is part of a great machine which controls him, and it is absurd to talk of him as being independent of it. He is ruled by great social laws that he can in no way control. One often hears people say that a workman should earn what he gets; the difficulty is for him, by any amount of industry, to earn what he needs. By far the greater number of men are bound to earn a wage which they cannot control. It is fixed for them by society. Now in a society which is free, where there is no organisation, where every man is free to get what he can for himself, the reward of the mass of labour – the many who cannot contrive and who have not combined – is set too low. Lately we have realised this, and we are augmenting the rewards of the mass of labour in a number of ways.

We have a great system of free education, we have free hospitals, clinics, Schools for Mothers; we have the Care Committee with free dinners for school children; we have Golders Hill Gardens – the pleasure ground of the people; we have museums and public parks with the free music of military bands. Whatever has been said about our system of free education, it has never been said that it pauperises the people. A man was never pauperised, never undermined in his independence by going into the London Hospital. I think this is because these great systems of public education and public care were given in the first spirit of giving. They were given so that the people might become vigorous. Youth is the title to education, sickness to healing. When a gift passes right into the people's lives, when it is available to everyone, when it becomes one of the rights of man to enjoy certain social status and amenities, then I think it ceases to become demoralising. No man was ever demoralised by his right to free air.

With regard to the feeding of school children and the gift of food. I think that if it were recognised that every child, just by dint of being a child, has a right to a dinner at school it would be a good thing. When a gift can be enjoyed by all without acknowledgement of poverty, when no caste is lost by accepting it, it is a good gift.

Nobody has the least hesitation about walking into Golders Hill Park, though if everyone had to make an affidavit at the gate that their income was under two hundred and fifty a year, lots of prosperous as well as unprosperous people would be kept out. When I suggest that the unfortunate middle classes should pay higher taxes and rates in order that dinner should become part of the curriculum of the elementary school, a howl will go up about diminished incomes. We have to remember that the rewards of the middle classes, like the rewards of the labourers, have been fixed by society; if society decides that it is better for it to spend its surplus on the feeding of children, we must learn a new piety and transposing old words say 'Society has given, and society has taken away'.

About private giving. If your gift is given in the good old way with tenderness and wisdom, the recipient will nearly always give you kindness and a good return. But the cadgers and the beggars have generally been undermined by the propitiatory spirit of the gift given to secure conformity to a religious idea or a theory, distributed in small circles to those who would subscribe to a creed or to a system. If the recipient has no sympathy with the creed or system, he has received the gift badly which was given in a bad way. I would have gifts given very intimately or with great kindness. I would have them given either by a friend or by the State.

THE PLATONISTS

Cecilia had a beautiful body but she also had a mind. She thought more about her mind than about her body — that was one of her charms. She imagined that she could make men do the same — that was one of her mistakes. She was tall, lithe, slim, just full enough in the hips and round enough in the body to save her figure from boyishness. Her face was beautifully proportioned like the face of a Roman matron. Her brow was modelled, her eyes were brown and oval, her mouth was firm and at the same time tender, her chin was round, she had quite an adequate nose, her skin was like cream and her cheeks were red. In the middle of the left cheek was a little blemish, a small red spot.

There was in her face no coquetry. Many beautiful women wear a beauty expression as a barber hangs out his pole. As if they would say: Be it known, by this special look of complacency, that our features are beyond reproach. The absence of this beauty expression had, in a measure, the effect of hiding Cecilia's beauty. People saw in her that expression of seriousness which is associated with the faces of women who are powerless to charm, and they looked no further. It came upon people suddenly that Cecilia was beautiful, and then it had all the joy of a discovery.

When she was twenty-one all this did not interest Cecilia. She was scarcely even neat in her dress. Personal adornment she took as a sign of an unemancipated spirit. She liked to dress as nearly like a boy as she could. And she read as she brushed her hair, which was arranged with Madonna-like simplicity. She read while she did her hair, she read always and she read everything. A child of her age, she had no opinions, or rather she had opinions in phases. She liked to talk about her phases, and she liked to talk about them to her men friends. She believed in the possibility of intellectual friendship between the sexes. She had lately been reading a German book which said: That there is no reality, but that everything is 'seeming'.

James discovered Cecilia's beauty almost at once. He was unaccustomed to looking much at women, either plain or handsome ones. But there was something in Cecilia that satisfied him. She understood his interests instinctively. The very negligence of her dress pleased him. James had a horror of the female with the dusting brush. He liked the sort of things that Cecilia said, and he also liked to watch her while she talked. James was without the modern disease of self-analysis, he did not examine his mind about Cecilia. But he felt pleased about her, and thought a good deal about her over his pipe at his lodgings.

These lodgings were sacred from the dusting brush. They were a chaos of undisturbed maps, papers, books, works of reference, Roman drainpipes, tiles and pieces of pottery for James devoted all his leisure to a certain branch of archaeology. This room was a horror and source of offence to all James' female relations. They longed to exchange order and a surface cleanliness for James' grimy, though scientific arrangements. James knew that women have no real sense of order but only an instinct against peace, but he felt that Cecilia would appreciate his room. She was so quick to understand the archaeological matters in which he was so interested. James had never stopped to consider the nature of the female mind, but now he too began to believe in the possibility of intellectual friendship between the sexes. It was with this in mind that he asked Cecilia to go with him on the river.

He took her to Pangbourne, and in the boat she sang, which filled James with quite an unusual pleasure. He felt exhilarated by the song and the beauty about him, and he pulled lustily while Cecilia talked to him about the German book and about nothing having reality but only appearance. James looked very hard at her. Cecilia also was exhilarated, she talked merrily enjoying so much the friendship of James. As she talked about her 'unrealities' she waved her hand towards a tree on the bank ahead which James could not see. 'That tree is not a tree' she said, 'it exists only in the mind. It is . . .' At that moment the 'appearance' of a branch hit James smartly in the back, the speed of the boat was arrested and Cecilia was thrown forward into his arms. It was then a strange thing happened about which James did not stop to examine his conscience, he kissed Cecilia upon the little red blemish in the middle of her cheek.

THE DEFICIT

I know some dull people. They live in a dull house, in a dull street in Bloomsbury, which has not always been dull. In this street are no boarding houses, no Swiss waiters, but there are to be found a few examples of the common black Bloomsbury cat. It is a sombrely distinguished street, a survival of the better days before the gates were opened to unprivileged traffic; when the city magnate could sleep in suburban silence and within sight of trees, twenty minutes walk from the Bank.

The street still knows the small city magnate, the master tailor, the merchant, the printer and the Jew. There is a leaven of people whose professions take them in the direction of the Strand. Among these is the head of the dull house. The dull front-door is opened by a mistress of dullness: so good a parlourmaid as almost to cease to be a woman. When I follow her up the staircase of the dull house I wonder if she ever carried any emotion in her thin bosom, and if she thinks at all.

This house has an evil effect upon me. I must behave well in it and yet it fills me with a spiteful profanity; I want to break its consecrated silences with the songs of the street; I want to destroy its tiresome orderlinesses and prepare it for the day of Judgement when even such interiors will be resolved into sticks and shreds.

I am led into a dull room. The furniture, inherited from a relative, is early Victorian in form, stiff and comfortless, but solid and costly. Over the mantelshelf is a picture by a reputable artist, some exhibitor at old Academies, it is without interest, almost without colour. There are reproductions of madonnas, reminiscences of galleries in Rome; these beautiful women are compromised by their associates, and seem to share the guilty ugliness of the tables and chairs.

There is everywhere a wonderful neatness. In this room Motion is dead: that cushion will always occupy just that position on that sofa, that paper-knife will always rest upon the Hibbert *Journal*. There are more rooms like this one. Downstairs is more of the relative's furniture, a sideboard as gloomy as a hearse and as big, mahogany chairs, a mammoth table and here a portrait of the relative which shows that he left behind him not only his mahogany but his long chin. I sit at this long table exchanging glances with the relative, and conversation with the inheritor of the mahogany and the chin.

I talk to the dull man about Switzerland, to his wife about the Church Congress, to their daughter about her Care Committee, and my mind is occupied with unlicensed wondering: how, in these surroundings, in this house, did these people ever manage to do anything so natural as to beget a child. What does it mean, all this dullness? I associate lack of animation with death. These people are prosperous, there is a public to whom they appeal; the man has made a considerable success at the bar; they are not even sterile, there is an elder daughter and somewhere a son. The human race gained fifty per cent on these grey nuptials. I cannot accuse these people of a fruitless marriage. And yet, as I eat their dinner, I feel they are my enemies. They must always play Saracen to my Christian; to vindicate my whole philosophy I must find them in the Wrong.

After dinner, I find myself alone with the dull woman. She is nearly sixty and is handsome, statuesque. She talks to me about children. She tells me how little she wanted maternity, how she grudged existence to the youngest daughter. She attributes the girl's want of stamina to this fact, and does so without apparent sense of regret or guilt. Her reason for grudging her youngest daughter existence seems to have been that she had given up her nurseries and sent away her nurse. She makes constant use of the word 'convenient'. I notice that the daughter of the dull woman, although she resembles her mother, is not beautiful. Here, at any rate, something has been lost. I am asked to go tomorrow to see the grandchildren of the dull people. I find them at tea. There is a small boy of three and a baby. The small boy is so dull as to appear to be mentally deficient. He spills his food and, still being unable to talk, screams. He is smaller than the average slum child of his age. He is plainly afraid of his grandmother; he cries and clings to his nurse, an over-trained servant, dull, and a poor chief friend for a little child. The dull woman expatiates upon the child's shortcomings without sympathy and without regret; she hopes that the mother of the little boy will not have any more children, and again makes use of the word 'convenient'.

It strikes me that this little dull boy is the deficit. These people had everything that is necessary for the making of a small boy. They had house room and milk and air and money, but they have neutralised these benefits with their dullness. And when all the resources of an elaborate educational system have been lavished upon him, he will not be so valuable as his long-chinned ancestor over the fire-place.

I have overcome the Saracen. To be losing ground with the generations is to fail eternally.

LONDON SCENES: THE NIGHT MARCH

As I stand at the bottom of the hill I am conscious of a faint insistent rhythm. It is a drum and fife band in the distance. That sound always stirs me with vague, half-understood emotions. Military music means nothing to me, I have always lived in times of peace, but my ancestors understood it. It is to me like a symbol of which I have forgotten the significance. I only know that it means something.

I look eagerly in the direction of the sound. Soon there is a swaying on the crest of the hill. This becomes a ribbon of marching men which the street lamps mottle with shadow and light. The light and the night and the wave motion of the swinging line give to the commonplace tune the appeal of great music, and in some way the sound of the music and the marching feet have a certain quality of silence. The sound and the scene no longer appeal to the eye and the ear, but only to the mind. They become like things vividly thought.

I see the faces of the first men. They do not speak. They are absent and pale as if their senses were asleep, they walk like somnambulists. By the side of the ranks walk many civilians all silent, all hypnotised by music and movement. Then come the horses walking in time to the music, and then a quick-firing gun – a toy ornamented with bright metal – so small, so neat and yet so deadly, suggestive of the powers of death and hell.

In the rear ranks the men are smoking, the blue-grey smoke ascends through the still air. The march seems like the march of ghosts. One of the ghosts raises his head and catches sight of me. He draws himself up and leers, very full of sex. The men pass. They turn the corner where a church shows its bulk against the London sky. I am left in the street with tears in my eyes. These men and that music mean little to me. But my ancestors, within me, remember them.

STUDIES IN TWO DIMENSIONS:
THE ADMIRABLE HOUSEKEEPER

The Admirable Housekeeper lived in a world of two dimensions. She thoroughly understood surfaces. She was as efficient as the powers who will bring about the millennium must be. There was perfect order on her surfaces; nothing was forgotten, everything was adequate and that is the two-dimensional word for beautiful.

If the Admirable Housekeeper had been as efficient in the three-dimensional manner as she was on her surfaces she might have changed something: reduced the infant death-rate, or altered the present superstitions about sex relationship. As it was she performed two doubtful social services: She kept a dull man solvent, and she provided his dull children with capital.

Neither the education, nor the family tradition, nor the instinct of the Admirable Housekeeper had given her a conception of the third dimension in life. She found the world ready for her. The prudence of the people who had begotten her had kept enough of their surplus to make the struggle for a living unnecessary to her. There had been nothing for her to create, nothing for her to alter. She had only to fit into the mould which incomprehensible forces had made for her. Her religion, her education, her morality, even the clothes she wore were ordered for her by these forces. Her ideas were very carefully arranged. Her mind was like a series of little regular boxes; ideas from one box never by any chance strayed into another box.

The one instinct that was strong in the Admirable Housekeeper was the instinct of imitation. Exactly what she imitated was determined by her ancestry and her temperament. All her desires were subject to this instinct, even the desire to reproduce. Marriage came to her as an opportunity to have a house of her own. Children came to her because children came to the married, it was almost a point of good form; there was no room in her scheme of things for ecstasy.

Pregnancy was a period merely of physical discomfort and an altered routine; it was a startling departure from the normal. She looked forward to motherhood with no spiritual exaltation, and she was very self-conscious about her change of condition. She took very little exercise because she was ashamed of being seen in an abnormal state of health. In order to make her condition as little apparent as possible, she wore tight clothes and a corset. In the pains of child-birth the Admirable Housekeeper glimpsed the three-dimensional world of strong anguish and ecstasy, of big debts and payments. Afterwards there was a reaction − almost like an atonement − the two-dimensional system settled on the new child.

The mother found him a nurse skilled in surfaces, who kept the child's body clean, and his clothes in perfect order. She prepared his food very slowly and with care, but, because of the two-dimensional system, she prepared the wrong food. The mother did not nurse her child, she had always been repelled by the sight of a nursing mother. If almighty God had, indeed, invented the serviceable breast of woman, he had thought better of it when he invented the feeding bottle! Unsuitable food went into the bottle, the very young infant was filled with starch. As a result his development was very medi-ocre, and he suffered just that amount of colic that can be expected in such nurseries. The Admirable Housekeeper did not dream the dream of the Jewish woman − she could not have mothered the superman.

When the child was two, it was discovered that he had a crooked leg, the starch had got home.

Immediately, the two-dimensional system got to work. Doctors and masseuses were engaged, physic was poured out, a great deal of human labour was expended and wasted, all because the wrong food had been put into the feeding bottle. Eventually the child's leg recovered, and his education began.

The Admirable Housekeeper atoned for having conceived her child by giving over his education exclusively to virgins. Later women were excluded from his scheme of things altogether, he was sent to a public school. When a great deal of money had been spent on him and lots of work, he turned out just as they had wanted him to turn out: very like other people. The Admirable Housekeeper never made a mistake in her calculations. The surplus at the bank steadily increased, she kept enough of the right sort of wine in her cellars, and her servants kept her house immaculate until they got gastric ulcers from overwork and not enough fresh air, and went to occupy nice tidy beds in the workhouse infirmary. Nothing went wrong with the Admirable Housekeeper's surfaces, but something went wrong with her body, and she died. Her children buried her with their two-dimensional feelings too deep for tears.

The poor body was borne into the ugly church where she had sat Sunday after Sunday for twenty-five years. In the pews were sombre, soberly dressed people who were taking the funeral very much for granted as if death were an incident in life. Their black clothes were the ceremonious symbol of grief, but there was no sorrow in their faces, but a curious expression of conscious well-being, as if each member of the company was congratulating himself on having resisted the common enemy a little longer, and felt he had drawn a prize in the lottery of life simply because he was not the corpse. The substantial oak coffin was carried into the church on the shoulders of six men – small tradesmen, the subjects of her little kingdom – looking very clean and conscious of their best clothes, wearing an expression of quiet joy as if they felt the distinction of taking part in the well-managed ceremony. After they had deposited the coffin before the altar and creaked on their tip toes to seats at the side, the clergyman reads the fine burial service, he looks like a mid-Victorian chemist and pronounces the word glory – glow-ry, but this does not matter to the dead.

The service is finished and the coffin is carried out while the organist plays 'O Rest in the Lord'. The assembly files out after it, and waits in the porch while the hearse drives off. Just before the procession starts, the sister-in-law of the dead woman leans forward to a friend and whispers an invitation to tea. It suddenly strikes her that this may be ill timed, she murmurs an apology and drops her eyes demurely. The expression soon fades, and she is plainly engaged with thoughts of tea. No woman follows the Admirable Housekeeper to the grave, she is deserted by her sex at this hour. The party on the church steps breaks into groups and becomes actively cheerful. There is a buzz of conversation, the plans of the bereaved family are discussed. Aunt Emiline – the richest of us all – says that she is glad to see that the children recognise their mother's death as evidence of the divine will.

If there is no joy in the two-dimensional world there is no grief.

NOTES

page line
number

3 3 'Snow', in *Poems* p. 44, Faber and Faber, 1935.

3 15 *Anna* was christened Edith Alice Mary and was known as Edith throughout her childhood, except that her father sometimes called her Anne as a pet-name.

3 22 *Paul Dehn*: a journalist who became a good poet and film script-writer. In his interview with Anna (*Sunday Referee, 12 June 1935*) he quoted her: 'My society exists to increase the imaginative side of women without spoiling their practical genius. Then we'll have you men where we want you!'

4 24 *Eliot Bliss*: Eliot Bliss' first novel *Luminous Isle* (Cobden Sanderson 1934) is to be re-issued by Virago Press Ltd in 1985.

5 11 *Richard Harris Barham (1788-1845)*: His *Ingoldsby Legends* published between 1840 and 1847 were illustrated by the three great comic illustrators of the time, Leech, Tenniel (of *Alice in Wonderland*), and Cruikshank (see p. 10). His grotesque poems satirised the more pompous aspects of the Church of England.

5 34 *James Brunton Stephens (1835-1902)*: b. Scotland, arrived

385

Australia 1866; tutor, schoolmaster and government clerk. He was a poet, novelist and humorist.

6 28 *George Allardyce Riddell*: created Baron Riddell of Walton in 1920. Founder and editor of the *News of the World*. A director of George Newnes Ltd and Arthur Pearson Ltd.

7 21 *David Garnett (1892-1981)*: This original novelist and lover of both sexes says he fell in love with Anna. She certainly impressed him, for years after he met her, he set down on three occasions his memories of her: in a foreword to her posthumous 'The Spirit of the Lawrence Women' in *Texas Quarterly* Autumn 1966; in an introduction to her *Selected Poems*, Chatto & Windus in 1971; and previously in his namedropping autobiography.

7 23 *'An Australian friend'*: This was Heather Sherrie who became a librarian at the Mitchell Library in Sydney. She attributes her interest in literature and the arts to the influence of Geoffrey Harper. Her special concern is with ecology and the environment. Her father was the editor of the local newspaper at Wagga, a town in Riverina in New South Wales, Australia, and later he worked on a weekly – *The Land* in Sydney.

    Wagga Wagga: A fine fat farming town on the Murrumbridgee River in Queensland, to which the railway had come in 1879. Wagga is Maori for a crow: the Maori language has no form for plurals, so adds a second Wagga to denote many crows.

9 40 *Harper Adams Agricultural College*: at Edgmont, Shropshire, founded in 1901.

10 5 *John Betjeman (1906-   )*: knighted in 1969, he became Poet Laureate in 1972. See the poem 'Slough,' in *Continual Dew*, p. 4, John Murray, 1937.

10 31 *George Cruikshank (1792-1878)*: probably the best nineteenth-century caricaturist, his illustrations of *Oliver Twist* have stamped themselves on generations of Dickens readers. Collections of his work can be seen in the British Museum and in the Victoria and Albert Museum. See also *Ingoldsby Legends*.

11 17 *Frank Potter R.B.A. (1845-1887)*: An underrated painter in his lifetime, W.B. Yeats recalls: '. . . at the Tate Gallery . . . I recovered an old emotion. I saw these pictures as I had seen pictures in my childhood. I forgot the art criticism of friends

and saw wonderful sad, happy people, moving through the scenery of my dreams. The painting of the hair, the way it was smoothed from its central parting, something in the oval of the peaceful faces, called up memories of sketches of my father's on the margins of the first Shelley I had read, while the strong colours made me half remember studio conversations, words of Wilson, or of Potter perhaps, praise of the primary colours, heard, it may be, as I sat over my toys or a children's book' (*Essays and Introductions*, p. 346, Macmillan, 1961). The Potter pictures were probably *The Little Dormouse* and *Girl Resting at a Piano*. See also p. 68. He died on the day his first major exhibition opened.

11 18 *Edward Aveling (1845-1887)*: This plausible wretch did useful work for the emerging labour movement, helped translate *Das Kapital* and even gained Engels' approval to sit as a Marxist delegate at the meeting in Bradford in 1883, when the Independent Labour Party was formed. (See Engels to Sorge, 18.1.1893.) GBS despised his dishonesty over money and people, but said he would trust him to die on the scaffold for his principles, even though he took his friars' purses with him. He partly inspired Dubedat in *The Doctor's Dilemma*.

13 28 *The Goossens family*: This formidable family was founded and continued by three Eugenes; a long-living lot. Eugene (1845-1906) was succeeded by his son of the same name (1867-1958), a famous conductor. *His* son (1893-1962) was even more famous, and also sired the great oboist, Leon, and the harpists Sidonie and Marie. (Another son, a horn-player, was killed in 1916.)

13 32 *G.B. Shaw (1856-1950)*: A short version of this may possibly be 'Economics of the Fine Arts', p. 276, *Collected Essays*, Constable, 1932.

14 5 Tensions that rose after the bloodily suppressed St Petersburg Rising in 1905 led to a deadly split in the revolutionary ranks of the S.R. Party in 1907. Many found exile in London: Lenin was the most eminent of the Russian leaders who visited them.

17 14 Peggy Chesters, Anna's first cousin on her father's side, writes, 'I remember seeing Mrs Patrick Campbell, Israel Zangwill and many others. May Mukle played the 'cello, and Anna sat down at the piano and sang her latest poem "I will pluck from my tree a cherry-blossom wand . . ."' . *Israel Zangwill (1864-1926)* was an influential man of letters, who fought for many progressive causes.

387

18 15 *Nina Hamnett*: painter and Bohemian, student at the Slade and contemporary of Augustus John: he said that she was a better draughtsman than he, and John did not joke about art. She wrote in her autobiography *Laughing Torso*, Constable (1932): 'We visited the poetess Anna Wickham. She lived in a beautiful old House in Hampstead. It had an apple orchard and Dick Turpin had lived there once. There we met Richard Aldington and his wife. They were Imagist poets. Richard had known Henri very well and had some of his work.

'In 1913 when I first met Anna Wickham I had influenza very badly. I was living alone and did not want to go home to the family. She was kind enough to invite me to her house and to look after me. I stayed in bed and had a room overlooking the garden. Several times a week D.H. Lawrence, his wife and Katherine Mansfield came to see Anna. Mrs Lawrence and Katherine sat by my bedside and talked to me. D.H. Lawrence sang hymns for hours in the drawing-room. This was not awfully cheerful. I had never seen him and was told not to get out of bed on any account as my temperature was nearly a hundred and four. One day I heard voices in the garden. I heard Anna's and a man's voice and got out of bed, and saw a man with a reddish beard walking among the apple trees talking to Anna. This was the only time I ever saw Lawrence and I never met him at all.'

18 37 *Oswell Blakeston*: now over eighty but still spry, concerned, and wickedly witty, a protean artist-novelist, poet and painter, who is also a first-class journalist and critic. In his youth he was a virtuoso on the mandolin (compare Anna's friend and lodger Malcolm Lowry's dexterity on the ukelele, which he proudly and affectionately called a 'tarapatch').

19 13 Kite balloons were similar to barrage balloons of the last war, except that they carried a basket to accommodate the observer. They were used for artillery spotting over land, or were flown from small aircraft at sea to locate enemy submarines.

19 30 *Princess Marie-José's Children's Book (1915)*: an anthology of poems, stories and drawings for children, the proceeds from which were used to provide milk, food and clothes for the babies behind the firing line in Flanders during the 1914-18 war. The President of the committee was the Duchess of Norfolk, the Chairman Mrs Haden Guest, Hon. Sec. Mrs Patrick Hepburn (Anna Wickham).

19 31 *Carmel Haden Guest*: from a distinguished Jewish family,

became a communist. Her husband, Leslie Haden Guest, was an M.P., and was made a peer in 1950. Their son David, a mathematician and Marxist philosopher, was killed while fighting with the British Battalion on the Ebro in 1935.

20 28 *1st Viscount Northcliffe*: Alfred Charles William Harmsworth may perhaps claim credit for launching *Comic Cuts* and *Chips*, but as a founding-father of yellow journalism must suffer odium for today's gutter press.

22 7 *Sir James Hopwood Jeans O.M., F.R.S. (1887-1946)*: Jeans became Secretary of the Royal Society in 1919. He would not have wasted his time had not Anna's husband been a serious astronomer.

22 7 *Sir Arthur Stanley Eddington O.M., F.R.S. (1882-1944)*: Director, Greenwich Observatory from 1906 to 1914, the Plumer Professor of Astronomy, and from 1914 Director of the Cambridge Observatory was another witness to Hepburn's status as an astronomer.

22 17 *Betty May*: a famous or notorious small-time club singer, a prodigious drinker, drug-taker and exhibitionist. She was a very nice woman, though wild.

24 18 In January 1928 Anna wrote to Natalie C. Barney: 'For the love of God don't tell me to write poetry. It maddens me − if you want me to write poetry let your will sleep in the storm of my energy. Don't ride all over the battle-field, stand on your hill and confer. If I am to write poetry I want you to help me in certain definite ways − *I want you to love my child*. Get ahead now and love my child.'

24 20 *Natalie Barney*: *Adam*, the periodical edited by Miron Grindea, devoted a number to her in 1963.

26 6 *Redonda*: a small island which M.P. Shiel, the poet, owned. He declared himself King of Redonda, and appointed John Gawsworth to succeed him. He ennobled me as Duke of Persopolis, and without my contributing to the island economy, too.

26 25 Anna's red-brick Victorian house in Hampstead came to be known as La Tour Bourgeoise by her friends in Fitzrovia. A Complaint Book was maintained for cheerfulness and as an umbrage-preventer. It was headed:
> The hope of houses and of nations
> Is in co-operations:
> Therefore we pray

Suggestions you will make,
For order's sake

26 35 *The Fitzroy Tavern*: a pub in Charlotte Street, Bohemian
centre in the twenties and thirties, it was known to its regulars
as Kleinfeldt's. This popular governor moved before the war
to Abbey Road, to a pub then called The Princess of Wales.
Post-war re-building has it re-named Lily Langtry.

27 20 *Beatrice Kean Seymour*: Her husband, William Kean
Seymour, wrote the parody of Anna's poem, 'The Cherry-
Blossom Wand', in *Punch*.

27 25 The constitution of Anna's 'League' is to be found in the
archives of Reading University. It reads as follows:

THE LEAGUE FOR THE PROTECTION
OF THE IMAGINATION OF WOMEN
Slogan: World's Management by Entertainment

That organised culture should sustain and stimulate
government.
The organisers of a nation's culture are its hostesses.
We have no political antagonism, but are generally
critical
of everybody, including ourselves.
We do not like the way Mussolini has organised his
colonial empire.
We do not like the way Hitler has managed his Jews.
And we don't like Stalin's effect on Russian poetry.

With regard to economics: there has been in point of fact no
economic peace since the Matriarchy. During the Matriarchy economic peace was exceedingly low, but it was the
only time in which 98% of the people could rely on getting
three meals a day.

The modern problem for government is Peace and
Plenty; and that is because the spirit of man has not dominated the machine, but the spirit of man is quite incapable of
dominating the machine. Man is a theorist. Woman is the
supreme organiser. The body of a woman takes in to itself
beans, beef and caviar and the yield is all the human life that is
or has been. The machine is in fact the material ghost of the
spirit of woman. The spirit of woman is liberated by the
industrial revolution. Man, the theorist, has materialised his
formulae in the shape of the machine. It is his tribute to
Woman in terms of imitation, and now her spirit is free
enough to use it.

390

The league will stimulate original work from women in the fields of economics, psychology and political theory, but, apart from this, the imagination of women can only be protected by the amused, and we, the committee, have gathered ourselves together because the state of the world does not amuse us and, therefore, we are not more amused by a woman's work of art than a man's work of art, and in the province of pure art we want to stimulate every sincere and interesting effort . . .

16th June 1938

(signed) Anna Wickham, Barbara Armstrong, Gwen le Gallienne, Maureen Forester Agar, Audrey Beecham (Sec), Carmel Haden Guest, Kate O'Brien, Charlotte Haldane.

27 37 The boys were known as the Two Madisons until they felt ready to venture into the arena of international cabaret. Matthew Norgate, a dramatic critic of the *Evening Standard* wrote, in January 1935, 'At the Holborn Empire I was delighted not only by the Arnaut Brothers . . . but by the Two Madisons and Sonia. This trio do a bit of most kinds of dancing, but what struck me most about them was the tap-dancing of the two men. Besides being beautifully timed this was notable for the fact that its exponents somehow made it interesting, and moved gracefully, especially as to the arms — phenomena I have never before come across in this sphere.'

27 39 *Olivia Manning C.B.E. (1911-1980)*: Her *Balkan Trilogy* (Heinemann, Penguin) is being serialised by BBC TV. Two of her earlier works — *The Doves of Venus* and *The Play Room* are to be re-issued by Virago Press, with introductions by one of her closest friends, the novelist Isobel English (Mrs Neville Braybrooke).

28 23 *Malcolm Lowry (1909-1957)*: His first novel, *Ultramarine* (1933), had been for the most part written while he was at Cambridge University. His world fame came later with *Under the Volcano* (1947).

29 22 Today we are much persuaded of the primary importance of the craft, the maker element, in poetry, but Keats seems to have shared Anna's view. 'If poetry comes not as naturally as leaves to a tree it had better not come at all.' (Letter to Benjamin Bailey, 13 March 1818.) She would certainly have agreed with him when he wrote, 'I do think better of womankind than to suppose they care whether Mister John Keats,

five feet high, likes them or not.' (Letter to Benjamin Bailey, 18 July 1818.)

30 2 In a radio discussion with L.A.G. Strong in 1941 he added: 'the point of having rules is that you can break them.'

32 35 'Of course, this state of consciousness is very rare; this joy and wonder at being alive, in a universe that troubles me no more and *is* no more, can only just hold; more commonly the opposite feeling prevails; what is light grows heavy, the transparent becomes dense, the world oppresses, the universe is crushing me. A curtain, an impassable wall stands between me and the world, between me and myself; matter fills every corner, takes up all the space and its weight annihilates all freedom; the horizon closes in and the world becomes a stifling dungeon. Language breaks down in a different way and words drop like stones or dead bodies; I feel I am invaded by heavy forces, against which I can only fight a losing battle . . . But in this anxious situation I do not quite give up the fight, and if, as I hope, I manage in spite of the anguish to introduce into the anguish, humour, − which is a happy symptom of the other presence − this humour is my outlet, my release and my salvation.' (Preface vol. i, VII-VIII: *Plays*: mostly translated by D. Watson, Calder and Evergreen, 7 vols, 1958-1967.)

34 1 *Ralph Hodgson (1871-1962)*: The poet of suffering animals.

38 18 *George Hepburn* remembers: At school, I had obviously been learning the poem by Byron called 'Ocean', and I was very proud of this. When I got home for the school holidays, to show off my new found knowledge I wrote on the kitchen wall, which was covered with writings, the first line of the poem:

'Roll on, thou deep and dark blue Ocean − roll!'

A day or so later, Anna wrote under my line the following short comment:

Only a friendly gentle soul
Will give the sea advice to roll
Because the sea has plainly its strong will
More set on rolling than on keeping still.
And Byron and our George, a couple of kind kings,
Have simple faith in their effect on things.
Roll on thou deep and dark blue ocean roll.

42 21 *C.B. Cochran (1873-1951)*: Knighted in 1948, he was a most celebrated impressario of light entertainment. *Anton Dolin (1902-1983)*: born Patrick Healey-Kay, premier danseur of

the Diaghilev Ballet. *Bud Flanagan (1896-1968)*: with his partner Chesney Allen, he adorned the Crazy Gang through three decades.

46 8 *John Keats, (1795-1821)*: See *Letters* (1895), p. 54.

52 17 Anna was congenitally untidy, but she loved order and deeply desired it. The Hepburns still have a small brown note-book (*see photograph*) titled 'Where Is It', the pages marked alphabetically, in which in Anna's handwriting all household possessions are listed and located, e.g.

cash-box	Drawer I	Chest A
cigar case	Drawer II	Chest A
collars (soft)	Drawer I	Wardrobe
collars (starched)	Drawer II	ditto

60 29 '*The Load of Hay*' on the rise of Haverstock Hill, Hampstead, was directly opposite Anna's grandfather Edwin's music shop. Used by waggoners in the eighteenth and nineteenth centuries to rest and water their horses, for a while it was re-named 'The Noble Art' (by a tenant devoted to the Fancy), but now flourishes under its old sign.

62 23 *Origin of Species* was published in 1859.

62 30 *Herbert Spencer (1820-1903)*: He coined the phrase 'survival of the fittest' and was influential among free thinkers of the period: he wrote: 'People are beginning to see the first requirement in life is to be a good animal.' This was in some years before D.H. Lawrence became a guru. His evolutionary philosophy seems to have escaped full comprehension by scientists and philosophers, but he always assumed he had predated Darwin by four years.

64 38 *Sim Reeves (1818-1908)*: a notable and popular tenor of the period.

70 18 *Dolly Radford* came from an aristocratic family, but married an artisan craftsman. She was a friend (and patron) of D.H. Lawrence as well as Eleanor Marx and Anna Wickham. Her younger daughter Margaret stayed sometime at 49 Downshire Hill during the 1914-18 war as a companion-cum-mother's-help.

98 14 *Alfred, Lord Tennyson*: died in 1892, aged 83.

108 12 *Charles Stuart Calverley (1831-1934)*: This prince of parodists may have influenced Anna in her light verse. She would have approved of his

O Beer, O Hodgson, Guinness, Alsopp, Bass,
Names that should be on every infant's tongue.

134 21 The Hepburn family was immensely proud of its lineage: two members of the family wrote books about it. One contains a family tree showing the descent from Charlemagne and Alfred the Great via Robert the Bruce and Bothwell. In a letter to Natalie C. Barney, Anna wrote, 'I have been fighting the spirit of Charlemagne for my imagination.'

151 16 *Miss E.G. Colles* was Lady Superintendent of the St Pancras School for Mothers in 1908 and 1909. She was the author of *The Pudding Lady* (1910). Her brother was music critic of *The Times*.

INDEX OF FIRST LINES